SPECIAL CHALLENGES
IN CAREER MANAGEMENT:
COUNSELOR PERSPECTIVES

SPECIAL CHALLENGES IN CAREER MANAGEMENT: COUNSELOR PERSPECTIVES

Edited by

Alan J. Pickman
Chase Bank, New York

LEA LAWRENCE ERLBAUM ASSOCIATES, PUBLISHERS
1997   Mahwah, New Jersey

The views expressed in this volume do not necessarily reflect those of Chase Bank or its management.

Lawrence Erlbaum Associates, Inc., Publishers
10 Industrial Avenue
Mahwah, New Jersey 07430

Cover design by Brian Whitehill

Library of Congress Cataloging-in-Publication Data

Special challenges in career management : counselor
perspectives / [edited by] Alan J. Pickman.
p. cm.
Includes index.
ISBN 0-8058-1856-1 (cloth : alk. paper). — ISBN
0-8058-1857-X (pbk. : alk. paper)
1. Outplacement services. 2. Unemployed—Counseling of. 3. Employees—Counseling of. 4. Career
development. I. Pickman, Alan J.
HF5549.5.D55S66 1996
158'.3—dc20   96-18079
                                     CIP

Books published by Lawrence Erlbaum Associates are
printed on acid-free paper, and their bindings are chosen
for strength and durability.

Printed in the United States of America
10 9 8 7 6 5 4 3 2 1

To Jan and Sarah—
With love, laughter, and many thanks

Contents

III INNOVATIVE APPROACHES IN OUTPLACEMENT AND CAREER MANAGEMENT

Preface

The practice of outplacement counseling continues to grow in complexity. Outplacement counselors are increasingly called on to respond effectively to a rapidly changing set of business conditions. In its formative years, the thrust of outplacement consisted of providing full service, individualized career planning, and job-search assistance to a limited number of senior executives. In later years, outplacement services were offered to a much larger and more diverse group of individuals. Programs changed, as well, to include group formats and, in some cases, time-limited services.

Most recently, outplacement professionals have come to recognize that their skills and expertise are of value not only to those corporate employees whose jobs have already been eliminated, but to those individuals who remain within their organizations. Such individuals, the "survivors" as they have come to be known, also need assistance in order to manage their careers more effectively. In recognition of this trend, the major professional association of outplacement professionals, formerly known as the International Association of Outplacement Professionals (IAOP) changed its name in 1994 to the International Association of Career Management Professionals (IACMP). Many of its practitioners began designing programs and delivering services in the areas of executive coaching, organizational development, and internal career management, to name just a few.

The growth and evolution of the field has presented many counseling challenges to its practitioners. Delivering high quality services to clients more diverse in their age, gender, race, income, occupational level, and areas of specialization necessitates a deeper understanding of the dynamics of the counseling process, a broader repertoire of counselor interventions, and more knowledge about job search and marketplace conditions. More attention is also being paid to issues surrounding the competencies and training required to deliver high quality career management services.

Furthermore, the increasingly competitive nature of a more mature industry has impacted the design and delivery of career management services. Innovative approaches and formats have been introduced in an effort to meet client needs and, thereby, remain viable as business entities. One of the major areas where innovation is taking place is in the application of technology to career management services. Although it is a field that has not historically relied heavily on technological innovations, there is a growing awareness that career management firms and their practitioners must become more sophisticated in this area in order to meet the rapidly changing needs of sponsoring organizations and individual candidates.

As a result of the many challenges faced by career management professionals, the need to think clearly about the services we deliver, the ongoing development of our professionalism and the changes in the labor market to which we must respond has never been greater. One of the best ways to accomplish this is to tap the knowledge and experience of experts in the field. These chapters are designed to accomplish this. The contributors to this volume represent established industry leaders with demonstrated expertise in their areas of special interest. In all cases, they bring a distinct and informed perspective to their discussions.

OVERVIEW OF CONTENTS

The volume is divided into three sections. The first section examines some of the more psychologically minded issues relevant to the practice of outplacement and career management. In chapter 1, I reflect on the satisfactions and frustrations of practicing outplacement counseling. I highlight the complementarity of the counselor's professional and personal roles. Locker discusses the impact of job loss and organizational change on individuals. She provides some very specific guidelines to assist career management professionals in distinguishing between those situations when a client's problems can be addressed properly in an outplacement context and those situations that require referral to a trained mental health professional. Chamberlain focuses on the importance of understanding the unique thoughts, feelings, and behaviors of each individual we counsel. This is necessary, she contends, in order to grasp the meaning of work in our clients' lives. Bowers is especially interested in issues surrounding professional identity formation in outplacement and career management counselors. She stresses the need for career professionals to have a firm fix on the roles that are most congruent with their style and skills. This enables them to present a clear picture to corporate sponsors, individual candidates, and to themselves.

The second section addresses the counseling challenges of several distinctive client groups. All the authors of these chapters have extensive experience in counseling members of their specialty populations and have been recognized by their peers as experts in their respective areas. They highlight many of the important considerations in understanding these clients and they all provide many practical suggestions for producing successful counseling outcomes.

Carsman begins the section with a discussion of reluctant networkers, those individuals who have a less than positive attitude regarding networking, despite the exhortations of their counselors and peers that networking is the most effective job-search method. The career development and job-search patterns of science and technology professionals is the focus of White's chapter. He sees a major role for career development professionals in assisting scientists and technologists in responding to rapidly changing marketplace, organizational, and managerial conditions. Lands describes the challenges in counseling older clients and emphasizes very strongly the importance for counselors of believing that older adults can continually grow, learn, change, and achieve. Lee draws on her extensive experience in counseling minority clients. Demographic statistics make it clear that minority group members will comprise an increasingly larger percentage of the individuals served by career management professionals in the years ahead. She provides rich case material on counseling African American, Asian American, and Latin American clients. Spanier sheds light on what she describes as the "helpless client syndrome." She provides a variety of innovative methods and approaches that are not typically employed with these candidates, but that can be extremely effective, if skillfully used. The special circumstances surrounding job loss among lawyers from large law firms is the focus of Allison's chapter. Throughout his chapter he weaves material gathered directly from interviews with outplaced attorneys. Gallagher, a major force behind the drive to establish competency standards for outplacement professionals, concludes the section by detailing the history and process of establishing recognized credentials in the field, with special attention on the formation of The Outplacement Institute.

Part III is a collection of chapters that discuss innovative approaches to a variety of outplacement and career management topics. Prichard begins the section with his comprehensive overview of the use of group formats and approaches to provide effective outplacement services. Lee follows with an examination of those individuals who might well have to pursue some form of self-employment, but who do not fit the typical pattern of decisive, resourceful, self-reliant entrepreneurs. He argues that career management professionals need to do a better job of helping these individuals pursue their "personal business ventures." Strewler, former President of the IACMP, reviews the evolution of career centers with special attention on the emerging partnerships between public and private organizations in delivering vital job search services to the workforce.

Carsman reviews the ways in which the proliferation of affordable computer and telecommunications products and services has impacted the world of career management professionals and their clients. He challenges practitioners to become more knowledgeable about technology in order to assist their clients more effectively. Strickland and Hayes, in separate chapters, discuss the growing service known as executive coaching. In their distinctive styles, both authors address such topics as the qualities and skills of successful executive coaches, the benefits of this activity for both individual candidates and their respective organizations, as well as the steps by which the coaching process is conducted. There is no doubt that business leaders are increasingly recognizing how individualized coaching can become a powerful tool for improving an executive's managerial performance. Cates discusses yet another area into which career management professionals are expanding their activities. He sees that survivor employees of many corporations have become career disillusioned and desperately need assistance in developing self-confidence and restoring some sense of control and direction over their careers. He urges outplacement consultants to broaden their vision. They have helped millions who have lost their jobs. Now, they need to seize the opportunities to function as career management consultants to those still employed. Axmith, a recognized industry leader in developing outplacement in Canada and Australia, concludes the volume by sharing his thoughts about the rapid pace of change in the global marketplace and the implications of these changes for successful outplacement practice.

ACKNOWLEDGMENTS

The writing of this book was a wonderful experience at several levels. Some of them were more easily predictable; others came as a very pleasant surprise. The quality of the contributions was not a surprise. I was convinced that I had assembled a group of the most distinguished and knowledgeable practitioners in outplacement and career management and asked them to write on their areas of special interest and expertise. I had worked closely with many of them over the years, and was at least familiar with the work of the others. My initial impressions were confirmed as the authors contributed, without exception, excellent chapters on the important topics of our field.

What was not so easily predictable was how much I would enjoy the process of working with them and the ways in which our collegiality and friendship would grow and develop. My relationship with each author was a little different prior to this project. Some are among the founders and current leaders of outplacement counseling and I have been appropriately respectful and impressed by their contributions over the years. Others have been my supervisors and teachers and I owe them a great deal. Others are among my most valued professional colleagues. Several of the authors have made very important contributions to the Chase Career Services Department. I am delighted to be able to provide all the authors with this visible platform for their expertise and talent.

As an editor, I learned that each author had a different style and needed to be supported in a different way. Some authors looked for more direction; others for less. Some had a clear conception of their chapter from the outset; for others, the process was far more gradual and evolutionary. Some were more confident about their writing skills based on prior efforts; others needed more encouragement. What was common to all was the high degree of professionalism that they brought to this venture. All were extremely thoughtful in their writing and committed to advancing knowledge in the field through their contributions. Without exception, they were cooperative and responsive to my comments and suggestions. Beyond all this, they were fun to work with! The credit for this volume truly belongs to them.

There are others besides the authors who deserve thanks. Once again, I cannot say enough about David Rottman, the manager of Chase's Career Services Department, and my valued friend and colleague. He continues to lead our department in a way that makes me feel very fortunate to be associated with it. He sees to it that our clients receive the most professional services available and he supports his staff, myself included, with a thorough commitment to professional development.

I want to thank the professionals at Lawrence Erlbaum Associates—Ray O'Connell, Sharon Levy, and Robin Weisberg. As with my first book, they were encouraging and responsive in all respects. I am delighted to be associated with them and look forward to our future collaboration. Thanks also to Perre de Clue Scott and Mike Thomas of the Career Services staff for their excellent and responsive administrative support.

Finally, I acknowledge Jan Gura and Sarah Pickman. Jan became my wife during the writing of this book. Her encouragement, expansive thinking, and high standards are a constant source of inspiration. Equally important, I am constantly made aware by her example that, even as I pursue such worthwhile projects as this book, I need to savor the adventure, spontaneity, and wonder of daily life. Finally, I thank my very special daughter, Sarah. She provides joy, laughter, and richness at every turn.

—*Alan J. Pickman*

Contributors

Gil Allison, MBA leads the Career Transition Practice at Brecker & Merryman, a human resources consulting firm that helps leading corporations and professional service firms develop and implement integrated human resources and communications strategies. His prior outplacement and career management affiliations include the John Crystal Center and J. J. Gallagher Associates. He has counseled executives from a variety of industries and has in-depth expertise in working with lawyers from major law firms and corporations.

Murray Axmith, MSW is founder and chairman of Murray Axmith Associates, Canada's leading outplacement firm, established in 1975. Murray is a charter fellow of The Outplacement Institute, and past president of the Association of Outplacement Consulting Firms International (AOCFI). He is also former chairman of the Professional Standards and Ethics Committee of AOCFI. Murray has written more than 100 articles on various career management topics and is a frequent speaker at industry conferences and seminars.

Sandy Bowers, MA has been working in the career management field for approximately 20 years. For more than a decade she managed Citibank's Career Services Department. She also maintained a private practice in career management and served as an adjunct professor at the New School's Graduate School of Management. Sandy is a founding board member of the International Association of Career Management Professionals (IACMP) and served as vice president of membership, and treasurer during the organization's first 5 years. She is currently working for Citibank in London with a focus on leadership staffing and management development for a global finance business.

Mark J. Carsman, PhD is an independent career management consultant with more than 15 years of experience providing outplacement and career management services to individuals and organizations. His prior affiliations include Mainstream Access, Fuchs, Cuthrell & Co., and the Ayers Group. Mark is an industry leader in the use of computer-based databases and on-line information services for supporting job searches. He is a former member of the board of directors and vice president of the New York chapter of IACMP. He is also a part-time instructor at New York University (NYU).

Charles W. Cates, PhD is founder and general manager of Enter-Change, a nationwide career management firm. He is a charter fellow of

The Outplacement Institute, and serves on the board of directors of the IACMP and is a member of the Executive Committee. Charles has presented outplacement and career management topics to numerous professional groups and has taught at several universities. He is active in assisting outplacement professionals who are looking to broaden their expertise and practice areas.

Letitia A. Chamberlain, PhD is director of NYU's School of Continuing Education's Center for Career, Education, and Life Planning, and co-leader of the school's Directors' Group. She is also an adjunct instructor in career counseling for graduate students in NYU's School of Education, Department of Applied Psychology. She has served on the board of directors for the International Society of Retirement Planners and the Retired Senior Volunteer Program. She has counseled and consulted adults of all ages in hospital, school, college, community, and corporate settings.

James J. Gallagher, PhD is the former chairman of The Outplacement Institute, the sole certifying body for outplacement professionals. With more than 25 years in the field, he is regarded as one of its earliest and leading practitioners. He is the founder and former chairman of J. J. Gallagher Associates. Jim was a founding director and president of the Association of Outplacement Consulting Firms International, and a director of the IACMP. He has published more than 100 articles on outplacement topics. Jim is currently retired from active practice and lives in California.

Gary E. Hayes, PhD has been a consultant and psychologist in numerous corporate settings during the past 8 years. He has designed and implemented management and organizational development programs for corporations, ranging from the international divisions of Fortune 100 companies to the domestic operation of start-up organizations with as few as 300 employees. In 1995, Gary co-founded and became managing partner of Executive Development Associates, LLC, a global human resources consulting firm. He is a licensed psychologist and psychoanalyst who maintains a private practice in New York City.

Anita Lands, BA is a corporate outplacement consultant specializing in late career and nonfinancial retirement planning. Additionally, she is associated with Chase Bank's Career Services Department and the outplacement firm of Lee Hecht Harrison. She is on the adjunct faculty at NYU, where she received the NYU Award for Teaching Excellence. Professional affiliations include board membership of the Retired and Senior Volunteer Program (RSVP) and founding president of the greater New York chapter of the International Society for Retirement Planning.

Mary Ann Lee, MA is currently a career development advisor at Deloitte and Touch, L.L.P., and serves on its diversity planning steering committee. Her prior counseling affiliations include Chemical Bank, Citibank, Chase Manhattan Bank, and Hong Kong Bank. She is an adjunct faculty member at NYU, where she teaches a course on multicultural issues in career development. She is a founding member of the Asian American Professional Women, Inc. Mary Ann maintains a private practice with an emphasis on assisting Asian Americans with career development issues.

Robert J. Lee, PhD has been president and chief executive officer of the Center for Creative Leadership in Greensboro, North Carolina since 1994. Previously, he founded and was the co-chairman of Lee Hecht Harrison. His outplacement consulting focuses on senior executives and individuals seeking to make important changes in their work lives. He is a charter fellow of The Outplacement Institute and a founder and past president of the Association of Outplacement Consulting Firms International.

Barbara Zuck Locker, PhD maintains a private practice in psychotherapy/psychoanalysis with individuals and couples in New York. She is the former director of the Employee Assistance Program at Citibank, where she provided organizational and management consulting to the bank's executives. She is an active member of NYU's postdoctoral psychoanalytic community, and has presented papers on such topics as managing organizational change, stress management, and the role of work in adult life.

Alan J. Pickman, PhD is a licensed psychologist with a broad range of counseling, supervisory, and administrative experience in corporate, university, and mental health settings. He is currently the senior outplacement consultant at Chase Bank's Career Services Department. He is a charter fellow of The Outplacement Institute and a board member of IACMP. Alan is also an adjunct faculty member at NYU, and maintains a private practice. He is the author of *The Complete Guide to Outplacement Counseling*.

Peter Prichard, MA is a vice president at Seagate Associates/OI, the world's largest career transition network, headquartered in Paramus, New Jersey. During the past 20 years, he has consulted with individuals from hundreds of companies using the principles outlined in his chapter. He has also trained more than 150 experienced career consultants in these techniques with special emphasis on innovative group approaches. Peter has presented at more than 150 national conventions, local conferences, and workshops.

Sheryl S. Spanier, MS   has been active for more than 20 years in the career counseling field in business, academia, and government. She was associated with pioneer firms in outplacement and is currently senior vice president at the Strickland Group, where she provides executive coaching and career transition services to senior executives. She serves on the board of the IACMP as Ethics Chair and New York City Regional Representative. She maintains a private practice assisting executives to manage, advance, and change careers.

Joan Strewler, MA   is founder and president of Career Dynamics, Inc. (CDI), based in Bloomington, Minnesota. She is the former president of the IACMP. Additionally, she serves on the Board of Governors of the Outplacement Institute and is a member of the Outplacement Industry Coalition. Joan is a former chairperson of the Ethics Committee and the International Chapter Development Committee. She is a licensed psychologist in Minnesota and a nationally certified career counselor.

Kathleen Strickland, MS   is the founder and chief executive officer of The Strickland Group, Ltd., a consulting firm that specializes in executive coaching and outplacement for senior executives. Prior to starting the firm 7 years ago, she was a partner at J. J. Gallagher Associates in New York, and a consultant for Murray Axmith Associates in Toronto. Kathy consults executives about a wide range of topics including communications issues, corporate politics, and women's and minority issues. She has clinical training as a psychotherapist and as an alcohol/drug abuse counselor.

Daniel White, MA   is a career and organizational development consultant specializing in working with scientists and technologists. He provides training and counseling to individuals and groups, helping them to develop the skills needed to enhance their careers. Dan is currently a vice president with QED, a human resources development consulting firm in New York. Previously, Dan served as a training and organization development director at Citicorp, where he counseled executives on adapting to rapidly changing business conditions.

I

PSYCHOLOGICAL PERSPECTIVES FOR CAREER MANAGEMENT PROFESSIONALS

1 Reflections on Being an Outplacement Counselor

Alan J. Pickman
Chase Bank, New York

The practice of outplacement continues to grow in complexity, posing many ongoing challenges to its counselors. Outplacement counselors have many different roles, which we must learn to play. At certain moments we function as strategic thinkers, organizational consultants, and trusted advisors to corporate executives. At other moments, we function as empathic listeners, accepting facilitators, and informative guides to individual candidates. At still other moments, we need to be analytical observers, knowledgeable information providers, and concise writers and editors. It helps to be a persuasive presenter, judicious sounding board, inspirational motivator, and shrewd negotiator, as well.

If this seems like a tall order, it is. Consequently, it is important to understand this complex activity as fully as possible. Although we could be content to understand the work of outplacement counselors solely in terms of an objective job description or a cursory review of tasks, it is my intention in this chapter to focus on the more personal and subjective experiences of being an outplacement practitioner. For example, what is it really like to do this challenging work day in and day out? What type of satisfactions, frustrations, and rewards does it bring? How are counselors affected by it? What keeps most of us coming back for more, or causes a few of us to move on to other activities? In what ways do we as counselors influence our clients and in what ways are we, in turn, impacted by our clients? These are some of the issues that are addressed in this chapter.

BLENDING OF PERSONAL AND PROFESSIONAL LIVES

The practice of outplacement counseling provides us with a distinct opportunity to develop personal and professional roles that complement and nourish one another. This stands in sharp contrast to so many occupations where individuals are called on to separate or compartmentalize work and personal roles. For outplacement counselors, the personal and professional roles are very much intertwined. Outplacement counselors are able to draw fully and richly on various life experiences to assist in counseling sessions. For example, the various jobs we have held, the managers for whom we have worked, the obstacles we have confronted, the disappointments to which we have been subjected, the transitions that we have successfully negotiated—all of these experiences can be tapped and can enhance a counselor's effectiveness. Conversely, the powers of observation, relationship building skills, effective marketing strategies, and knowledge of the world of work developed as outplacement practitioners can certainly be very useful in relating to family, friends, and associates. This interplay of personal and professional lives can be very rewarding for counselors.

Another very important dimension of this personal and professional role complementarity is what we can learn about our own strongly held beliefs through our counseling work. Our moral imperatives, personal values and core beliefs often find their way into our sessions. Sometimes they are expressed directly, whereas at other moments they are imbedded in our comments. The following is just a sample of some of the themes that counselors have been known to introduce into sessions:

- Feeling powerless is a state of mind.
- You have less to lose than you think.
- If you do not advocate for yourself, nobody else will.
- Corporate life is not fair.
- Preparation and practice are key.
- If you do not expect anything, you will never be disappointed.
- Money is important, but it is not everything.
- Change does not occur without risk.
- Everything worth doing is difficult.
- We are all afraid of being wrong.
- There is little to be gained in remaining stuck in the past.
- Learning more about yourself is always worthwhile.
- Asking for help is not a sin.

As these themes suggest, important expressions of ourselves can easily find their way into counseling sessions. However, we need to guard against introducing these themes blindly or indiscriminately. By carefully reflecting on and understanding our counseling behaviors, we can learn a great deal about our individual values, attitudes, and beliefs. This will then enable us to choose our interventions more carefully and with a greater likelihood that they will be of benefit to our clients.

Learning about our values, attitudes, and beliefs is a step in our professional growth. However, in order to maximize personal growth, we must also learn to integrate the understanding of values, attitudes, and beliefs into our personal lives. It is very often the case that we are not as effective or knowledgeable in managing our own career as we are in assisting others to manage theirs. Who among us can say that he always "practices what he preaches"? When it comes to our own careers, we sometimes ignore the very same advice that we give to clients. For example, do we always manage our own careers in the proactive ways that we encourage our clients to do? Do we manage both our direct reports and our own managers as effectively as we might? To what extent do we seek out professional development opportunities? To what extent do we take on assignments that involve some risk and that require development of new skills? To what extent do we remain abreast of the latest developments in our field? To what extent do we regularly expand our network of contacts? To what extent do we negotiate assertively on our own behalf? To what extent do our outplacement organizations attract, retain, and develop their employees?

These are just some of the questions that underscore that, like our candidates, we also have careers that need to be managed effectively. Most of us could probably acknowledge, safely, that we do not always follow the very sound advice we give to clients day after day. We often fall short in adhering to our own words. Although it would be easy to treat lightly the discrepancy between what we preach and what we practice for ourselves, to do so would be a mistake. It robs us of credibility with our clients and renders us hypocritical in our own eyes. If the discrepancies persist and widen, ultimately our effectiveness as agents for change is compromised. So, it is very important to keep in mind that the intertwined nature of our personal and professional lives is a double-edged sword. On the one hand, it holds out the opportunity for personal growth and rich satisfactions. On the other hand, it challenges us to maintain the highest standards of excellence and professionalism.

There are many other benefits that the career provides for its practitioners. Financial gain and professional prestige are certainly among them, although outplacement counselors are not likely to ever be among the very highest occupational groups along these dimensions. What we do have, however, are very substantial opportunities for personal growth through our work.

We also have the capacity to learn a great deal from our clients. Each client brings with him or her the sum total of their accumulated knowledge and experience. We learn a great deal about the work that people do and the organizations within which the work is done. In a given week, we may learn how a marketer strategizes about an upcoming campaign, how a general manager motivates staff, how a training professional delivers a new program, how a human resources executive implements new policies and practices, how a data processing professional applies the latest technological innovations, or how a clerical employee copes with the sameness of repetitive tasks. In addition, we learn a great deal about how corporate decisions are made and how corporate cultures differ from organization to organization and from industry to industry.

Experienced practitioners know that what we learn from one client can transfer to our work with other clients. If we remain alert and attentive to each client, we can often find ourselves introducing in a later session material and information learned in earlier sessions. Our clients truly have a lot to teach us. If we become excellent students of them, our future work is enhanced.

For example, Jonah H. was a client whose job-search experiences I often pass along to other clients. Jonah was a reluctant networker, but an excellent writer and a resourceful researcher. His functional background was in direct marketing. In addition, his life circumstances were such that he was willing to relocate anywhere in the United States for a suitable position. Despite my repeated efforts at stressing the benefits of networking, as most outplacement professionals advocate, he was reluctant to do so. Instead, he conducted a job-search campaign that consisted primarily of direct mail. He drafted dozens of well-researched targeted letters and sent them to appropriate corporate officials. He also sent out scores of broadcast letters to corporations and executive recruiters across the country. As a direct marketing specialist, he was accustomed to relatively low rates of positive response. However, he also was confident, that if he sent out a large enough number of letters to a broad enough territory, he would find some available positions. He turned out to be correct, and identified six to eight positions and ultimately received three desirable offers. Jonah taught me the importance of recognizing that job-search approaches can be tailored to work well under special circumstances, even if they appear to go against the conventional wisdom.

Another benefit of working as an outplacement practitioner is the nature of relationships that we can build with our clients. We are positioned to be the "good guys" in the job loss scenario. Most of us have had the experience of being asked by those not in the field how we can tolerate dealing continuously with such a painful and depressing activity as job loss. What is not always clear to the uninitiated is that we are positioned to be seen by candidates as the ones with the "white hats." We are the ones who can help individuals turn their situations around, to find opportunity in the face of apparent crisis. Furthermore, in many cases, we are able to counsel individuals for the duration of their search, culminating in the acceptance of an even better new position. There is something enormously satisfying about seeing our efforts contributing to such a concrete, measurable, positive outcome.

Judy S. was such a client. A woman in her early 30s, Judy was a graduate of a prestigious New York business school. At the time of her graduation from business school, she felt that many of the best, brightest, and most ambitious students were pointed toward investment banking. She wanted to be among them, and landed a job at a major New York bank. Although she worked in the investment banking area for 7 years earning a VP title and substantial financial rewards along the way, she did not find it satisfying. In the aftermath of her job elimination, we did a thorough assessment of her interests, skills, and style. As a result of our discussions and those she had with valued colleagues and friends, she became convinced that a more creative job marketing financial products and services would be more to her liking. She conducted a successful job-search campaign and landed a new job elsewhere in her organization. The job was clearly a better match with her interests, temperament, and style. She felt that she was now able to make a career-related decision that was based more on her needs, rather than those of others. She was delighted with her change in direction.

There are also satisfactions that stem from being helpful to others in ways that might be more difficult to measure, but are, nevertheless, experienced by both counselor and client. For example, we know that many times we have assisted individuals in coping with difficult feelings around loss, rejection, and self doubt, to name just a few. We know that we have helped individuals become much more knowledgeable about their skills, interests, style, and values. We know that we have helped individuals to think about ways to manage their careers more effectively and to plan for their future more wisely. These can be enormously satisfying experiences.

For example, Joel Z. was a 42-year-old male referred to me in connection with a complicated family business situation. The original owners of the business were two brothers. One of the brothers had two sons, both of whom were now active in running the business. The second brother had a daughter who did not enter the business. However, some years after her marriage to Joel, he did enter the business. Joel's relationships with his cousins-in-law were always somewhat strained. However, when the business was profitable, the differences were smoothed over. In recent years, the business fared more poorly. The cousins felt they could not afford to carry Joel and his substantial salary. So, with a good deal of anguish and guilt, they decided to make the necessary business decision to force Joel from the business.

He was referred to me after his ouster. Initially, he was quite angry and resentful, as was his wife, daughter of one of the original owners. However, as time passed, Joel acknowledged that he had never felt comfortable in the business, and that although it met his financial needs quite nicely, it left him feeling quite unfulfilled in other ways. During the course of our self-assessment exercises, he talked with great enthusiasm about his volunteer activities working with children and teenagers, both in his synagogue and in other community activities. He also described his long-standing interest in American history. He eventually decided to return to graduate school for a master's degree in education with the goal in mind of teaching social studies in elementary school. At last report, he was progressing splendidly toward his goal with a degree of enthusiasm and excitement that he had never experienced in the family business.

Outplacement candidates vary enormously in terms of their prior exposure to counseling professionals. Some have not only undergone prior career or outplacement counseling, but have benefited from psychotherapy with a trained mental health professional as well. They are fully aware of the potential benefits of counseling. Others have had no prior experience with counseling of any type. They arrive full of questions and doubts about the potential benefits of outplacement counseling, or any form of counseling, for that matter. The fact that their former employer is sponsoring the activity only adds to their suspicion. Yet, when the outplacement counseling work goes well it can alter substantially the individual's view of professional counseling. Hopefully, it leaves the client with the distinct impression that seeking out a well-trained, skilled, empathic, professional counselor in the face of life's problems and challenges can be a valuable and productive course of action. Outplacement counselors can, justifiably, take great pride in their efforts, especially if they result in clients' attitudes toward helping professionals being modified in this way.

Another source of satisfaction derived from outplacement counseling is the opportunity it provides for becoming knowledgeable about a wide range of topics. At the same time, it also holds out the opportunity to develop special niches or areas of expertise based on our own special interests. In terms of broad knowledge, there are many topical areas that are relevant to the work of outplacement practitioners. Among them are current and future sociological trends, business news and current events, human resources practices, psychology and counseling theory and practice, and job-search techniques. Many practitioners, especially those who like being involved in multidimensional activities and projects, find it very much to their liking that they are called on to be knowledgeable about so many different areas. The challenge of being broadly based in this way enables outplacement practitioners, at their best, to be seen as up-to-date, versatile, and well-informed. Being seen as esoteric and "ivory towerlike" is hardly a prescription for success in the field.

On the other hand, in addition to being broad based in our knowledge, outplacement practitioners can also develop niches or areas of expertise that are consistent with our special interests. This provides an opportunity to feel that the work allows for highly individualized self-expression. For example, there are practitioners who have developed expertise and distinguished themselves in such areas as delivery of specialized group outplacement services, working with special populations such as preretirement clients, minority clients, scientists and technical professionals, or entrepreneurs.

STRESSORS AND FRUSTRATIONS

Outplacement counseling is not all satisfactions and rewards. For counselors, there are stressors and frustrations as well. The stressors fall into several different categories: individual and dyadic, organizational, and cultural.

Individual and Dyadic Stressors

Individual stressors are those that are located within an individual. They are person-centered stressors. For example, those drawn to outplacement counseling and other forms of counseling often take pride in their commitment to helping others. However, working closely with others on a constant basis is emotionally demanding. In order to avoid becoming overly stressed, practicing professionals must develop consistent methods of stress reduction that work for them. Some counselors might find this difficult to do. It may be because they do not recognize their own symptoms of stress, or it may be that they respond to their stresses in a manner that is nonadaptive or not healthy.

For example, one outplacement colleague always felt she had to have the "right" answer in response to the questions and inquiries of her clients. Striving to always be right created a great deal of stress for her and eventually contributed to her becoming much more defensive and threatened when clients asked challenging questions.

Another set of stressors are those that take place at the dyadic level. They emerge from the interactions of the counselor and client. Counselors have different styles and different sets of needs. The same is true for clients. Most experienced counselors know that there are certain types of clients who are more stressful for them than others. For example, one outplacement colleague places great importance on his role as a helping professional. He switched to outplacement from corporate human resources, where he did not feel he had sufficient opportunity to be of genuine assistance to those he served. He worked very hard to accomplish the transition from human resource generalist to outplacement counselor. He thought he had arrived in a role where everyone would appreciate his genuine commitment to helping. Subsequently, he found it very stressful to work with help-rejecting clients; those individuals who frequently had a "yes, but ... " response for his interventions or who had a "yes, I will" response for him, but then never followed through with any of the ideas on which they seemingly had agreed.

Organizational Stressors

Another set of stressors are those that are organizational in nature. These stressors are related to the working conditions under which outplacement counselors operate. Some stressors are more common for those outplacement counselors who are full-time members of a firm. Other stressors are more common for per diem counselors. For example, for those affiliated full-time with a firm, stressors include:

- What are the expectations regarding the size of a caseload the counselor carries?

- How manageable and realistic are the expectations?
- To what extent is there organizational support and recognition for feelings of overload?
- To what extent is there a culture that allows counselors to acknowledge openly that there are certain clients with whom they are struggling?
- Is such an acknowledgment met with collegial support and efforts at assistance, or is it responded to as if it reflects inadequacies and limitations on the part of the counselor?
- To what extent is there variety in the job for the counselor?
- Is there an opportunity for taking on special projects, or is there an unbroken string of one-to-one counseling sessions?

For per diem counselors, stressors include:

- How predictable are their assignments?
- How steady is their income stream?
- To what extent do they feel as valued and respected as the full-time counselors?
- To what extent do they feel in control of their career and its direction?

There have been a number of recent developments in the field that have further impacted outplacement counselors around these organizational stressors. First, outplacement professionals are increasingly called on to do as much, or more, with candidates in less time. Sponsoring organizations are increasingly sensitive to the price of outplacement services. Many of them are no longer as able or willing to spend as much on outplacement services as in the past. They are interested in shorter, less expensive programs and the "unbundling" of services that previously had been included under one comprehensive price tag. Consequently, counselors find themselves having fewer sessions and less contact with individual candidates. This happens even though, from a strictly counseling point of view, the counselors often think the candidates need more, not less, assistance. Yet, the formally agreed on services are limited. This can be frustrating for individual counselors, especially if they value the ability to form long-term and intensive relationships with candidates, and/or feel a professional obligation to provide whatever assistance is warranted.

A second organizational change is financial. Given the aforementioned pricing pressures exerted by sponsoring organizations, outplacement firms, as business entities, are finding their profit margins narrowed. Although there are any number of possible management responses to such a development, one that has been implemented by some firms is to reduce the compensation paid to their counselors. This seems to impact especially the per diem counselors, many of whom have seen their daily rates decrease rather substantially, at least for some of those at the national outplacement firms.

An additional organizational stressor concerns opportunities for professional growth and development. There is some sentiment among certain outplacement practitioners that their organizations are not doing all that they can to promote professional staff development. According to this line of thought, outplacement firms need to support their own professionals by providing more, not fewer, opportunities for staff development. These opportunities can take many forms including counselor supervision, seminars on relevant counseling topics, and support of staff involvement in such professional associations as the International Association of Career Management Professionals (IACMP). Some practitioners feel that although their organizations are to be commended for their commitment to servicing candidates and sponsoring organizations, they fall short in doing as much as they could to develop and enhance the skills of their own staff professionals.

Cultural Stressors

A final set of stressors are those that are cultural in nature. Outplacement services take place in a larger context, and are influenced by social, economic, and historical factors. Most counselors would agree that the average job search takes longer than it did several years ago. Right Associates, a leading national outplacement firm, has documented this trend. They found that, in 1988, the average length for an executive job-search campaign was 25 weeks. By 1993, the average length of a search campaign was 32.25 weeks, an increase of 29% (J. Aron, personal communication, February 1, 1994). Consequently, counselors work with clients for longer periods of time. Frustrations can build. Disappointments can mount. In addition, there are other marketplace factors that are stressful. Many candidates are constantly confronted by reports of job market "gloom and doom" and can become easily discouraged about future prospects. Other candidates are convinced that this will not be the last time in their careers that they will face job elimination. This, too, can be very disheartening. Further, many candidates are forced to take jobs at smaller organizations that they view as less prestigious than their former companies.

There does not appear to be any quick end in sight to the economic difficulties that have led to so much downsizing in recent years. Marketplace instability is international in nature. It affects organizations in all industries. There are no safe havens to which clients can be directed. These conditions complicate the career planning and job search efforts of the candidate and can lead to great stress for candidates. They can easily have the same effect on counselors.

An additional and related cultural stressor concerns the rapid pace of social and technological change taking place throughout our national and global economies. These changes are certainly not easy to manage for many of the candidates seen in outplacement. Many long-service employees joined their organizations when organizations were more stable, jobs were more secure, and proactive career management was less critical. Outplacement practitioners are regularly called on to assist individuals in responding to the emerging realities caused by the rapid pace of change. It can be a stressful aspect of the job, as some candidates struggle mightily with these changes.

In addition, as mentioned previously, personal and professional roles are very much intertwined for outplacement counselors. Not only are we required to assist candidates in responding to these emerging realities, but we must respond to them ourselves. We must manage to stay abreast of how labor markets and occupations are changing in order to be of maximum assistance to our candidates. Also, at the same time, we must remain abreast of developments in our field in order to manage wisely our own careers. There can be moments when it feels like the "merry-go-round" of rapid change never stops or slows for us as professionals. We need to face the changes daily, either for ourselves or for our candidates. Like any occupational group, there are some of us who embrace rapid change and welcome it as a source of stimulation and growth. There are others of us who prefer a more deliberate pace of change. Yet, whatever our own individual style or temperament, we are regularly called on to assist a wide range of individuals. As a result of these ongoing cultural changes, the potential for counselor stress is great.

In summary, outplacement counselors have many different roles that we must learn to play. Providing outplacement counseling services is a complex professional activity that brings with it many satisfactions and rewards. One of the major sources of satisfaction stems from the complementarity of our professional and personal roles. Other satisfactions include the ability to form gratifying relationships with candidates, the opportunity to learn a great deal about careers, and the chance to focus on topics that are of special interest to us.

There are frustrations and stressors that accompany practicing outplacement counseling as well. The stressors can take place around a variety of issues including those related to the counselor–candidate dyad, organizational pressures, and cultural changes. Understanding more fully both the satisfactions and frustrations of this professional activity will enable counselors to continue their growth and development as skilled and dedicated practitioners.

Job Loss and Organizational Change: Psychological Perspectives

A well-accomplished woman I know lost her job some months ago at a prestigious financial services institution. The job discontinuance, coincidentally, coincided with her 60th birthday. This may have been an insignificant coincidence, but the institution's severance policy guidelines deem the onset of the 61st year as qualification for retirement. My vibrant, "young," employed, involved friend suddenly found herself "retiring."

The issues that the nomenclature raised were myriad. Yes, it was wonderful to have the richly enhanced severance package that comes when a job "goes away," especially at the point in life when one qualifies for retirement. On the other hand, could this woman suddenly make the psychological transition from active employee to retiree? Even though the appendage "retiree" has a much more positive connotation than "unemployed," it is replete with psychological consequences.

Recently we met. She gave me an update on her new life. Although rich in love, activities, friends, family, and interests, she, nevertheless, described her life as somewhat adrift and "discombobulated."

"Why?" I asked, "is it not possible for you to savor this well-earned freedom to enjoy all those nonwork aspects of yourself? You are 60 years old and have worked all of your life. There are so many things you've wanted to do!"

"Well," my sage friend replied, "we just got back from Europe. It troubled me to fill out the customs declaration form. I did not know how to respond to the question which asked for my occupation. After all, we are, in the eyes of the world, what we do. Aren't we? I no longer have an occupation."

Yes, I agreed. In the eyes of the world we are, indeed, what we do. At least, we are what we do for paid work. When we no longer do that work, our very being is called into question. It raises issues of identity, self-esteem, belonging, and purposefulness.

Expanding on this theme, this chapter focuses on the psychological effects of unemployment and, in a closely related vein, the emotional

13

reactions employees face in response to organizational disruptions and changes.

Although this chapter is not intended to adequately train outplacement professionals to do comprehensive psychological assessments of clients, it is designed to provide some helpful guidelines for counselors to more completely understand the impact that personal, emotional, and psychological factors will have on their outplacement clients. It is also intended to encourage outplacement professionals to think more comprehensively about these issues and to be more aware of signs of psychological problems that may affect the job-search process. In addition, this chapter provides some guidelines for distinguishing between those situations when a client's problems can be addressed properly during the outplacement counseling process and those situations that require referral to a trained mental health professional.

Finally, this chapter also discusses the individual and organizational consequences of institutional change and disruption. Historically, support services such as outplacement have been aimed at those individuals who have lost their jobs. A strong case can be made that the "survivors" of change, those individuals still employed after many others have "disappeared" following mergers or downsizings, are also at risk, personally and professionally. Careful organizational analysis and planning for change points toward a need to provide services for this population as well.

THE ROLE OF WORK IN ADULT LIFE

To understand the psychological effects of organizational disruption and/or job loss on the individual, counselors should first have knowledge of the role of work in people's lives. Work is the single most time-consuming activity of adult life. Given the profound importance of work, remarkably little attention has been paid to it in the psychological literature (Czander, 1993; Grey, 1989).

Psychological theories relating to work have come more from the domains of social, developmental, and vocational psychology, rather than from the psychoanalytic tradition. They have tended to focus on issues of career selection and career development at various stages of adult development. Very little has been written about the intrapsychic meaning of work for individuals, even though no less an authority than Freud seemed to acknowledge the importance of work. Erikson (1950) said anecdotally that Freud felt *lieben is arbeiten* (love and work) to be the central activities of human life. It is curious that he then devoted almost no attention to *arbeiten*. Perhaps, he found love the more compelling topic, but it is noteworthy that most individuals tend to define themselves more in terms of what they do for a living and less in terms of who they love or who loves them.

One's work responsibilities are usually physically, mentally, and emotionally demanding. They require great amounts of time and energy on the job. Also, there are few individuals who do not at least sometimes think about, talk about, and/or worry about work, if they are not actually working, during their so-called leisure time.

In the 1970s, educational theorists and academicians were predicting that the technological revolution would create a leisure society. Technology would enable people to get their work done in much less time than before. They predicted that people would be ill prepared to handle the vast amounts of free time; time made available as a result of these technological efficiencies. Doctoral programs were established to train counselors in leisure studies to prepare them to help people learn to use their unstructured time constructively. It is almost humorous to contemplate the folly of this point of view in light of the reality of work patterns in the 1990s.

Individuals work more than ever. At no other time since the Industrial Revolution have people worked as many hours a day for as many days a week. Days off from work and hours spent sleeping have declined nationwide. The technological revolution has made every place a workplace. Fax machines, cellular phones, and laptop computers have given us all home offices—even car and beach offices. This omnipresent "virtual office" has further blurred the lines between work and leisure, making us all, more than ever before, linked closely to what we do.

Our well-being at any given time is impacted by the interplay between how we feel about our personal life and our work life. The times when we feel really great in life are usually the times when we are not having problems in either area. Conversely, we tend to feel the worst when both are not going as well as we would like.

We tend to derive an important measure of self-esteem from work. Identity is also related to our work. We are defined by others, and frequently define ourselves by our occupational roles. At a cocktail party it is typically only a matter of moments before we are asked, "What do you do?" The question is never answered by a lawyer, accountant, psychoanalyst, or auto dealer with the response, "I'm a great mom or dad." Pity goes out to recently excised corporate employees, our outplacement clients, at such a social event.

How frequently is our self-definition publicly exclaimed as a job title? Stereotypes, assumptions, and even comic associations abound around any number of occupational choices. The *New Yorker* publishes entire books of doctor and lawyer cartoons, which we deem appropriate Christmas presents for our physician and attorney friends. Clearly, self-esteem is externally, as well as internally derived. Our work titles, the location of our offices, and other seemingly external factors, influence how we feel about ourselves and how others view us.

Work, at its simplest level, fulfills our basic needs for food, clothing, and shelter. It is only when these basic needs are assured that individuals are free to pursue the fulfillment of higher level needs (Maslow, 1950). We can then look to work as a vehicle for more creative forms of self-expression. Work also provides psychological structure and a sense of purpose.

We also derive security from work. The security is not only material but social as well. Work is a major area of social connectedness and social support. It is an ironic fact of life in outplacement that clients are cut off from a principal source of social support at a time in their lives when they need it most.

Work has an important connection to family life. Our status in the family is largely influenced by the ratio of our roles as breadwinner and caretaker. Needless to say, the life of the family is drastically altered by the loss of an income, and this change is exponentially increased if it is the sole income. Given the importance of work in every aspect of adult life, what happens to individuals when things go wrong at work?

ORGANIZATIONAL UPHEAVAL AND INDIVIDUAL JOB LOSS— PSYCHOLOGICAL CONSEQUENCES

Articles frequently appear in the popular press on the changing social contract between employers and employees. The notion of "womb to tomb" employment, once a staple of American culture, is increasingly an archeological artifact of that culture. The only constant in the workplace appears to be change.

As this cultural change is taking place, employees' assumptions about their role in the workplace are also changing. Workers no longer associate good performance with job security. They do not believe that loyalty to a company will be reciprocated. Employees feel less of a sense of belonging to a work culture and more of a sense of being there temporarily subject to the winds of change.

Although change may be good for a company in the long term, it can often be devastating to individuals in the short term. Organizational change causes workplace anxiety. An entire jargon has arisen, at least in part, in response to this anxiety (Locker & Epstein, 1994). Its intention is to minimize the psychological effects of a tumultuous workplace. For example, individuals are no longer "terminated" as in the old jargon. They are now "downsized" and entire workforces are "made available." The euphemistic terminology of downsizing takes the event out of the realm of individual experience and places it in the context of a societal event. It is important for outplacement counselors to remember that our clients do not feel downsized, they feel terminated! It does not matter how many others were similarly "downsized," "re-tooled," "re-engineered," or "right-sized." Most individuals who lose their jobs in a corporate staff reduction still experience the job loss as a personal blow, even when they are told that the job has "gone away."

The *survivor syndrome* is a paralytic combination of relief and guilt experienced after living through a catastrophic event. It is a phrase used in psychological literature to explain the somewhat puzzling behavior of catastrophe survivors who often experience guilt rather than elation. In the popular 1994 film *Fearless*, Harrison Ford portrays a man who survives an airplane crash in which many others have perished. Life as he knew it before this event is over, and he is consumed with doubt about the meaning of life and guilt about his own survival. This dramatization depicts something that behavioral scientists have long known—surviving an event that others have not survived leaves one in conflict. "Why did I survive?" It also leaves doubt. "I came so close. Next time will I get another chance?"

The phrase, survivor syndrome, has in recent years been applied to those workers who remain employed following massive downsizings or corporate takeovers. These workers, the survivors, often find that their ability to function in a highly creative and productive way is compromised once they recognize that they are working in an environment where their own employment is not secure.

Similarly, *merger anxiety*, a syndrome seen in senior level executives, those most responsible for decision making, is brought on by fear of being eliminated during an acquisition or merger. When these individuals are threatened, they do not perform at optimal levels. This, of course, has organizational as well as individual consequences. Sometimes, once seemingly confident executives exhibit a paralysis in decision making. They would rather do nothing than do something wrong. Some individuals do not work as hard because they experience a loss of loyalty to the company; or they respond in an opposite way. They refuse to miss even one day of work for fear it will cause them to appear extraneous. Employees waste time listening to rumors and worrying about their futures. They become concerned about having to accomplish more with fewer resources and they fear being inadequate to the task. Survivors frequently feel they survived by mistake, rather than because of their own abilities. They fear being found out as impostors.

A 47-year-old male, a high-level manager in a major publishing company, was distraught over the prospects of a merger with another publishing house. His career had spanned more than 20 years, during which time his company had been acquired by a much larger firm. At the time of the acquisition, many of his colleagues were released as "redundant"—their jobs taken over by their counterparts in the acquiring firm. This manager believed that he survived only because his job counterpart was nearing retirement age and chose the severance package over staying with the newly merged publishing house. The manager harbored feelings of being second rate, not really good enough, and something of a misfit in the new entity. When rumors began about another merger, albeit with a smaller firm, his earlier anxieties resurfaced and he sought psychotherapy. He described his work environment as demoralized and felt pressure to perform in an exemplary manner in every interaction to prevent appearing anything other than essential.

If individuals in a merger environment eventually do lose their jobs, this definitive event usually follows a long period of uncertainty that has already impacted and often eroded their internal sense of security and well-being about work. Sometimes feelings of suspiciousness toward the company bordering on paranoia are experienced.

Anger, anxiety, and depression are predominant features of early response to job loss. Often, denial is exhibited. Then, once individuals accept the job loss, their self-esteem is often shaken. Sometimes, self-blame and doubt take over as individuals personalize the loss. Whether a worker is transitioned to outplacement because a job has actually gone away, or whether that worker has, in fact, been viewed as a less than optimal performer and/or "fit" often seems irrelevant to the recently released employee.

Issues of shame and guilt in the face of job loss frequently affect relationships with family and friends. A 38-year-old mid-level manager in a production company kept his unemployment secret from his wife for the entire time of his severance period. He dressed for work each morning and commuted to Manhattan from their suburban home. He did not reveal this deception to his outplacement counselor. Finally, he had to face his wife when his checks ran out. Outplacement counselors should not assume that things are fine at home and need to remember to ask about what is not being talked about.

Although this is an extreme case, it is important to note that, for many people, life and work are inseparable and without work their very existence is called into question. Depending on how much their identity has been derived from work, individual outplacement clients will experience changes around issues of self-definition and self-importance.

EVALUATING THE PSYCHOLOGICAL STATUS OF THE CLIENT

Understanding the individual's psychological response to job loss is essential in evaluating the psychological health of the outplacement client.

As Pickman (1994) pointed out, the role of outplacement counseling is to help clients " ... face job loss with renewed self-confidence, to learn effective job search strategies and techniques and to conduct a successful job search campaign" (p. 67). Pickman also noted that in order for the outplacement process to be successful the counselor " ... must determine the extent to which candidates are ready to engage in an outplacement process" (p. 67).

It is true that most outplacement professionals are not trained mental health clinicians. Even for those who are, it is important to recognize the appropriate boundaries of the outplacement counseling relationship. Individuals who are coming for outplacement or career counseling are not expecting psychotherapy or psychoanalysis and any presumptuousness on the part of the counselor can have negative results.

However, at the same time that career management professionals need to be ever mindful of the parameters of their particular counseling contracts, it is also true that being aware of clinical issues will be very helpful in dealing with clients. Preexisting physical, systemic, interpersonal, emotional, or psychiatric problems can certainly be uncovered or heightened by job loss.

To this end it is necessary for counselors to understand the client in context. An assessment of readiness for counseling should include:

1. An assessment of the client's functioning prior to the "trauma" of job loss.
2. An evaluation of the client's social support, strengths, and outside work interests.
3. A clinical assessment of the appropriateness of grief and mourning.
4. An exploration of the possible need for a psychotherapy referral or psychiatric evaluation.

ASSESSMENT OF PRIOR FUNCTIONING AND SOCIAL SUPPORTS

As noted earlier in the chapter, job loss is one of the great stressors of adult life. *The Diagnostic and Statistical Manual of Mental Disorders (DSM-III-R)* of the American Psychiatric Association (1987), ranks job loss as an acute stressor, comparable to marital separation and miscarriage in terms of its impact on adult life.

There is a wide range of individual response to such an event. A good predictor of how an individual will respond to such a stressor would be past behavior. Is the person a "hot reactor" or a "cool reactor"? Does he or she express feelings verbally, or physically through psychosomatic illness? What is the individual's physical and psychological health status?

Does the individual's culture allow for expressions of anger, anxiety, and sadness? Who will hear the client's complaints? The vast literature on social support and stress reduction supports the notion that social support will help a person through a crisis.

A 33-year-old female attorney was devastated when she was told she would not make partner in a major New York law firm. She had relocated to New York City 8 years earlier, leaving family and friends, in pursuit of her partnership aspirations. During her years in New York, she had focused on career and made few friends. She socialized mainly through late night snacks and midday "gym dates" with fellow associates. Her world had grown so small after 6 years in New York that she sought psychotherapy at age 31 to increase her ability to socialize and to become more receptive to the possibility of an ongoing relationship. Despite having actively initiated the psychotherapy treatment, she frequently canceled sessions because of job demands. She came to recognize that she was not yet ready to give up her single-minded pursuit of partnership, even for appointments that might help her pursue her other goals. She left therapy after 6 months.

The decision by her firm not to offer her a partnership was attributed to a cutback in her area of specialization. Although she was given salary and some lead time to find another position, she was also given a clear timetable for leaving the firm. She became deeply depressed and soon returned to treatment.

One complicating aspect of this situation was that she had almost no social support network outside of work. Her meager support system completely fell apart when she was separated from the work environment. The absence of a support system made her "recovery" that much more difficult.

This vignette highlights the need for counselors to know what supports exist for clients and how the supports will be impacted by job loss. Counselors might want to be mindful of the following considerations: (a) does the client have a loving supportive relationship? (b) what type of family life does the client have? and (c) is the prejob loss relationship already taxed, or is it one that the client can rely on for comfort and security?

The client's financial status is also very important. What about financial obligations? Is severance and/or savings adequate, and for how long? Career management professionals should be acutely aware of the financial status of clients because an individual preoccupied by concerns about day-to-day life management and financial obligations will have particular difficulty facing the higher level demands of an active job search. Another consideration is whether the individual has a serious substance abuse or gambling problem. A person with inexplicable serious financial problems might be facing such a problem.

It is useful to evaluate how closely the individuals were identified with the corporate culture from which they have been removed. This is also a place to find out about the clients' interests other than work. What activities connect them to the outside world or to their own inner resources? What nonwork activities provide a sense of fulfillment and accomplishment? For example, an individual who has spent his work life longing for more time to pursue his avocational interest in photography is a better candidate for forced early retirement than a colleague who has never attended a class or workshop on a topic unrelated to his field of employment.

ASSESSMENT OF GRIEF RESPONSE
AND POSSIBLE NEED
FOR MENTAL HEALTH REFERRAL

It is important for counselors to distinguish between appropriate grief and mourning and pathological grief and mourning. Anxiety about the future, anger at the former company, and some depressed affect are certainly normal responses to job loss. However, prolonged extreme feelings of despair, a sense of hopelessness about the future, and loss of interest in formerly pleasurable activities are signs that an individual has experienced a more serious pathological depression and that a psychotherapy referral should be considered.

If an individual's depression or anxiety seriously impairs functioning, a psychiatric evaluation should be arranged. Feelings of hopelessness that may include suicidal ideation are always to be taken seriously. Prudence dictates that in such instances outplacement counselors contact the appropriately trained individuals in their career management or outplacement organization. To help counselors with this difficult assessment process, here are some guidelines:

1. In appropriate grief the client may experience mood swings ranging from relatively good humor to depressed affect. A more disturbed reaction would be a client who has long periods of hopelessness and expresses a sense of not wanting to go on.

2. Most people who lose their jobs will question and evaluate their own self-worth and lose some confidence. More problematic are individuals who can no longer see anything valuable about themselves and question whether they are worthwhile. Such individuals might also feel unloved, become more fearful of interpersonal connections, and express paranoid ideas.

3. Mild depression will cause a loss of interest in pleasurable activities, sleep and eating disturbances, some fatigue, and possible difficulty in getting along with others. If someone cannot find pleasure in any activities, completely loses humor and the ability to enjoy life, has a serious weight gain or loss, reports chronic insomnia or an inability to get out of bed, groom themselves, or keep simple appointments (dentist, car repair) unrelated to a job search, this is cause for concern.

4.   Indecisiveness, poor judgement, and pessimism about the future are also characteristics of those who have recently experienced a serious organizational upheaval and/or job loss. More problematic is when these signs remain prolonged and debilitating and seriously influence a person's functioning at home, at work, or with the counselor.

Although no one of these symptoms alone may constitute serious danger, a combination of several of them could be cause for concern. If the counselor feels that any of the client's responses are extreme or prolonged, and if the client does not seem to be able to move forward in the counseling process, then a consultation with a mental health clinician is in order.

Situations that might possibly involve individuals harming themselves or others are especially sensitive and worrisome. It is not unusual for a newly unemployed person to say, for example, "I'm going to kill myself." Although this statement must always be taken seriously, it is important to be able to discern whether a client is seriously depressed or just expressing an exasperated sense of frustration. History of emotional illness, prior suicidal ideation, lack of a support network, and the expression of an intention or plan should be cause for serious concern by counselors and might well be the basis for immediate intervention by appropriate professionals. These cases are rare in outplacement and career management work.

Similarly rare, but also noteworthy, are cases of individuals who appear intact and high functioning when employed but who demonstrate a serious deterioration in functioning when faced with job loss. These situations are more likely to occur when individuals experience the workplace as "home" and are almost completely dependent on their paid employment for a sense of self-definition and purpose. These clients present particular problems in the outplacement office because they frequently substitute the "holding environment" of the outplacement offices for the security of the workplace. The danger is that these individuals are unable to regroup and pursue other employment. They become as dependent on the counseling offices as they had once been dependent on the job.

MANAGING PSYCHOLOGICAL ISSUES
AND THE JOB-SEARCH PROCESS

Although I have briefly touched on some severe cases that might present themselves to career management professionals, the vast majority of clients are appropriate for the task at hand. A model that is helpful in assessing psychological readiness for counseling is illustrated in Fig. 2.1.

The model reflects an interaction between expressing feelings about the losses and changes one has experienced and an ability to move forward in the search process. First, individuals must have an environment in which to express these feelings and a place where the psychological impact of these feelings is understood in order to be able to move forward. However, if individuals are stuck in the feelings without sufficient opportunities or structures that facilitate forward movement, their psychological problems will increase, not decrease. On the other hand, if individuals are asked to move forward without sufficient opportunity to express themselves and work through their feelings, the same result can occur.

SUMMARY AND CONCLUSIONS

Pickman (1994) pointed out that a number of social and economic factors have contributed to the increased need for outplacement services. Along similar lines, I believe that the increased demand for psychologically oriented counseling services in industry, including outplacement, can be attributed to the gradually developing awareness among many corporate managers that the emotional life of their employees is quite relevant to the "bottom line."

Beyond outplacement, progressive companies have begun to recognize the impact that organizational change can have on employees and have begun to pay some attention to those still on board following job eliminations. Having a job in an environment where others have lost theirs does not necessarily make an employee feel happy and secure. Recognition of this has prompted many companies to offer additional support to those who remain in place. The proliferation of stress management and organizational change management programs and the expanding presence of employee assistance programs attest to this trend. There is also an expanded role here for career management professionals. They are needed

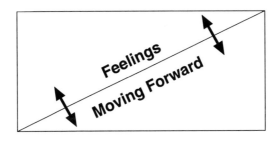

FIG. 2.1. Moving forward feelings.

to focus on the organizational upheaval that leads to job loss and on the effects of the upheaval on those who survive.

In closing, this chapter is designed to encourage career professionals to think beyond the goal of placement and to understand clients within a broader context. Counselors must be fully aware of the important role that work plays in the lives of their clients. As noted earlier, contemporary psychology and psychoanalysis have paid much more attention to love relationships and much less attention to the vital role of work in adult life. It is long overdue for work issues to receive the full attention that they deserve.

It is evident, by now, that work lives are inextricably intertwined with personal lives. Individual identity is more than ever defined by occupational title. In such a context, recently unemployed clients as well as those subjected to organizational upheavals must contend with issues that are rich in psychological complexity. Career management professionals face new and challenging opportunities in assisting individuals in responding to these events.

REFERENCES

American Psychiatric Association (1987). *Diagnostic and statistical manual of mental disorders* (3rd ed., rev.). Washington, DC: Author.

Czander, W. (1993). *The psychodynamics of work and organizations.* New York: Guilford.

Erikson, E. H. (1950). *Childhood and society.* New York: Norton.

Grey, A. L. (1989). The analytic career: Identity changes through adult work roles. *Contemporary Psychoanalysis, 25,* 641–662.

Locker, B. Z., & Epstein, D. (1994, March). *Working within the corporate culture and subculture: The psychoanalyst as corporate and organizational consultant.* Paper presented to the Psychoanalytic Society of the New York University Postdoctoral Program, seventh biennial conference, New York.

Maslow, A. (1954). *Motivation and personality.* New York: Harper & Row.

Pickman, A. J. (1994). *The complete guide to outplacement counseling.* Hillsdale, NJ: Lawrence Erlbaum Associates.

Counseling the Person: Psychological Aspects of Career Counseling

3

Letitia A. Chamberlain
NYU Center for Career, Education, & Life Planning

UNDERSTANDING THE PERSONAL FACTORS

On the face of it, career counseling seems like a simple idea and one easily understood by counseling and career management professionals. The counselor helps individuals make career plans, decisions, and changes. More specifically, and perhaps more broadly, the counselor helps clients seek and get jobs, resolve difficulties experienced in the workplace, and move their careers in the directions they want. Sometimes, that means helping clients pick up the pieces when jobs are lost or plans derailed. Sometimes, it means helping them breathe new life into "tired" work situations. In the simple, although not simplistic, version of counseling, the counselor helps clients sort things through, assess themselves and job market realities, develop options, make decisions, construct action plans, and effect transitions from where they are to where they want to be.

As any experienced counselor knows, however, not all counseling proceeds in this orderly and mutually satisfying way. The counselor can feel stymied; the client frustrated. Sometimes this is the result of job market realities that are just plain distressing. After all, workers in today's job market have to cope with changes in the workplace of a magnitude that may not have been experienced since the Industrial Revolution. Other times, the inability to "feel good" about the work of career counseling has to do with complex factors that clients and counselors alike must consider: (a) increasing employer demands for academic credentials and technical skills, (b) the economic difficulty of sustaining a desired lifestyle, (c) the realities of discrimination in the workplace, (d) the frequently difficult task of balancing family time and, (e) the demands of 60- and 70-hour work weeks. These realities make it difficult to sustain a satisfactory work life and a career that continues to provide both fulfillment and sustenance.

The counselor working with individuals on issues such as these draws on knowledge, skills, and concepts related to the work-world realities, career planning, development, assessment, decision making, job search, and the counseling process. Counselors also need an understanding of the "personal" factors that affect the individuals with whom we work and concepts that enable us to gain the information we need to work effectively with them. It is this latter task in which I have been particularly interested over the past several years; the challenge of using the personal understanding of a client to enhance the career counseling process. It is my experience that for some of our clients progress will not be made unless the counselor understands and addresses personal issues in the counseling process.

Definition of Terms

First, however, I would like to say something about the meaning of the word *personal*, and why I choose that word instead of others. In one sense, of course, counseling of any kind is personal. That is, as the dictionary tells us, it "pertains to" or is "characteristic of a particular person." The dictionary goes on to state that *personal* is used to distinguish the characteristics of an individual, as opposed to the characteristics of "things." Yet the literature of career counseling is filled with arguments on how much of career counseling involves personal counseling and how much it involves "career" counseling, as if careers could be defined as something distinct from the person "living" the career.

In using the term *personal* in this chapter, I do not intend to address the professional arguments regarding the definitions for personal and career counseling. Rather, I am distinguishing those aspects of counseling that seem particular or unique to the person, rather than characteristic aspects of career paths, career planning, career development, decision making, occupations, job market realities, or the many other data to which the counselor and client attend as they work to resolve problems through career counseling. Personal in this context refers to the psychological realities of the client, to the layered meanings for that client of "work" and "career." In choosing to describe this aspect of counseling as personal or psychological, I mean to underscore that the issues with which I am concerned in this chapter have to do with the unique thoughts, feelings, and behaviors of the particular person we seek to help.

I am not concerned here with the facts, the realities, the situation or career of the client, nor even the role of client values, interests, skills, priorities, or preferences in the counseling process. I am addressing a simpler yet more complex topic: namely, the ways in which clients perceive their work, their lives, their roles, themselves—their personal psychological realities. The clarification of these personal meanings, I believe, can positively affect the counseling process, and in some cases, progress cannot be made without examining these personal realities.

Broadening the focus of the counseling in this way can, in some cases, provide challenges to the counselor and client alike, and can frequently, and paradoxically, provide a focus for the counseling that otherwise might "miss" the real concerns of the client. I have avoided as much as possible references to either personality issues or clinical issues to avoid suggesting that the issues discussed here are either as broad as the "person" or as medical (illness requiring treatment) as the "clinic."

At the risk of seeming pedantic, I would like to clarify two other terms: namely, work life and career. Over the past several decades, a number of writers have suggested that career development specialists focus on people's lives rather than careers (McDaniels, 1977; Super, 1957). Richardson (1993) pointed out that a concern with work rather than career allows us to focus on the multiple roles and contexts within which individuals carry out their occupational lives. Outplacement professionals, of course, are primarily concerned with people in the context of employment. Even when employment is the primary focus, professionals who take a broad view of the person, one that includes the person in all of his or her life roles, have a greater chance of understanding their client's employment situation, and can more effectively help clients make decisions related to career, employment, job, or occupation. In some cases, an understanding of the personal concerns or roles of the client is a necessity if progress is to be made.

The idea that work is related to the developing self, over time, is not new. Careers have been defined in terms of a pattern of some or all of life's roles over time (Gysbers & Moore, 1975; McDaniels, 1984; Minor, 1986; Super, 1976, 1984). For many, the concept of career implies a commitment to a particular field of work, to an occupation, or to a particular place of work. Just 40 years ago, Donald Super (1957) pioneered the Career Patterns Study, and broke ground by viewing career as the implementation of one's self-concept over time. His view of a career existing within a developmental framework and changing over a person's lifetime is now commonly accepted.

The current focus on work in the context of life, and the increasing recognition that paid employment is only one of many important life roles, sets the stage for our current acknowledgment that career counseling will likely involve the counselor in some discussion with our clients of their multiple life roles, and broaden our focus to work within the context of a lived life.

Super himself has suggested that for most people there may be as many as seven, eight, or nine roles simultaneously performed by a person at the peak of a "life career" (Super, 1984, p. 33). These roles may be either tangential to or overlap with paid work or occupational roles. Career counselors, focusing as they do on the role of paid work and the issues related to this role, may be unaware, in some cases, of other life roles enacted by their clients, or may see these roles as appropriately tangential to the counseling process. However, it may be that in some cases focusing on these tangential roles may illuminate, in the long run, the career-related problems that brought the person to counseling in the first place.

Careers, as they are actually experienced by the individuals who enter our offices, often have different characteristics than those described as ideal or even as typical careers. Career development specialists recognize that for some clients, careers are decidedly not viewed by them as implementations of self-concepts. They may not even by viewed as the major life role career counselors assume them to be. For example, paid work may play a role that is not clear at first glance. Motivations may be extrinsic, not intrinsic. Or, the motivations may have little to do with the job. Plans may never have been made. Goals may be obscure. Seemingly successful careers sound hollow when described to the counselor. Clients appear to have made unconscious choices, or not perceived that they ever had choices to make. The client may seem unable to make a commitment. Self-concept may be negative. Too narrow a focus on managing or developing a career may lead us down a road where we avoid an examination of their work lives in all the rich complexity of actual experience. The person who comes to us for help may not need to be fully understood in order for us to guide and advise him. But for some clients, the counselor will need to examine the psychological fabric in which work-life reality of the client is woven before counselor and client can determine what the next moves should be.

To understand this psychological fabric is to fully understand the meaning of work in our clients' lives. This fuller understanding of the meaning of work for our clients is what I refer to as the psychological context for a career. Ways to explore this context and the potential fruits of that exploration are perhaps best understood through example and illustration. The people referred to in the following pages do not, in fact, actually exist as described. They are composite examples, created from actual cases. What is true about them are their psychological realities, and the processes through which their progress was made. None of these cases are unusual. If the reader recognizes them, it is because we have all met and talked with people like these.

PSYCHOLOGICAL CONTEXT

Clients come to us as whole persons. They have full lives, fulfill many roles, and have complex personalities. They have lived over time, in many spaces, and have organized their internal experiences according to the meaning of these experiences, including the work experience. The personal meaning of work for any person is not at first apparent to others, including the career counselor, and may not be entirely clear to the client. Discovering, with the client, the meaning of work experiences can be one of the very satisfying processes in the work of the career counselor. I have come to believe that this meaning can best be understood as the "psychological context" for the current career dilemma that the client experiences. By this I mean the matrix of meanings in which the work, job, or career is embedded.

This context can be understood in terms of three aspects of life for the client. The first is developmental; the ways in which the client has changed over time, the transitions he or she has experienced. In other words, this refers to the changes experienced and often described by the client as stages, or chapters in his or her life story. The second theme is also developmental but refers to growth in terms of the self, a unique self-definition, or sense of identity that each person creates. The third aspect refers to the situational aspects of the client's life. What roles, responsibilities, and relationships dominate the internal world of the client? With what social groups does he or she identify? Family, ethnicity, race, sexual orientation, nation, class, religion, generation, geographic region—these are typically relevant in counseling. The important identifications are those that dominate the thoughts and feelings of the client, not the demographic characteristics that are statistically accurate.

The ways in which these experiences of change, identity, and social context are perceived and organized by clients create the psychological context within which their jobs, work, and careers are experienced. Understanding this context can become a useful focus of counseling when we reach an impasse in our efforts to help a client; when we find what seems obvious to us as counselors does not match the clients perceptions, or when we have other indications that a fuller understanding of the client may be required in order to resolve whatever problems are left unresolved.

A CAST OF CHARACTERS

In order to illustrate the quality and flavor of this kind of exploration, I introduce a cast of characters, whose stories, I hope, illustrate the ways in which an exploration of the psychological context of the clients' presenting problems can contribute to an "unblocking" of an impasse in the counseling process. I am not illustrating success stories but rather, how the clarification of the undercurrents of meanings for the client can be used to further the counseling, to unlock impasses, to identify the next steps that must be taken with or without the help of the counselor. Such explorations may at first seem irrelevant or at least not a direct approach to the counseling problem. They are, rather, ways of counseling the person, and integrating the multiple strands of meaning associated with work, life, and career for that person.

The first client is Bud. A friend had referred him for career counseling because he was questioning everything about his work and his marriage.

At 40 years of age, with a wife and two children and a highly paid position in a bank, Bud was concerned that he might soon be a candidate for job termination due to technology-driven across-the-board cuts. In a matter-of-fact tone, Bud described his distaste for the work he did and said he wanted to make a radical career change.

Earlier that year, Jack had called and said that he wanted advice because he had recently sold his successful business and was having trouble deciding what to do next. A middle-aged, soft-spoken, intense man, Jack lived in a wealthy community in New Jersey, and made it clear when he called for an appointment that the idea for counseling originated with his wife, although he was willing to give it a try.

Rose's career in law had been a successful one. Now in her late 30s, her position was about to be eliminated. She decided to try career counseling, despite her reservations. She needed help, she said, deciding what to do next. She had never been very gratified by any of her several positions in law and seemed to have no expectation that she would in the future.

Margaret was not quite sure whether she should see the counselor who specialized in job search or the one who would help her reevaluate career goals. Unemployed for more than a year, she had lost her management job when her company merged with another. She had been very depressed, and had no idea what she wanted to do. She thought a radical career change might be the answer.

Why am I focusing on these particular clients? Perhaps because in each case I had had the experience of wondering if we had gotten "off track"—whether, in fact, anything positive was happening—when a "surprise" occurred in the counseling. The road these clients traveled was circuitous; it was not always clear whether the detour would lead back to the main road. The surprise occurred when client and counselor arrived at an answer to a question that had not been clearly formulated at the outset. Formulating the right question turned out, in the end, to provide the answer to the career problem with which we had started.

In each case, the turning point in the process can be understood in terms of the psychological context of the client's career. As we all know, satisfactory resolutions are often reached without having to explore psychological context at all. However, those are not the cases being discussed here. For these clients, the reformulation of the "right" question to ask grew out of explorations and understandings of their life and career development, the clarification of their self-definitions or identities, including an occupational identity, and the examination of the social, family, and cultural contexts that shaped the experiences of work for the clients. Not surprisingly, each person's psychological space contained elements of all three dimensions: development, self, and context. In each case, however, the exploration of one factor led to the others and opened up the doors to discovery much as a step down one side road can ultimately lead to a whole new vista, not seen when that first step was taken.

Jack

Let's get down to cases. Jack provides us with a good example of the way in which the exploration of the client's psychological context led to a reformulation of the questions the client asked himself, and the problem he wished to resolve. Jack's difficulty deciding what he would do next had multiple causes. He was experiencing difficulty navigating the developmental issues posed by his ending the career he had developed first as a corporate manager and then as a businessman in his own partnership. He was experiencing a crisis of identity and self-definition as he confronted the fact of his aging, the fact of his wealth and independence, and the fact that he no longer had a set of expectations, rules, or guidelines for making his own choices. Finally, he was conscious of his social context: his relationships with his family and his neighbors, and he felt diminished in both. He felt a lack of respect from his suburban neighbors because he was unemployed and associated a lack of status with the loss of an occupational identity. The burden of having to assume domestic roles also left him feeling both guilty and depleted.

As he explored his feelings regarding his life, his past, his struggles, and his current pain, Jack moved from a position of choosing among alternative forms of employment (self-employed, new partner, consultant), to a quest for self-definition. Given freedom of choice, which he now had for the first time in his life, could he allow himself to explore his "inner terrain," as well as the external world and its many possibilities? Such a journey was one that he both relished and feared.

As he talked about having arrived at this peculiar point in life, where he was so wealthy that it was an embarrassment, deep fears had emerged. He felt that he was at the end of the road he had followed in life. He was alive and well, restless, unfulfilled, and without direction.

Highly conscious of his age, a feeling enhanced by the death of his business partner, the parenting challenges posed by his adolescent daughter, and the desire of his wife to get a job, Jack had no set roles to perform. Work had always defined his tasks, and now he felt terrified at the lack of structure and the growing realization that it was he who was to set the tasks and define the roles.

As counseling proceeded, he asked himself why this was so scary, and began to construct a different description of his life stage. At the conclusion of the counseling, he would describe his present stage as one where he was emerging from a long dark tunnel, and now could see the blue sky opening up at the end of the darkness.

When the sky's the limit, the question of what to do now can no longer be framed in terms of finding a next job. It is, rather, a question closer to this: "Who am I really, and what is it that I want to do before I die?" The realization that his stage in life involved this opportunity and this danger was Jack's turning point. Once he began to describe his current stage of life in terms of where he had been and where he wanted to go, he opened himself up to an exploration of his current feelings. Jack tamed his terror with the excitement he felt about making his own choices. He could now formulate goals and desires hitherto unexplored, and enjoy an independence that he had not experienced even while he succeeded in life as an independent businessman.

Bud

The convergence of development, identity, and context, all aspects of personal meaning, can be seen in another case, both similar to and different from Jack's. Bud, at age 40, also experienced himself as a man struggling to define himself anew after a lifetime of self-definition that no longer fit. Bud had been alcoholic since he was 17 and in spite of being successfully in recovery for 5 years, still defined himself as a drunk who had somehow managed to work, to rise in the ranks of his company, to assume greater responsibilities over the years, to earn a six-figure income. He did not regard himself as a success, however, but rather as a man who had been lucky, a Black man succeeding in a White world, and one who felt he had no significant achievements in life except becoming sober. Bud stated his problem at the beginning of counseling as one of identifying alternate forms of employment outside of the finance industry (in which he stated he had no interest). He was not in immediate danger of unemployment, but saw the "handwriting on the wall."

As the counseling progressed, however, it became apparent that Bud was already engaged in a significant process of discovery. A year before he came for counseling, he and his wife had embarked on what he described as fruitful meetings with a psychotherapist. In his therapy, Bud stated, he discussed his marriage and his family life, and examined some of his basic assumptions about being a good husband and good father. In career counseling, Bud also entered eagerly into an examination of his basic assumptions and the ways he had managed in the work world. He talked about his failures and achievements in school, the army, and in the bank where he had achieved career and monetary "success" devoid of any feelings of accomplishment and despite his personal difficulties with alcohol. The developmental themes for Bud began to emerge as he looked at himself in the work world. He began to assert his authority on the job without being preoccupied with how others saw him, and to realize that he wanted more from his job than just "scraping by."

Bud's central quest, in his therapy and in his career counseling, appeared to be one of self-definition. In terms of career, this meant exploring for the first time what it was he really liked to do, what skills he wished to emphasize, and in what positions he felt he could best define himself. Because Bud defined himself first as the head of a family, as a husband and a father, and because achievement in a career mattered little to him outside of its relationship to his role as head of family, he talked about the work-related issues with which he was concerned in terms of his ability to work at a job that he liked that would compensate him sufficiently to maintain his family life. The social context of Bud's career was central to its meaning for him. He was first a husband and father, and then a worker. He had siblings who looked to him for support and guidance. He was the child who had "made it" and felt a responsibility to his immediate and his extended family. He was also a member of the community of recovering alcoholics, and a Black man in a White world. Bud valued these roles, and took seriously his responsibilities to each of the social units that constituted his world.

When Bud had explored this psychological terrain, he reformulated his questions to focus on his quest for self-definition, and the exploration of what he might do to insure that his next steps in the work world might reflect his increasing desire to succeed on the basis of skills and goals rather than luck and happenstance. He realized as counseling proceeded that before he could decide to leave his field, he would have to open his eyes to the wider world in which he worked; that his focus had always been narrow because his interest had been simply "getting by." When he did, he decided that obtaining educational credentials would be the surest way of increasing both his skills and his job security.

Both Bud and Jack struggled with issues of identity that reflected their stage in life, the events and situations of their lives, and their personal quest for self-definition. Interestingly, the two women I recalled were able to answer their career questions by exploring the personal meaning of work in their lives.

Rose

Both Rose and Margaret came to counseling asking: "What do I do next?" For Rose, a lawyer, 39 years of age, the question was precipitated by the impending elimination of the position she had held for several years. For Margaret, who had lost her job a year and a half prior to counseling, the question represented the first step she was able to take as she pulled herself out of the depression the layoff had created. In each case, however, the question was transformed in the process of counseling through an almost inadvertent line of questioning that related to family life, both past and present, and to questions of identity and self-definition. Self-definition for each of these women involved learning to distinguish their own preferences from those of their fathers.

Rose had been an outstanding law student, and, by any standard, had an extremely successful career. It was difficult at first to determine exactly why she had come for counseling. She said she needed to explore alternatives within law in order to be prepared when her position was cut. She needed no guidance in this exploration, however, showing up at each session with a long list of leads she had pursued, possibilities she had or would explore, and decisions she had reached. The puzzling aspect of her presentation of her feelings about work was that she evidenced little enthusiasm for law, had never been very fulfilled in any of her positions, yet clearly believed that this was the right field for her. It seemed that the problem was simply where to go next, and she clearly stated that she did not really have an expectation that she would find anything more satisfying than a law career, and each week she proceeded nicely to identify options and explore them.

How then did any other perspective emerge? In a line of questioning that involved discussion about family expectations, Rose revealed that her father wanted to be a lawyer, that he had never been satisfied with the level of achievement in his own career. She had always felt that her achievement had been very important to him. As Rose continued in counseling, she discussed her conflicts over her wish to succeed as a lawyer (a wish that could easily be fulfilled if it were merely a matter of intelligence, opportunity and know-how) and her wish to have another child. The developmental stage for Rose involved both personal age and career stage. If she were to have another child, this was the time. If she were to achieve new heights in her career, now was also the moment. The decision became a source of conflict, however, because what was also involved was the question of self-definition. Through discussion of the meaning to her of her work, it became clear that the direction her law career should take was not the direction her father would view as the most successful. The question then became: Whose career and whose life was it anyway?

In addition, it was clear that fulfillment in her family roles was critical to her sense of self. As she clarified the meaning of work in relation to her stage of life, her sense of self, and her roles in both her family of origin and family of choice, the question that she struggled with emerged. The broader social context (broader than family, that is), in which Rose was raised and in which she lived contributed to her conflict. She came from an achievement-oriented social class where it was taken for granted that if you had the ability, you rose to the top. She had the abilities. She needed "permission" from a counselor not to rise.

Margaret

Margaret, on the other hand, had already risen to the top of her industry. A successful marketing specialist, she had won the admiration of family and friends by being inordinately successful in a highly competitive business. It was easy to understand the depression that followed her loss of position. In her early 40s, Margaret had experienced nothing but success. She rose to the top in every enterprise she undertook. After her divorce 5 years earlier, Margaret's job had become not just the central activity in her life, but the central meaning in her life as well. She worked long hours, and took great pleasure in her achievements. In her view, she *became* the job.

Embittered by her loss of position at the height of her career, Margaret came to counseling asking what she should do. She knew that the one thing she did not want to do was what she had already done in the same field. An engaging, gentle-mannered woman, Margaret thoughtfully mulled over possibilities, but as she progressed in counseling, her attention kept returning to her early loves: music, art, literature, learning. Eventually she came to the themes that led not to the answer to the questions she brought to counseling, but to the breakdown of the impasse she reached each time she reviewed what she might do and why it would not work out. Once again, Margaret's story illustrates the importance of exploring psychological context and the meaning of work within that context.

Here is what emerged. In response to a question about her family of origin, Margaret reflected on her family's values and stated that, in her family, being a visual artist was the only thing that really counted. In particular, she described a father who had considerable artistic talent, and brothers who entered arts-related professions. She also described an unhappy childhood, and briefly stated that she had spent a lot of her childhood feeling that she was a disappointment and a failure. Her lack of talent was further evidence of that failure. Fortunately, Margaret had a therapist with whom she could discuss these family dynamics. What was especially interesting was that in the process of this digression, Margaret realized that she had never done what *she* wanted to do.

The realization deepened. Eventually she concluded that she had always aimed to gain the approval and acceptance of others. Even though her family had little respect for business success, they admired her because she had risen to the top. She had money, status, and, finally, respect from the family who had denied it to her before. As a child, she had always felt unworthy and disconnected from her family. At last, through her employment she became a kind of celebrity.

In counseling, we examined the meaning of work in her life and career. Tracing the developmental theme provided one source of insight. Margaret's career was central to the meaning in her life, and that career had come to an abrupt halt. One path had ended, and the next move had to be made based solely on her own choice. She worked as a freelance consultant in her field but wanted to make a change to something more meaningful. As we explored the reasons for her difficulty generating possible options, it became apparent that she did not experience her successful career as reflecting her own interests, values, or sense of self. By tracing the developmental path her career had taken, we were brought directly to the question of self-definition.

Margaret's undeveloped sense of self became evident when she was unable to answer questions about her own likes and dislikes, her preferences, her wishes. As we talked, it became increasingly evident to us both that she had always experienced herself as a "good girl" who did what was expected, who was capable and hard-working, who would always rise to the top of whatever organization she was in, but who had never chosen *where* she wanted to be. As counseling proceeded, Margaret asked herself new questions: What was it in life that she really wanted to do? What were her own interests and needs? Whose career was it? Was it really okay to earn less and enjoy more?

As we discussed these questions, Margaret reflected not only on the role that work had played in gaining her family's approval, but also the added rewards of acceptance and respect within her social context. She was looked up to both on the job and off. She enjoyed being in control, having a high income, and being viewed by others as successful. She almost forgot that she did not like her work, or her industry, and had little respect for her achievements.

As counseling progressed, Margaret gradually began to pay attention to the nonwork aspects of her life, and by doing so put paid employment in its proper place. It became something she wanted to do in order to feel productive, to earn an income, and to express her interests. She reevaluated how much income was "enough," and began to feel that her job did not have to provide the only avenue for self-expression, identity, and acceptance. When Margaret took the "loading" off the job, it became easier to explore the ways in which she could earn the money she needed and, at the same time, engage in activities that would provide her with the sense of involvement and the enjoyment that had been missing throughout her life and career.

DISCUSSION

Successful outcomes in counseling do not always require an exploration of the psychological context of clients' concerns, and the personal meaning of work in their lives. The question, then, arises: How do we know when to explore these meanings and this context? I have found several indicators that can signify that attention must be paid to the personal meaning of work for the client.

One is the persistent introduction by the client of personal data, and the frequent reference to particular nonwork events, issues, people, or self. Jack's references to his poverty, age, teenage daughter, and wealth were openers for fruitful exploration of his life transitions; the meaning of work in his life, and the way he perceived his present state. Bud, who consistently referred to the fact that he was "just a drunk"—a recovering alcoholic 3 years sober—allowed the counselor to address the issue with him directly. We directed the counseling, temporarily, away from the career problem—the job that would soon be eliminated—and toward the problems inherent in shaping one's identity for the first time in middle age. Margaret began her story by talking about her father and her brothers, and comparing herself unfavorably to them. Her sessions were filled with references to these early years, but not until they became a focus for discussion did important insights emerge.

Another indicator is the conspicuous lack of any personal data, even when one might expect it. No personal data was introduced by Rose, despite her having stated that she had never been happy in her work. When the counselor asked more questions about personal matters, Rose acknowledged for the first time that she was struggling with the question of whether to have another child and whether it would limit her current career. Rose, it turned out, wanted to shift the focus of her work, and also to shift her attention toward her family. However, in career counseling she felt she must only discuss the career questions. Her view shifted when the counselor identified the connections between work and nonwork roles in her life.

So, what can we learn from these stories? Perhaps we can use them to illustrate the importance of exploration and discovery in the counseling process. When the client asks the counselor, "What do I do now?", the counselor needs to discover, with the client, just what constitutes "now," keeping in mind that now can only be defined by distinguishing it from "then." Once the now is understood, the "to be" can be constructed. No one who enters our counseling offices comes to us free of a past or a future. They are all from somewhere, and on their way to somewhere else. How they perceive their past and future will likely have much to do with how they perceive the present. The perceptions themselves are grounded in the fundamental sense of self each person carries with him or her, and these self concepts shape the visions the individuals have of themselves and their futures. Finally, the grounding of our clients in time, place, and the fabric of human relationships, serves as the ballast, supports, and constraints as they move forward in their quest for answers to questions that are continually changing.

REFERENCES

Gysbers, N. C., & Moore, E. J. (1975). Beyond career development—life career development. *The Personnel and Guidance Journal, 53*, 647–652.

McDaniels, C. (1977). leisure and career development at mid-life: A rationale. *Vocational Guidance Quarterly, 25*(4), 356–363.

McDaniels, C. (1984). Work and leisure in the career span. In N. C. Gysbers & Associates, *Designing careers* (pp. 558–590). San Francisco: Jossey-Bass.

Minor, C. W. (1986). Career development: Theories and issues. In Z. B. Leibowitz & H. D. Lea (Eds.), *Adult career development: Concepts, issues and practices* (pp. 17–39). Alexandria, VA: National Career Development Association.

Richardson, M. S. (1993). Work in people's lives: A location for counseling psychologists. *Journal of Counseling Psychology, 40*(4), 1–9.

Super, D. E. (1957). *The psychology of careers*. New York: Harper & Row.
Super, D. E. (1976). *Career education and the meanings of work*. Washington, DC: U.S. Government Printing Office.
Super, D. E. (1984). Perspectives on the meaning and value of work. In N. C. Gysbers & Associates, *Designing careers* (pp. 27–53). San Francisco: Jossey-Bass.

4 Identity Formation in Outplacement and Career Management Counselors

Sandra Bowers
Citibank, London

Unlike the majority of counseling disciplines that offer specific routes to professional development, certification, and identity, career and outplacement counseling has, since its inception, allowed entry from the widest variety of sources. From the beginning, outplacement as a counseling occupation was open to all who believed they had the skill to assist displaced executives, who could be credible to corporate clients as well as counselees, and who could effectively market their qualifications. Individuals entered the field from backgrounds in executive recruiting, social work, information management, counseling psychology, business management, health care, training, teaching, school psychology, marketing, college career centers, organization development, administration, and military service to name several routes, but by no means all. In fact, many of the earliest counselors were executives who had themselves been outplaced and who sought to use their coaching skills, business knowledge, and management experience to assist others in their transitions.

Outplacement was, and still is, a counseling field requiring no specific or advanced degrees and no narrow band of credentials. Individuals came to it with PhDs, MBAs, MSWs, and MAs of great variety, BAs in many disciplines, and even with no formal college degrees at all. A knowledge of business and an ability to relate to senior executives was the most important requirement for many early counselors.

Settings, too, were varied and numerous. An outplacement counselor could work as an independent practitioner, a small business owner, a career consultant within a large corporation, or a staff counselor for a career management firm.

Although this variety added enormous richness, depth, and broad expertise to the field, it also resulted in confusion and marked differences in how the outplacement counselors saw themselves and how they viewed their work. Was outplacement a business or a profession? Were outplacement professionals coaches, counselors, teachers, trainers, or simply peers sharing knowledge of the best way to job search? Where did outplacement counseling end and psychological counseling begin? Were there deeper issues being tapped within the counselor–candidate relationships and were counselors qualified to deal with them? And where, exactly, did outplacement and career counselors fit in the ranks of other counseling professions?

These are questions that I personally have struggled with since I entered the field in 1980. To answer them, one needs to explore the many roles of an outplacement counselor. Unlike many other counseling professions where the relationship is more singularly focused, the roles of an outplacement counselor change and take on a different weight at different stages of the outplacement relationship. Since 1993, we have had some guidelines through The Outplacement Institute as to how these roles might be categorized.

The Competencies Standards present a daunting profile of a multiskilled professional able to shift from a marketing and management role, to a one-on-one counselor with assessment expertise, to a subject matter expert in job search imparting this knowledge to individuals or to various size groups. Then, the practitioner often shifts to a career management and executive development coach. What is not addressed by these categories is the meaning of each role to the practitioner and its place in the whole of one's professional identity. With such a complex menu of possibilities, it is critical that outplacement professionals have a firm fix on the roles most congruent with their style and skills and that this grounding allows them to present a clear picture to the corporate candidate, the counselee and, most importantly, to themselves. Let us explore the roles, one by one, and the questions each raises for our view of ourselves.

THE ROLES OF THE OUTPLACEMENT COUNSELOR

Consultant to Corporations and Organizational Candidates

Outplacement counseling differs from most other counseling professions in the way in which it is initiated. Most often, the first interaction is not with the counselee, but rather with the referring source, usually a corporate manager or human resources professional who is making the determination about what services the counselee should receive and how much the sponsoring organization is willing to pay for the services. This interaction can be as simple as a presentation by the outplacement professional of the services that will be offered to the counselee. Sometimes, however, it also entails working with the corporation on their career development or downsizing strategies including a determination of who will be included and affected, coaching management on proper communication, and even working with individual managers on how to conduct a termination session. Although in some outplacement organizations this contact is made through a marketing person rather than a counselor, the skills required to advise the organization and "make the sale" are necessary for most counselors.

How does this interaction impact a counselor's identity? It often depends on the person's background. Those from a background in management, strategic planning, or organization development will take naturally to this role, embracing the opportunity to have an impact on the organization's effectiveness, profitability and, in some cases, even survival. For other counselors, particularly those who come to the field from a psychological counseling background, this role presents a conflict—a necessary, but unpleasant, activity they must get through in order to assist the counselee. Still others see it is a challenge—adding a business dimension to the outplacement profession that is unavailable in other counseling fields and that makes outplacement more interesting to them. Many who have embraced the full scope of an outplacement practice's professional requirements, view the role as an important up-front opportunity to assure that career management and outplacement services are delivered properly, terminations are done fairly and humanely, and that those affected are given the best possible services available. They see each party, known and unknown, as their client, all in need of counseling. As such, the marketing transaction becomes a counseling session, designed to minimize the pain often experienced by everyone involved. It is this view of the organizational consulting role that allows many counselors to maintain their sense of personal integrity.

Consultant to Candidates on an Individual Basis

Whereas it may seem that this is the core role for most outplacement professionals, it is important to consider what this role actually entails and to begin to challenge some of the common assumptions about the role. For many of us, the opportunity to work one-on-one with candidates in transition, and often in distress, provides the essence of our professional identity. Looking more closely at this role, however, one begins to see subsets that are key differentiators. What type of candidates do I prefer to work with? Am I more comfortable with short-term counseling interactions or do I prefer the opportunity to build solid, long-term counseling relationships that enable me to touch some deeper, personal issues? Do I see myself as a strategist, working on the broad reach of an individual's career goals or as a subject matter specialist and teacher, guiding candidates through a disciplined process leading them to their next jobs?

Some counselors prefer to work only with senior, smart, motivated candidates and they see themselves as partners in the development of the candidates' next career steps. They provide vision, expertise, and advice to a receptive audience, who is willing to respect the counselor's authority and act on their recommendations. Other counselors develop an identity built around helping the less sophisticated candidates who need gentle step-by-step hand-holding through the entire process. They enjoy seeing the process unfold over time as candidates discover their own capability. Still others gravitate to candidates who are likely to encounter long and difficult job searches and pride themselves on staying with these candidates as they slowly overcome their personal and professional obstacles and become more marketable job searchers and more productive professionals.

Most counselors who work one-on-one with candidates work, or have worked, with all of these types of candidates and many more. But, over time, most counselors not only develop preferences, they develop a sense of themselves and their place in the field, which is built around those preferences. Understanding and claiming the preferences is essential to the formation of one's professional identity.

Consultant to Candidates on a Group Basis

Probably more than many other counseling disciplines, career transition and outplacement counseling offers practitioners an opportunity to work regularly with groups. There are many types of group activities that are part of the career transition process and the wide variety offers counselors an excellent opportunity to find or develop a special niche. This enables them to differentiate themselves, both within the field and within their own minds.

Groups can be formed as one-time events for a morning, a day, or 2 or 3 days with the goal of imparting specific job search related information in the most efficient or cost-saving way possible. Although there is interaction and sharing that takes place in these short-term groups, the group leader is primarily responsible for teaching content, facilitating learning, motivating through information, and leaving participants with a sense of calm and control based on a knowledge of how to proceed. Although content is important here, above all, the group leader must make the material interesting and easy to learn. This requires not only an ease with the subject matter, but a bit of "show biz" as well. The best leaders of these types of groups find the perfect balance between the two. Because these groups are time limited, there is often very little long-term connection between the group leader and the participants. Some counselors enjoy this type of activity more than others. They love the special twist they alone bring to their material. Others find these groups routine, repetitious, and tedious, and they miss the ongoing relationships that can be formed with other types of groups and with individual candidates.

There are other types of groups that offer connection and ongoing relationships, though not to the same degree as working with individual candidates. Support groups, "attack" or "focus" groups, networking groups, and ongoing groups, made up of homogeneous job searchers, fall into this category. These groups offer counselors a chance to facilitate individual expression within a group setting as well as to guide group interaction. They also offer counselors the opportunity to see candidates "in action" and to get a different sense of what issues might be impacting their job search. Each of these types of ongoing, interactive groups requires special skills of group facilitation. The leader must know how and when to intervene, how to encourage participants to share without fear, and how to manage the conflict that might emerge in one of these groups. This is a skill not available to everyone who becomes a career transition counselor, nor is it a skill everyone wishes to develop. As with other professional activities, it is important to know both your interest and abilities in group formats.

Assessment

Between the extremes of counselors who refer all assessment exercises to a dedicated assessment center or professional and those who do only assessment and feedback but no ongoing counseling, there is a wide variety of assessment knowledge, training, certification, and skill among outplacement practitioners.

If assessment can be categorized as the process by which counselors gain an understanding of candidates on many dimensions and help the candidates gain an understanding of themselves, then all counselors do assessment to some degree. There would be no way of helping candidates manage career transitions without getting to know them and their needs.

What differentiates counselors here is the comfort level they experience with sophisticated assessment tools and techniques and standardized psychometric instruments, the amount of training they have received in administering and interpreting instruments that require certification, their preference for standardized instruments versus interview-based assessment, the degree of insight they bring to interpreting the available data and, finally, their skill in sharing those insights with the candidate. It takes both interest and practice to gain expertise in the use of assessment tools and many outplacement counselors prefer to rely on their growing relationship with the candidate rather than to use more formal assessment methods. They believe that through well-developed interview techniques, they gain a better understanding of the candidate's many personal dimensions and through regular interaction, they get a full picture of a candidate's character. Others, having gained comfort and success with a certain approach or instrument, lobby for that approach as the "best."

Still others use a complex battery of standardized instruments as the foundation for future understanding, an outline to be filled in through the ongoing relationship. However, just as with the other competencies, it is important here to claim one's preferences in assessment, to know one's limitations, to understand how many different ways there are to arrive at the same ends, and to present one's capabilities honestly and accurately to the corporate customer, the candidate, and the field.

Job-Search Training

Unless counselors have carved out a very narrow and specialized niche for themselves (assessment, marketing, information management, delivery of specific group content), it is impossible to practice in the field of outplacement without being able to do job-search training. Job-search training encompasses every process and subject necessary to conduct an effective job campaign. It is separate from the individual counseling and assessment competencies in that it focuses on the external marketplace and on action versus reflection.

Starting with helping a candidate plan a job-search strategy, job-search training takes a candidate through each of the critical elements for mounting a job-search campaign: setting targets, doing research, preparing a resumé, developing and using a network, tapping the formal job-search systems, presenting oneself effectively in networking conversations and job interviews, and, finally, negotiating the job offer. Although there is a mountain of practical knowledge a counselor must master in order to be skilled in this competency, it is a part of the outplacement counseling discipline that is embraced by many counselors. They enjoy the strategizing, the problem solving, the focus on maneuvering skillfully in the external marketplace. This is the part of outplacement counseling that comes closest to running a business, to managing a staff, and to coaching junior staff members.

In some instances, there is a great divide between those counselors who handle this part of the counseling relationship effectively and those who are more skillful in helping candidates explore their inner world through assessment and self-reflection. Clearly, the learning and counseling style required for each of these aspects of outplacement counseling are vastly different, as is the counselor's approach to the candidate. In the initial counseling and assessment phase, the counselor is a reflective guide, allowing the candidate's awareness to emerge through self-discovery, thereby enabling candidates to claim their own insights. In the job-search training mode, the counselor is a teacher, actively sharing her or his special expertise and knowledge with the candidate and frequently encouraging candidates to trust the counselor's way of doing things, rather than trusting their own natural style or instincts. It is, therefore, especially important in this phase that counselors stay current with all the latest trends, marketplace data, and employment information. Furthermore, they need to know where and how to find tangible information on industries, fields, companies, and job categories, and they need to be able to convince candidates of their expertise in order to impact their job-search strategy. Not every counselor is willing to take on this challenge. In fact, market and industry data is one of the most underexplored aspects of outplacement training. This often poses a dilemma in hiring an outplacement counselor. Does one hire a savvy business person or executive recruiter and train this person in counseling skills, or does one hire a person with strong counseling skills and train him or her in business disciplines? And, how realistic is it to expect one counselor to be all things to each candidate? These are questions for industry leaders but they are also questions for individual counselors in forming their identities.

Career Counseling

It would seem that everything we have talked about so far constitutes "career counseling." How, then does one separate this competency from those already mentioned? Although the differences may be subtle, career counseling is that part of the outplacement counseling discipline that addresses long-term career goals and strategies and that assists candidates in looking beyond the next job to the management of their careers over their entire work life. Here, the focus of counseling knowledge shifts from aligning the candidate's skills, interests, values, and personal style with the next career move and looks more at the skills, interests, values, and personal style necessary to succeed in specific job and career choices either in the present or in the future. Although this expertise certainly comes into play in working with a candidate's immediate job search, a different perspective and time horizon is required when dealing with long-term career and life and work planning. In addition, the counselor must posses a very broad knowledge of jobs, careers, industry and corporate cultures, and various career and life stages and strategies, both conventional and unconventional. In this competency, it is the counselor's role to introduce the candidates to options they may never have thought to explore and to free them from the restraints—lack of vision, fear, inertia, negativism—that might keep them stuck in unsatisfactory jobs and career paths. For the counselor, it often requires imagination, daring, creativity, resilience, and an almost missionary zeal to challenge candidates' narrow views of the future and to inspire them to take risks with no certainty of the outcome. Not all counselors can do this work well. Those who can often find it difficult to work with candidates stuck in long and difficult job searches. Again, it is these subtle differentiations of role and style that help each of us find our special niche in this amazingly diverse professional discipline.

FINDING OUR OWN SPECIAL IDENTITY

What actually is "professional identity" and what is its importance? In some ways, forming and claiming a professional identity is practicing what we preach. Although we often encourage and assist our candidates in defining their special niche, the "unique selling proposition," we frequently do not expect the same of ourselves. We either expect ourselves or are expected by others to be able to be equally effective in all of the outplacement competencies in working with all types of clients and in practicing in all types of settings. Because this is rarely possible, many counselors feel inadequate in some portion of their work. Having a strong sense of your particular skills, style, and expertise does not mean that you must work in that area alone, or that you cannot or should not go beyond your comfort zone. Many counseling disciplines are divided into specialties but practitioners frequently work outside of the boundaries. A couples or family therapist sometimes works with individuals; clinical psychologists conduct groups as part of their one-on-one therapy practice; substance-abuse counselors deal with a variety of addictions. Knowing yourself and your preferences, however, gives direction and focus to your work. It allows you to specialize and excel in those areas in which you excel. It also allows corporate clients and candidates to have a clear understanding of what you can and will deliver. Furthermore, it enables you to develop an enduring confidence in those skills you use well and enjoy and a tolerance for doing some things less well without being overly self-critical.

It has been difficult for outplacement counseling to see itself as a unified profession with practice standards that cut across all affiliates. The acceptance of The Outplacement Institute, its Competencies Standards, and its certification process has helped, but we are still a field struggling to reconcile the need to be both a profession and a business. There are still gaps in our own ranks between those who focus on one or the other, between those who believe in strict professional "credentialing" and those who believe that professional identity springs from the business organization with which you are affiliated.

Our strength has been our inclusiveness, our willingness to embrace practitioners from so many different backgrounds and with so many different skills. As a field, we must continue to seek that diversity but, as individuals, we will benefit both from broadening our view of the profession and from bringing more focus to our view of ourselves.

In 1980, when I was still new to the career counseling field, I attended an American Association for Counseling and Development (AACD) conference in Washington with several of my new-found colleagues. The keynote speaker at that conference was Richard Bolles, and he spoke to us as fellow professionals, not as novices. At that time, the career counseling field was deeply fragmented and Bolles spoke to those divisions with vision and eloquence. Using the analogy of the blind men viewing an elephant, he delineated the competing views of what career counseling seemed to be at the time—recruiting, job-skill training, job-search coaching, life and work planning—and spoke of how each group held firmly to the belief that they were doing the most needed work. In the end, he said, we are all dealing with the same thing. We are all seeking to help individuals regain their self-esteem in the face of displacement and career uncertainty. As such, we are all in the same profession, the profession of healing. That speech was a seminal moment for me in forming my own professional identity. It is a view of myself that I have carried with me ever since and it has enabled me to embrace, fully, parts of our profession and to minimize others with the clear knowledge that whatever I choose as my focus will be a part of my mission to help heal.

I believe it is time for each of us to claim our own part of the elephant, knowing that without the parts, the whole is not a living, breathing, very alive being.

II

COUNSELING SPECIAL POPULATIONS

5 Helping the Reluctant Networker

Mark J. Carsman
Career Management Consultant, New York

INTRODUCTION

If there is anything career consultants can agree on, it is that networking is a hugely important tool in career change and job search. Equally noncontroversial among career consultants is the view that clients who avoid or underemploy networking are hurting themselves and their efforts. Indeed, this belief in the value of networking within the career management profession verges on being the equivalent of divinely communicated doctrine.

This is why most consultants and virtually all published guidance in the field urges, exhorts, and cajoles clients to embrace networking as a central part of their job search and ongoing career management practices. Despite this overwhelming emphasis on networking, a disturbing number of clients refrain from or underutilize networking.

This situation can be very frustrating to the well-intentioned consultant, especially when the client's other activities are proving unproductive. This frustration does neither party any good and can threaten and even destroy the consultant–client relationship. This often happens when the consultant becomes, or comes to be perceived as, an unhelpful "nag" or when the client is, or comes to be perceived as, uncooperative or not truly motivated to achieve expressed goals.

This chapter focuses on some alternative ways of looking at this situation that have proven to be productive for both consultant and client.

NETWORKING RELUCTANCE: A PRACTICABLE DEFINITION

The way one defines or labels a given matter often determines whether (a) the matter is viewed as a problem at all, (b) it is a severe or trivial matter, (c) it is important to fix, and (d) its solution can or will be possible and how one will attempt to resolve it.

51

By way of analogy, consider the probable reaction by both the attending physician and the patient in reaction to the following diagnostic labels: *highly treatable, chronic, malignant, refractory*, and *terminal*. One label may lead to hope, activity, and healing; another could lead to despair, inactivity, and death. It is the same with the use of labeling in networking.

I have found the terms *networking reluctance* and *reluctant networker* to be more descriptive of reality and, more importantly, of great usefulness in dealing with what are more typically called *non-networkers*. As a diagnostic label, non-networkers connotes clients who do not and will never network. In contrast, the reluctant networker or networking-reluctant client is one who might never network at all, or might do it all the time (albeit uncomfortably), or something in between.

The term also embraces people who overtly and actively reject networking, as well as those who passively or covertly reject or define the networking process to suit their personal needs and discomforts; as when they redefine networking as sending resumes to people instead of trying to gain a personal contact. The breadth and inclusive nature of this definition is valuable in that its lack of specificity encourages a problem-solving frame of mind and approach to the matter in each case.

Networking reluctance has other benefits, as well. It has been my experience that this term is relatively nonjudgmental, carrying little in the way of negative semantic baggage for the client. Clients are comfortable describing themselves, and being described as a reluctant networker or having networking reluctance. On the other hand, many clients object to or appear uncomfortable with being called a non-networker. They sense the social undesirability inherent in that label and the implicit need to defend against it, because it casts them as being contrary to what most people appear generally to accept as "good."

In summary, networking reluctance or reluctant networker are terms that provide clients with a socially comfortable way of indicating a less-than-positive position regarding networking, without provoking the need to defend and further entrench such a position. These terms, therefore, facilitate open discussion, creative thinking, and experimentation with new ideas and behaviors. Non-networker or similar labels tend to be taken as an indictment that, in turn, spawns defensive behavior and attitudes and locks clients into their current views and behavior.

NETWORKING RELUCTANCE STEMS FROM MANY SOURCES

As one would expect, the basis for and expression of networking reluctance differs for each individual. Nevertheless, certain themes have emerged repeatedly in my experience with this population over many years. For purposes of this discussion, I offer six categories: *conceptual, social skills, ethics, distorted thought processes, cost–benefit issues,* and a *sense of urgency.*

Conceptual

Networking-reluctant clients often have invalid or counterproductive concepts or theories regarding what networking is, the way it is supposed to be done, its social acceptance and appropriateness, its difficulty of execution, and its actual value on a net-cost basis. Here are some highly typical responses to the question that I have asked to self-acknowledged reluctant networkers over many years: "The trouble with networking is ... ?"

- Networking is a con game; it's just a sneaky way to get in front of a decision maker.
- Networking involves telling lies to people.
- Networking involves taking advantage of people, their contacts, their time and goodwill. It's a one-way relationship.
- Networking is like begging for charity or a handout.
- Networking is only for extroverts; it only works when you are good with people.
- Networking requires a large initial pool of contacts; it's not for someone who does not have a network.
- Networking involves telling people you are not looking for a job, when you are.
- Networking involves asking people for information you do not care about, when you really want job leads they have or even a job with them.
- Networking is a very slow way to get a job.
- Networking is a very difficult way to get a job.

These and similar negatively tinged comments were elicited from networking-reluctant clients who had received professional career guidance on networking, as well as from the general public whose knowledge of networking came from varied and uncertain sources.

The difficulty in dealing with conceptual barriers to networking is that one cannot easily tell whether they represent actual matters of concern or confusion, or whether they are rationalizations for other barriers to networking. Some conceptual barriers are valid (networking is not an easy process), whereas others are not so valid (networking is like begging for charity). In any case, though, if left unresolved, they are likely to impede or impair the client's networking activity.

Social Skills

Many networking-reluctant clients lack, or lack confidence regarding, certain social business skills central to the practice of successful networking. Many of these individuals are often, but not always, psychological introverts as defined, for example, by Jung (Fordham, 1966). Even those within this group who do have sufficient social skills and polish lose confidence when placed in novel or unfamiliar situations. Areas of weakness or uncertainty frequently encountered include conducting small talk, making introductions, shaking hands, active listening, maintaining eye contact, using appropriate body language, and telephoning skills.

Ethics

Networking-reluctant clients frequently express a great concern with ethical issues that relate to networking. They appear genuinely distressed at any behavior that they view as dishonest, deceptive, or manipulative. For these clients, any "gilding of lilies" or bending or distorting their view of the truth is not acceptable. These are the clients who will blurt out in networking contexts: "I am unemployed. Do you have a job?" After getting a negative answer, they will move on without attempting to make further discussion. For these clients, networking must be taught, planned, and conducted in a way that does not invoke or augment any feelings of dishonesty, or they will reject networking.

Distorted Thought Processes

Networking-reluctant clients tend to use emotional reasoning or "cognitive distortions" in their contemplation or conduct of networking.

For example, many of these people will not begin to network because "no one will want to talk with me." Such "fortune telling" of a negative kind, when accepted uncritically, produces the result that no introductory phone calls are made and networking ceases.

Other common cognitive distortions include:

- "No one (or Mr. Jones) will want to help me" (fortune telling or mind reading).
- "I will be embarrassed—and I could not stand that" (fortune telling or overgeneralizing).

These errors of thought either arrest the networking process at the very outset or inhibit or derail it, once it starts.

Cost–Benefit Imbalances

Many networking-reluctant clients reject networking because they view the cost of doing networking to be substantially greater than its probable value or benefit to them. This conclusion is reached either by inflating the perceived cost of networking and/or deflating the probable benefit expected from doing it.

For example, such clients may ascribe very high personal costs to doing networking. They focus on the loss of face, humiliation, discomfort with meeting strangers, wasting job-search time better spent in some other activity like contacting employers or recruiters. They may also view networking as a chancy and uncertain process, given that it is often a very indirect path to a goal. Under these conditions, it is easy for them to truly believe that networking is a good and useful activity in principle, yet logically conclude that they ought to be doing something else instead.

Sense of Urgency

Some networking-reluctant clients have no patience for long-term or long-range activities or strategies. They want action now and want to pursue only those activities that are seen as the shortest distance between two points. Networking is often viewed as a rather indirect and uncertain path between one known point (the client's current undesired position in life) and no specific end point. In this context, networking is seen as a potentially useful tool for creating happy accidents or building a foundation for the future. However, unless networking can be shown to be of immediate pragmatic value, clients concerned with this issue will often decline to engage in the process.

TYPICAL MISTAKES CAREER CONSULTANTS MAKE WITH THE NETWORKING RELUCTANT

Career consultants may inadvertently make matters worse with networking-reluctant clients. It might be argued that their behavior toward the client may, in certain circumstances, actually cause networking reluctance to occur. These errors or missteps may often be traced to our own blind spots, unstated and unexamined operating biases, and styles of functioning and communicating.

Acting Like an Extrovert When Dealing With Introverts

As a group, career management professionals are often socially, if not psychologically, extroverted. They tend to have well-developed skills and are comfortable socially in both familiar and unfamiliar situations. For most of them, networking may be a "natural" skill and orientation. It is rarely a burden.

Extroverted career management consultants must be vigilant to the possibility of forgetting or not fully realizing just how difficult these social behaviors could be for certain others. A lapse of sensitivity and empathy in this regard will create an insurmountable gap between such a client and consultant regarding networking, if not everything else in their work together.

Assuming That an Acquiescent Client is a Networking Believer

Consultants must never assume that "what they see is what they get" when meeting new clients. Many extroverted-appearing adults are often introverts who have learned to act extroverted in certain professional contexts. Even mature, successful professionals who appear to be at home in an extroverted world can be intensely and uncomfortably introverted when deprived of familiar surroundings.

Many networking-reluctant clients will not challenge the consultant regarding networking. They may not do so for many reasons, including a nonconfronting personality or a desire to be cooperative or to be liked as clients. They might also be intimidated by authority. Such attitudes often make networking difficult for them, as well. If clients' views on this subject are not drawn out in a gentle and permissive context, they are likely to remain hidden and not subject to change.

Relying on Subjective and General Reports of Client Activity

Many networking-reluctant clients will knowingly provide exaggerated reports of their activities. They do this for many reasons. Some do it to please, pacify or avoid angering the consultant. Others will innocently report their activities in qualitative and highly subjective ways. A self-report of doing lots of networking could turn out to be making two introductory telephone calls in the prior week. For that client, two calls might have represented a Herculean effort.

For some clients, the standard weekly activity logs may prove intimidating or daunting, that could lead to deception or avoidance of the consultant's involvement. It is necessary to create and use methods of reporting that provide sufficient detail for analysis, and are conducive to making candid client reports. Such reporting may have to be tailored to the needs and personality of individual clients.

Failing to Explore Individual Client's Attitudes Toward Networking

Many career consultants fail to explore initially, on an individual basis, the views and attitudes of their clients toward networking. Even when attempted, some consultants may do so in a manner designed to solicit agreement or compliance to the consultant's perspective, rather than to gain the heartfelt views, expectations, and concerns of the client. Failure to understand and deal with client concerns at the outset serves to weaken the consulting relationship and loses an opportunity to handle networking issues before they become problems.

PRACTICES THAT HAVE HELPED NETWORKING-RELUCTANT CLIENTS

What follows are a number of techniques and perspectives that I have found to be useful in forestalling or helping with active expressions of networking reluctance. It is not an all-inclusive list and readers are encouraged to extend the list through their own efforts in working with a population that is both needful and appreciative of help with this problem.

Assume Nothing About the Client

Assume that the client knows nothing about the process. They may have inadequate or imperfect knowledge or they might be uncomfortable admitting to their perceived failings. Start at "ground zero" and work up from there.

Foster Open and Free Expression of Negative Feelings and Concerns Regarding Networking

Many career consultants, and especially those who work in an agency setting with a large case load, feel too rushed and busy to actively solicit problems or concerns about networking, or other matters, from their clients. Under those circumstances, it seems much easier and more sensible to tell clients what to do and, in the absence of active disagreement from them, move on to the next matter or client. To actively invite a client to discuss what they think and feel about the guidance provided, especially their concerns, seems like inviting trouble and work where it does not exist. Nevertheless, a troubled or uncertain client will probably not heed the "doctor's" advice and will likely require more attention and be more troublesome than necessary in the long run. In these matters, the consultant will pay now, or risk paying later.

Help People Adapt Networking to Their Personality and Not the Other Way Around

Reluctant networkers are often introverts or people with low-key, nonassertive personalities. The typical scripts and prescriptive behaviors common to most presentations on networking often seem too "blatant" or "pushy" to those clients. In such cases, it is important to emphasize that many styles are appropriate and successful in networking and then willingly revise those scripts to accommodate their sensitivities.

It would be better, still, to provide a variety of scripts and materials at the outset of networking presentations in order to legitimize and demonstrate a broad range of styles and networking behaviors suitable to many temperaments.

Reward the Quality of Networking Efforts, and Not Just Results

Even when networking is conducted productively and effectively, it sometimes feels like hard work for almost everyone. By definition, it is almost always extremely difficult for the networking reluctant. For them, the journey is not always its own reward. It is, therefore, especially important to provide consistent and appropriate extrinsic rewards, primarily by consultant praise and encouragement, for every meaningful step taken by networking-reluctant clients.

In the early stages of networking, rewards might be granted for performing enabling objectives, such as creating a list of contacts, or developing a script. In later stages, rewards might follow when more challenging, longer term goals have been reached. Using principles established by behavior modification psychologists, the client and consultant could agree on appropriate extrinsic rewards for accomplishing mutually agreed-upon goals, as well as penalties for not doing so.

Use the Power of Positive Peer Pressure

Reluctant networkers are frequently unsure about or especially concerned with what is or is not socially acceptable behavior regarding networking. They may not trust any one person's views in these matters, even that of a professional consultant. In addition, they often lack a lengthy contact list at the start of the process.

Being in a support group gives the client additional sources of information and validation regarding the networking process. Such a group could uphold the fundamental validity and social acceptance of approaching and seeking to network strangers; something highly important to most networking-reluctant clients. Because networking-reluctant clients often lack contacts of their own, involvement in a support group provides an instant gain in personal networking resources through access to combined resources of the group.

Despite the advantages, many networking-reluctant clients will not want to be in a group, given their underlying discomfort with dealing with strangers in this context. Nevertheless, greater participation can be achieved if the group is portrayed and structured as something that would be helpful and not potentially embarrassing to them.

For example, I have conducted a course at New York University's School of Continuing Education for a number of years. It has been titled "Networking for Non-Networkers" and "Networking for Shy People." The course catalogue description attracts networking-reluctant individuals who believe that networking could be valuable and who feel that this group program is designed for them and their way of thinking. Under these circumstances, they not only choose to come, but pay to do so and participate quite actively.

In contrast, most of the job-search and support groups I have encountered in outplacement settings tend to be designed and conducted by networking enthusiasts with little obvious sensitivity to the needs and perspectives of the networking reluctant. Such groups may even be named in ways that are likely to intimidate or repel the networking reluctant, such as a "job attack group."

However formed, it is very important that the composition of the support group be evaluated with the networking reluctant in mind. The group need not be a networking-reluctant group; it should not, however, be a group that is dominated by those for whom networking presents little challenge. The group leader must be sensitive to the networking-reluctant client for whom this activity is particularly difficult and even threatening to their self-esteem.

Help Clients Reframe Their Views of Networking

Many networking-reluctant clients see networking as a manipulative, deceptive process by which the networker asks for favors or charity in the manner and position of a beggar. Given this perspective, it is vital to work with the client to come up with a way of networking people that will be, in their view, more of a mutual exchange of value. For example, the consultant can stress the idea of giving something back to the networking host on an immediate and extended basis. Provide clients with a new model that is consistent with their orientation toward honesty and nonmanipulative behavior.

Initial presentations on networking by consultants should emphasize the mutually beneficial nature of "proper" networking, as opposed to referring to it only after objections are raised to other rationales and techniques.

Teach Methods for Coping: Managing Stress

Networking is hard work and can be stressful to all. Networking reluctants may incur greater amounts of stress. They would be well served by learning to identify and handle their stress. At a minimum, consultants can be helpful by identifying this as a potentially important issue and by helping clients to find or create appropriate avenues for stress reduction and recreation. Help here could include referring them to stress management programs provided by other professionals, when necessary.

Teach Methods for Coping: Cognitive Behavior Modification

Networking reluctance often stems from illogical or faulty reasoning, also referred to as cognitive distortions. It is often very helpful to all networkers, reluctant or not, to learn to recognize common forms of cognitive distortions and to learn how to recognize and manage their own errors of thoughts. Most people have typical, repetitive errors of thought. Many networking-reluctant clients have been helped by creating a chart of their common thoughts, along with rational challenges to them. "No one will ever want to see me" is challenged by "I can never be sure who will or will not see me. I know some people have, so why wouldn't someone else see me, too?"

Provide Concrete and Varied Forms of Instruction

Helping clients to network properly involves teaching people new concepts and skills. Learning styles vary with individuals; some people are comfortable with conceptual or abstract presentations, whereas others require more concrete forms of information. Some learners do well with information that is visual; others auditory. As a general principle, therefore, it is good practice to provide training using a variety of modalities. Experience with networking-reluctant clients suggests that concrete forms of instruction (modeling, scripts, audio- and videotapes, role-playing) are particularly instructive and motivating for this group.

Use Successive Approximation Techniques

The attainment of small steps is easier and less threatening than "going for the gold" right from the beginning. Encourage clients to take any reasonable step in networking and reward it. Initial successes will be more likely and more quickly attained, and the client will be encouraged to persist to greater challenges and more meaningful results.

Use Objective Sources of Information
to Legitimize the Networking Activity

Many networking-reluctant clients are very uncertain about the appropriateness of networking. They need high degrees of assurance on a continuing basis as to what behavior is considered either socially acceptable or ethical. They may not accept their consultant's view as being sufficiently authoritative in their case. Or, if they do, their confidence may waver easily. Consultants should understand that this need for other sources of assurance reflects more on the client, and should not be taken as a personal affront or indictment of their competence.

It is, therefore, important for the consultant to provide a wide range of objective and credible support for networking, such as newspaper articles and testimonials from current or former job seekers. One of the benefits of a job support group is that it can be a continuing source of information that credibly legitimizes networking activity.

Be Authoritative, Not Authoritarian

It is all too easy to present to clients as if there is one best way to do networking. In fact, some career management consultants may actually believe this to be the case. Unfortunately, this posture engenders or exacerbates networking reluctance in certain clients, especially if they are uncomfortable with certain aspects of networking techniques being presented to them. If there is only one satisfactory way to network and they are uncomfortable with one or more aspects of the appropriate model, they may skip networking altogether.

In addition, an authoritarian posture is likely to be especially counterproductive with networking-reluctant clients, especially those who are decidedly introverted, shy or nonassertive. Such clients will feel decidedly uncomfortable about expressing concerns or opposing views that, if expressed, might be addressed satisfactorily.

It is important to provide a range of possible actions (including the less than ideal), to the client along with the trade-offs involved with each. Clients could, therefore, make informed choices with which they are comfortable. The underlying idea here is that some, even less than ideal, networking is better than none at all.

Be Creative and Flexible Regarding
Approaches to Networking

Some consultants have been trained to use certain training techniques and specific, formulaic approaches to networking. These probably work extremely well for the majority of the clients for which they were designed.

The reluctant networker is, by definition, the exception where standard techniques are concerned and the consultant must provide alternatives.

In this context, it can be productive for consultants to accept and respect the client's preferred approaches to job search and then seek to enrich them to the greatest degree possible. For example, most networking reluctant clients are interested in doing impersonal, direct mail types of job search. In such cases, it may be possible to get candidates to add "I will call ... " at the end of all or some such letters, as part of the process of gaining responses to the letters. Once accomplished, such follow-ups to letters, when encouraged and supported by the consultant, could be used as a springboard to a more conventional form of networking.

Although many clients may be reluctant about contacting people by phone, these same clients may be quite enthusiastic about reaching out to people via the computer keyboard. Networking opportunities and job search resources are expanding greatly in cyberspace. Abundant and increasing opportunities for virtual networking exist on many commercial online services such as CompuServe and America Online, as well as numerous sites on the Internet. Many career interests and professional orientations are represented and online "meetings" are easily arranged and conducted among strangers. Indeed, that is the norm in that environment and not the exception. In monitoring online activity, I found that it is not uncommon for those involved to end up with referrals to people for in-person forms of networking and job interviews.

Remain Optimistic and Realistic

As a group, the networking reluctant can present great frustrations and challenges to both the skill and fortitude of career management consultants.

Some individuals within this group may never accept networking as something in which they will engage. Others, and one never knows who, will surprise us by starting off negatively and then turn into exceptional networkers. Realistically, the majority of the networking reluctants will probably retain some measure of reluctance. Yet, with patience and creativity, the consultant can help most clients network better than they would have done on their own. Furthermore, the consultant can help clients to achieve lasting and valuable personal and career growth, for when clients confront and defeat their networking demons, they often confront and defeat other demons within themselves.

REFERENCE

Fordham, F. (1966). *An introduction to Jung's psychology*. Middlesex, England: Penguin Books.

6 Career Development Counseling With Technologists and Scientists

Daniel White
Quality Educational Development, New York

UNIQUE CHARACTERISTICS OF THE SCIENCE AND TECHNOLOGY PROFESSIONS

Clients often ask, "Are scientists and technologists really different than other working people?" The answer is both "yes" and "no." The work cultures of science and technology are somewhat different than other work environments. They are often based on the solitary work of writing software, designing equipment, or performing experiments. Because the work requires intense individual effort, these professions tend to attract people with intellectual temperaments, strong concentration abilities, and introverted styles.

These traits, along with some unique characteristics of the science and technology job markets, create the foundation for this chapter on the career development and job-search patterns of science and technology professionals. The observations in this chapter are drawn from more than 10 years experience as a consultant, trainer, and counselor for science and technology organizations. Most of the clients referred to in the chapter are computer systems developers, biologists and chemists, and technical managers from a variety of industries.

Although this chapter highlights some unique aspects of these technical professionals, it is important to note that there are also many similarities to other corporate professionals. Some of these commonalties are the need to be treated with respect, the need to see some result for their efforts, and the need to learn and grow.

Determining how truly different technical professionals are can become a moot issue. More important than provable differences is the professionals' belief that they are different. As career consultants, it is important to respect these feelings of difference. This respect builds more trust and rapport than any analysis of similarities or differences.

Autonomy is a very important component of the scientific culture. Most scientists and technologists have grown accustomed to considerable

63

freedom of thought and action in their work life. Their high regard for autonomy affects many aspects of their career, including management, personal development, and counseling or mentoring relationships. This characteristic creates some special career challenges as well.

Scientists and technologists are accustomed to working on long-term projects in which they determine where they are going and how they will get there. When they feel this familiar sense of control on a project, they can be very disciplined, creative, and resourceful.

Career transitions are long-term projects; but they can become confusing and frustrating to technical professionals because they lack clear structure or identifiable progress checks. One way a counselor can help is to create some structure within the transition process. Most technologists will respond to this kind of approach with renewed motivation and dedication.

Building Rapport With Technologists

Scientific professionals possess a great deal of technical knowledge. The average layperson understands little of their work. It can be a great asset for a counselor to listen intently and ask genuine questions about technologists' descriptions of their work. Even if the counselor has no technical background, asking the most basic questions about the technologists' work goes a long way toward building rapport.

Scientists often enjoy teaching others about what they do. "Talking technical" can also give the counselor valuable information about the technologists' skills, interests, and values. The counselor can then help the professionals to better understand the skills they possess, and those they do not possess.

The self-reliance of the technical work culture can be another barrier to effective career counseling. Until very recently, much of the work in scientific research and development, computer systems development, and engineering has been performed by skilled individual contributors, working by themselves at their desks, in their labs, or at their computer terminals. These professionals have become accustomed to generating and implementing their own ideas. Seeking help from others can be seen as a sign of weakness or incompetence. A counselor may need to be patient with a technical client; waiting for opportunities to help, in small ways at first, then in bigger ways when more trust is established.

Introversion

The Myers-Briggs Type Indicator (MBTI) defines introversion as a preference for the inner world of observations and impressions. This contrasts with extroverts who prefer the external world of social interaction and expression. Because the science and technology professions require a great deal of solitary concentration, they attract many introverts to their laboratories and workstations. Scientists and technologists spend a lot of time in an imagined world, manipulating constructs or molecules.

Although the introverted style is well-suited to scientific work, career transition is another story. Most career management and job-search efforts require a lot of social activity. Building a network of relationships and presenting oneself effectively are the "stuff" that job searches are made of. These activities bring fear to the hearts of many introverts.

How then, can introverts master these extroverted activities to further their careers? One answer lies in changing perspective. From one perspective, "selling yourself" and "small talk" are foreign and unwelcome concepts to introverts. But, if they can view these activities as research into their career marketplace, technologists can develop a greater sense of comfort and enthusiasm for networking. Most introverts like researching, gathering information, and seeking understanding. If they apply this intellectual curiosity to their career management, the social interaction will "come along for the ride" with their research.

Counselors can help their introverted technical clients by repositioning networking as research. This reframing is not mere trickery, for good networking really is market research. By approaching their contacts with genuine curiosity, and by formulating meaningful questions, many introverts can overcome their fears and become successful networkers.

Assessing Style to Differentiate in the Marketplace

Knowing oneself is a benefit at work. On the job, self-knowledge enables individuals to choose roles that use their strengths. It can also signal when to avoid certain roles that may surface weaknesses or when to become hyperdiligent when performing a nonpreferred role.

Similarly, in a job transition, it is important for individuals to differentiate themselves by describing their strengths and work style. Following are descriptions of four different personality and work styles of technologists, linked to the kinds of tasks they prefer. These are based on observed correlations between MBTI types and reported skills and work preferences. They have not yet been statistically validated.

1.   Idea generators, or Intuition-Thinking (NT) individuals, are strong analysts who are scientifically or mathematically creative and enjoy developing new ideas. Intuition-Thinking-Perceiving (NTP) individuals like to generate hypotheses, but may not follow through in conducting experiments to test them. They may jump around, looking for new opportunities to create. Intuition-Thinking-Judging (NTJ) individuals

exhibit strong experimental design skills. They are good implementers and strive toward closure in their activities.

2.   Efficiency experts, streamliners, re-engineers, or Sensing-Thinking-Judging (STJ) types are very detail oriented and like to develop ways of improving existing systems. Their proficiency in finding and eliminating errors makes them effective at quality assurance.

3.   Scientific and technical networkers, or Extraversion-Feeling (EF) workers, can maintain a multitude of relationships, assimilate all that is going on, and coordinate activities.

4.   Coaches, teachers, or Extraversion-Intuition-Feeling (ENF) individuals, like to inspire others, brainstorm, and champion new cultural and personal values.

Every scientific and technology organization needs people with different styles. The value of stylistic diversity comes from professionals who approach their work from different points of view. If scientists can articulate their style, and explain how it can benefit an organization, they are on the way to convincing others of their unique value.

One computer scientist used his style as an efficiency expert to guide his next career move. He had worked in a variety of project management positions in a large bank. His field had become quite crowded with computer-systems project managers. In assessing his skills, he clarified his strengths in designing work flows and analyzing their smallest details to enhance efficiency. In planning his search, he decided that the best way to differentiate himself in this competitive market was to play from his strength. He researched the trends in his field, reviewed his past accomplishments, and started describing himself as a reengineering specialist. Within a few months, he secured a long-term consulting assignment on a large reengineering project.

SKILLS: TECHNICAL AND TRANSFERABLE

Every person possesses a number of skills. Some skills are very situationally specific, such as programming in COBOL or performing x-ray crystallography. These technical skills are critical to most jobs. They are the skills discussed in most job ads and interviews.

However, taken by themselves, technical skills are very limiting. A technical skill enables an individual to do basically one thing. The COBOL programmer may not be able to write code for PCs, or analyze a complex system. The crystallographer might not be able to design a new molecule to fit an active receptor.

Most people have another layer of skills that underlies their technical skills. The programmer may have strong analytical skills that enable him or her to break down any system into its logical, component parts. The crystallographer may have great pattern-recognition skills that enable him or her to determine the shape of a molecule given incomplete data. We refer to these underlying skills as "transferable" because they can be applied in a number of different situations.

Most working people are quite aware of their technical skills as they are the names of the tasks they perform daily. In science and technology, people tend to focus a great deal of attention on technical skills because they represent tangible human currency in the hard science professions. They may also dominate because technical professionals prefer seeing themselves as possessing concrete, indisputable skills, rather than the fuzzier, more human, transferable skills.

In a crowded marketplace, many competitors possess the same technical skill sets. Technical professionals need to find ways to differentiate themselves from their competitors. It is transferable skills that describe the real differences among professionals. For example, one x-ray crystallographer might be strong at interpreting and precisely calculating x-ray diffraction angles. Another crystallographer might have a gift for intuitively visualizing molecular shapes from a few points. These professionals possess very different skills that could be valued differently in different organizational environments.

Given the rapid pace of change in science and technology, transferable skills have a much longer shelf life than technical skills. In the computer technologies, specific software skills have a life span of approximately 3 to 5 years. By way of contrast, the underlying transferable skills, like analysis, research, error finding, or leadership, can be useful for a lifetime. Science and technology professionals, who understand their core transferable skills and regularly update appropriate technical skills, will have an advantage in the job marketplace of the future.

Retraining

Transferable skills are critical to defining one's career. Specific technical skills are needed in every job, as well. The level and complexity of technical skills required by most technical jobs can make it difficult for professionals to make career transitions. For example, a UNIX computing environment needs information technologists with UNIX skills. A gene therapy discovery program needs scientists with knowledge of gene therapy techniques.

Many scientists and technologists encounter a career problem upon completing a project of long duration. If their project was based on technologies that are no longer current, the professionals find themselves behind the times, with skills that are not very marketable. If their organization is financially flush, it can fund their training period on a newer technology project. However, if their organization is financially stretched, the professionals may need to fend for themselves.

This leaves the professionals with two short-term strategies. The first is to retrain in a new technology. The second is to seek employment in one of the firms that is still using their old technology.

Seeking employment with the old technology is obviously a risky choice because it might leave the professional even less marketable in the future. For this reason, many in this situation are choosing to retrain themselves. Most technical professionals who retrain learn the new skills that will make them current in their field. For information-technology professionals, that can mean studying object-oriented programming (C++) or the new Windows operating system. For medicinal chemists, it can mean learning computer-based molecular modeling. For telecommunications engineers, it can mean training in local area networking systems.

For some, retraining represents a rebirth in their career. Many technologists have spent several years working with the same technology. Although they have become expert at applying it, they may not have learned truly new skills in years. Reinvolving themselves in the learning process can rekindle their self-esteem, creativity, and optimism.

A computer technologist, whom we call Ed, experienced a rejuvenation in his career as a result of his retraining. Ed had spent 15 years as a computer technologist, starting by programming financial reports and moving his way up to managing the development of systems and applications at a large bank. He specialized in a particular brand of popular minicomputer hardware and software. His job at the bank was eliminated during a large-scale layoff. As he began his job search, he began to recognize that the industry was moving away from minicomputers toward PC-based local area networks (LANs), reducing the demand for his technical skill set.

He wanted to stay in his field. He liked information technology. He was good at finding practical computer solutions to business needs. However, he felt that his skills were becoming obsolete. He had not undertaken any major training since entering the computer field 16 years earlier.

He decided that it was time to update his skills. The first task in his retraining effort was to do some research to determine what new skills he should learn. His initial research had two goals. First, he wanted to determine what skills were currently in demand in the marketplace, and were likely to be in demand in the future. Second, he wanted to determine which of these skills best matched his interests and abilities. After conducting information interviews with a dozen people and reading many magazine articles, he decided to retrain in LAN design and management. (In some ways decisions about retraining are like investing in the stock market. The investor gambles that his or her informed view of the future will come to pass.)

With some more research, he found an institution that would train and certify him in these new technologies. He even found a funding source for his retraining. The Department of Labor's Job Training Partnership Act (JTPA) has set aside funds for retraining "dislocated workers." He was put on a waiting list for this funding but soon decided it was more important to start retraining right away than to wait the 3 months for the state funding to come through. (Other clients I have worked with have been able to use JTPA funding within a matter of weeks.)

He worked very hard during his 3-month retraining program. He attended classes, studied, and practiced daily. During his training, he described a feeling of excitement in learning that he had not felt since he was in college. He also felt a renewal of his self-confidence that had gradually been diminishing during his corporate career. He passed his certification with flying colors, and restarted his job search.

He reported that people responded differently this time around. He felt that they were more eager to help him now that he had marketable skills. He also believed that they noticed his renewed confidence and enthusiasm. Someone asked him if he had been to a spa or a religious retreat.

His investment paid off. Within 1 month of completing the training program, he found a position utilizing his new skills. The position originally paid a little less than his previous position. However, 1 year later he was back up to his previous salary level, with continued prospects for growth.

THE CHANGING JOB MARKET

In the last two decades, scientists and technologists have maintained a strong position in the job market in most industries. The economy's dependence on technical products in the 1970s and 1980s created a steady demand for computer professionals, pharmaceutical scientists, chemists, and other technical professionals. Their job security was enhanced by the barrier to entry that has formed by the technical training needed to function in these fields. When technical professionals did change jobs, most found new jobs easily through recruiting agencies and newspaper ads.

When downturns hit their industries, the supply of talent started to exceed demand. Many technologists were surprised at the difficulty involved in finding a new job. Defense engineers were the first to be affected by these economic changes. This was followed by heavy-industry engineers in the 1980s, financial services computer professionals in the early 1990s, and pharmaceutical scientists in the mid-1990s. Not until they became affected by these economic shifts did many technical professionals need to face a very competitive marketplace.

One of the major differences between an accepting job marketplace and a competitive one is the importance placed on communication and marketing skills. In an accepting marketplace, technical and analytical skills are the primary selection criteria. In the ultracompetitive marketplace, building relationships and handling organizational politics become just as important.

Many technology professionals have underdeveloped these skills in favor of learning science and technology. The training, work life, and the self-selection of technical professionals reinforces this tendency. It often requires long, solitary hours in a lab, at a desk, or at a computer terminal. It tends to attract people who prefer to spend much of their day working by themselves with ideas and facts. Their scientific culture has traditionally reinforced this tendency by placing less emphasis on social skills than the cultures of sales, marketing, or business management.

EMPATHY SKILLS FOR ANALYTICAL PEOPLE

Science and technology professionals are trained to deal rationally with logical phenomena. Attending to psychological issues is rare in scientific work cultures. Therefore, the more psychological and personal elements of career management may seem foreign to most. A counselor can help scientists relate to personal values and emotions by portraying them as logical constructs. These "soft" concepts can become more real to the technologist by seeking to understand the logical, cause-and-effect relationships between values, feelings, and behaviors.

Individuals who rely primarily on logic to make decisions often have underused skills at empathizing with others. The MBTI typology positions the logic of the "thinking type" and the empathy of the "feeling type" at opposite ends of the decision-making dimension. Although the thinking and feeling preferences are fairly evenly distributed in the population, the thinking preference dominates in the science and technology professions. This is to be expected, considering the degree to which these professionals use logic and analysis.

The scientific professions both select for people from Thinking dominance, and reinforce it through work requirements and culture. This phenomenon has created an environment in which many professionals have underdeveloped empathy skills. Thinking-dominant people are often so concerned with being logically and analytically correct that they become unaware of the impact of their behavior on others.

Because career transition is such a people-intensive activity, the counseling process can provide a timely opportunity to build empathy skills. This "empathy training" can begin with developing awareness of the role of empathy in organizational life. Often, technical clients can be helped to recognize the missed opportunities and soured relationships that resulted from overdependence of their thinking function.

Once clients recognize the importance of empathy, they can begin to build empathy skills. Clients can engage in empathy exercises in which they first try to guess the feelings and attitudes of others. They can review past experiences seeking to better understand the needs and reactions of others. They can also look at upcoming events, focusing on empathizing and building relationships with significant others.

The counseling relationship, itself, can serve as a laboratory for strengthening empathy skills. The counselor can point out, in real time, instances when a technologist seems to be oblivious to the counselor's reactions. Together, they can make a project of becoming aware of the reactions of others. They can also experiment with new, more empathic behaviors. This focus on personal development not only speeds up the client's career transition, but it also can transform the transition into a period of significant personal growth.

TO BE OR NOT TO BE A MANAGER

During the "go–go" years of computer technology (1970–1990), the industry needed large numbers of managers to supervise the growing population of technologists. The economy needed managers to direct the development of software and hardware to automate the transactions, the record keeping and consumer interfaces for banks, insurance companies, and other data-intensive organizations. To meet this need, many of the technologists with decent communication skills were promoted into department management and project management positions. Many of the professionals recruited into these positions were technically competent, but did not necessarily possess the managerial skills or values characteristic of managers of other business functions.

As these industries start to contract, they need fewer managers. Many of these technical middle managers have become downsized. In seeking new jobs, many face the difficult decision between remaining managers or refocusing their careers on senior technical or consulting positions. This decision is made more difficult by the status and pay differences between managerial and technical positions. (These differences persist, even in organizations with dual career tracks.)

A midcareer self-assessment can be an effective approach to making this decision. Many career consultants use a model that examines the match between the characteristics of the person and the job. They begin by assessing the skills, interests, values, and style of the professional. Then, they examine the relevant characteristics of the managerial job, looking for the degree of overlap. Fortunately, many managerial jobs have similar characteristics.

The generic managerial job characteristics fall into five major categories:

1. Interpersonal skills.
2. Administrative skills.
3. Technical/conceptual skills.
4. Managerial values.
5. Personal style.

Following is a list of characteristics of managerial work that I have used as a checklist. Prospective managers can review this list, and determine how well they fit.

Interpersonal

The interpersonal demands of most managerial jobs favor the following skills:

- Team players versus loners—Individuals, who are skilled at knowing when, how, and whom to include in making decisions and sharing information tend to make the best managers.
- Skills at negotiating, leading, and motivating—Knowing how to get through to others, gain their interest, and tap their enthusiasm, is a critical skill for managers.
- Good communicator—Good managers are links between their team and the organization. They have an interest and skill at sharing a great deal of information.
- Ability to maintain good relationships—Managers need to have effective relationships with their staff, their peers, and their senior management.
- Ability to handle conflict—Organizations are rife with competition. Good managers can deal face-to-face with conflict, and attempt to shape its outcome.

Administrative

- Project management skill—Good managers can delegate tasks to appropriate staff, and track their progress on these tasks.
- Like making decisions and solving problems—Managers deal with an inordinate number of problems. Good managers do not mind this intrusion. They enjoy rolling up their sleeves and using their best judgment.

- Understand organizational structures, resource allocation—Good managers seek to understand the unique and sometimes quirky way their organization operates. They learn to "play it" to pave the way for their team's success.
- Good at administrative details—Much of a manager's job includes writing reports, preparing budgets, tracking financials, and organizing information. Managers need to have an interest in doing this, otherwise their team will suffer, and their credibility will be diminished.

Technical

- Play the dual role of a technical professional and manager—The best technical managers balance their managerial tasks with attempts to stay current in at least one aspect of their field. This enables them to make good decisions, and to function as a coach, as well as an administrator, to their staff.
- Balance loyalties—to the technical discipline and to the organization.
- Identify with organizational big picture—Because managers are liaisons, they need to understand the organizational mission and the direction of the technology and the market.
- Have the respect of peers—One of the values of staying current is the continuing respect managers earn for their technical knowledge, as well as managerial skill.

Values and Motivations

- Enjoy power—Managers do have more organizational power than pure technologists. The best managers enjoy authority, responsibility, and the act of influencing others. Managers also need to relate well to those above them in the organization. Overall, they need to be comfortable with power.
- Comfortable with taking risks—The manager's job involves many risks and decisions. Managers who worry too much about each risk are likely to suffer a great deal of stress.
- Able to handle a lot of responsibility and pressure—The buck stops at the manager's desk. Managers also must serve as role models for work ethic and quality standards. Managers who cannot make the necessary time and energy sacrifice will be less than effective.
- Content with fewer friendships at work—This topic has been much written about. Having best friends in the department sets the stage

for favoritism and bias. The old saying goes: "A manager needs to be respected, not loved."

Personal Style

- Extroversion versus Introversion—So much of a manager's job is communicating and relationship building that extroverts seem more comfortable in the role than most introverts. This might seem prejudicial but it is backed by research. This is certainly not absolute, as there are many fine introverted managers who have learned to deal with the tension of spending much of their day communicating.
- Able to empathize with others—Management is primarily about communicating with a multitude of others. The best managers understand their positions, and respect their emotions and values.

Skilled counselors or mentors can help technical professionals understand the specialized requirements of management. It has different tasks and challenges than technical work. The decision to return to, or stay on, a technical career track can be an important decision in a professional's career. It can mean the difference between satisfaction and frustration. Counselors can help their clients make the difficult decision of following their true selves, rather than pursuing the organization's or society's ideal of status and power.

OUTSOURCING AND ENTREPRENEURING

Outsourcing is another phenomenon of the current economy. In the 1970s and 1980s, the corporate trend was to keep many functions in-house. By the early 1990s, the trend began to shift to a "leaner and meaner" philosophy. Organizations began to focus all of their energies on their core competencies by outsourcing some of their less central functions. For example, several pharmaceutical companies have outsourced their clinical trials function, and many banks have outsourced their data processing and transaction processing functions.

The transition to outsourcing does not necessarily reduce the net number of jobs in an industry. It merely moves them from one organization to another. Many of the scientists, technologists, and other professionals whose jobs have been outsourced are seeking employment in the organizations that are taking over their functions.

The phenomenon also creates a fertile environment for entrepreneurs. The large organizations who are outsourcing functions are looking for reliable, efficient firms with whom to partner. Because these functions once operated in-house, the large organizations need outsourcing partners who can work well with their operations and culture. Outsourced technologists with an adventuring spirit can make excellent vendors for their former employers.

Many former employees of large organizations are beginning to see the benefits of becoming an outsourcer to their former employers, and their former employers' competitors. They perform essentially the same type of work, with the added challenge, freedom, and potential earnings of running their own business. For many of these entrepreneurial technologists, the situation provides a midcareer growth that had been missing in their former corporate employment.

These entrepreneurial opportunities can run the gamut from one-person consulting operations to multimillion-dollar businesses with dozens of employees. For example, a data processing manager was laid off by his bank in 1991 in an effort to reduce their programming-related expenses. He noticed that his bank was contracting with some off-shore applications development firms at rates well below the U.S. market. He used his own overseas contacts to co-found another overseas development shop. He now runs the U.S. side of the operation, selling and managing relationships with at least four commercial banks.

Another budding entrepreneur is a medical doctor who lost his position in a large pharmaceutical firm as a result of its decision to outsource the clinical testing of new drugs. He determined that, even though his former employer had outsourced much of the clinical trial management, they still needed someone to manage the clinical data. He was skilled at collecting, analyzing, and reporting the large amounts of data generated by these trials. In his market research, he determined that several competitors were also interested in this service. So, he started a business providing this service to several pharmaceutical companies.

CONCLUSION

The scientific and technological professions, like much of the rest of the economy, are undergoing significant changes as we enter the late 1990s. The core technologies have grown more complex at the same time that the career marketplace has become increasingly global and competitive. These changes have placed tremendous pressure on a group of individuals who had been relatively protected from such changes.

The professions are now in a transition. The principles of career management that guided science and technology professionals are changing, as are organizational and management practices that affect them. Career development professionals can play a major role in assisting scientists and technologists to respond to these changes. This assistance can take a variety of forms, including a more comprehensive assessment of their skills and style. Counselors can also help scientists and technologists deepen their understanding of how changing market conditions will impact their future career development.

7 Counseling Older Adults

Anita Lands
Chase Bank, New York

INTRODUCTION

Corporations continue to downsize. Individuals at all levels and ages are impacted. Although it is difficult for individuals at any age or stage of career development to face job loss, it is particularly complicated for older adults, those in their 50s, 60s, and 70s.

There are special challenges and considerations in working with older clients around issues of job loss and career management. Counseling older clients is both similar to and different from counseling younger clients. Most similar is the counseling process itself; most different are certain of the issues which impinge on the counseling process and the counselor–client relationship. This chapter addresses a number of these issues.

When working with older clients, counselors play multiple roles, including motivator, facilitator, and sounding board. However, the primary role is often a combination of advisor, guide, change agent, and partner. In keeping with this primary role, it is valuable to establish a relationship of equality from the outset. Although older clients value the expertise of counselors as career management professionals, the clients bring their own expertise as well. They bring the knowledge, experience, and wisdom of their years. Therefore, the counseling relationship, process, and results are all enhanced by using a partnership approach and by ensuring that both counselor and client tap into each other's strengths.

Moreover, in counseling older clients, there are two principles that are critical to success. They are:

1. A belief that people can, and do, make changes at any age.
2. A belief that an older person's life circumstances are factors to be taken into account and are not prohibitive constraints to action.

CHARACTERISTICS OF OLDER WORKERS

Older adults are by no means a monolithic group; rather, quite the opposite is true. Research has shown that as adults age, individuation continues. Therefore, as counselors we must be free of inappropriate

77

generalizations and treat all clients in the unique manner that they deserve.

Workers aged 55 and older represent the fastest growing sector of the labor force. Career management professionals will be seeing more and more older clients. What are some of the major characteristics of older workers?

One can expect these older clients to be smarter, better educated, healthier, and more productive than their predecessors. They will have much to offer the world of work. They will be able to continue working longer and probably will need to continue working to some degree to fund an extended life.

Older workers belie the limiting stereotypes and myths operating in the labor market, many of which have been refuted by surveys and studies, including a major 1993 report by the Commonwealth Fund (1993), a national foundation that conducts independent research on health and social issues. Older workers are typically motivated, loyal, adaptable, and productive, with strong work ethics and habits, including consistently better accident and absentee records.

Older workers value their work for many reasons beyond the financial rewards of a pay check and benefits. The reasons include continued learning and skill development, a sense of identity, self-worth and purpose, feelings of contribution and achievement, and social contacts. However, older workers might also have experienced some form of age discrimination in the workplace that has contributed to feelings of frustration, doubt, discouragement, and possibly even paralysis.

Therefore, as counselors, we need to be creative and flexible in our thinking and problem solving with such clients. We must be open to a broad range of possibilities. More importantly, we must convey to our clients that they need to be creative and flexible as well. At the same time, we need to assist them by offering realistic and practical approaches to dealing with issues.

A major difference in counseling older adults is that noncareer issues have to be taken into account to a much greater extent. Often, even as job or career shifts are occurring, older clients are at a stage in their lives when finances, health, family, housing, and other lifestyle and life-planning considerations impinge on work-related decisions. Moreover, emotional issues often enter the counseling picture to a greater degree. In any event, both noncareer and emotional issues affect how older clients think about options and make choices. Counselors need to be sensitive to and be prepared to address any of these issues within the counseling framework.

ADULT DEVELOPMENT AND ADULT LEARNING THEORIES

It is helpful to take a brief look at some theories of adult learning and adult development, and how they play a role in counseling older clients.

According to Knowles (1980), adult learning revolves around the adult learner being self-directed, using one's own experience as a resource, learning from life tasks and problems, and being motivated more by internal incentives than external ones.

Characteristics of the successful adult learning process include an environment that is trusting, nonjudgmental, reciprocally respectful, collaborative, and supportive. The process also involves (a) a mutual assessment, including a diagnosis of needs by the facilitator (in this case, the counselor); (b) joint planning and setting of objectives; (c) independent study and experiential techniques for new learning; and (d) evaluation by the learner through collected evidence by peers and facilitator. On a practical level, older adults need to see the relationship and relevance between what they learn and their own lives, or they will not act on it.

As for adult development, there are a number of applicable theories, especially those of Erickson (1963) and Chickering (1981). They maintain that adult development progresses through several phases in later years, as it does in earlier ones. Each phase requires the successful completion of life tasks. Among the life tasks that are addressed within the context of later adult stages, is finding work, paid and/or unpaid. Here again, older adults tend to grow in ways that impact their lives pragmatically.

Both adult learning and adult development theories serve to underscore the reality that older adults are capable of continued personal growth throughout their lives. Understanding these theories and their practical applications, appreciating their motivational value, and integrating them into the counseling process can enhance the counselor's success with older clients.

KEY CONCERNS

There are a number of key concerns that can arise in counseling older adults. These concerns might be the client's explicit reasons for seeking counseling (e.g., job change, job loss, retirement), or they might be implicit, "the issue behind the issue" (e.g., concerns about age, self-esteem, remaining productive). Part of a counselor's success will depend on the counselor's ability to identify through early discussion and assessment the concerns of older clients and to help them respond effectively to these concerns. Beyond that, counselors can counter clients' possibly negative images and feelings by building in positive experiences during the course of the counseling process. A brief overview of recurring concerns of older adults follows.

Age and Aging

As everyone knows, our population is aging. Moreover, due to better medical care, improved diet and exercise, and changed attitudes, people seem to be much younger. What it means to be 50, 60, or 70 years old today is dramatically different from even one generation ago. Yet, many myths and stereotypes still abound about age and aging. Frequently, older adults themselves accept and internalize these myths and stereotypes, even when they run counter to their own personal experiences. Additionally, as stated earlier, they may have met some form of age discrimination in the workplace or job market, and fear that they will do so again.

In dealing with this issue, counselors need to be aware of reputable studies and statistics about age, aging, and older workers, which refute many of the limiting stereotypes. More importantly, we need to be free of age-related biases ourselves and to project that message to clients. Furthermore, we have to help our clients to separate fact from fiction and to encourage them to draw on their own experiences and resources to counter the potentially negative effects of an ageist society.

As an example, a former client, a management information systems professional in his mid-60s, was laid off during a reorganization by an international news service. Despite his track record, special expertise, and personal vitality, he had major misgivings about embarking on a job search due to his age and his concern about potential discrimination. Our discussions focused on distinguishing age-related realities from age-related myths. These discussions appealed to his objective, analytical nature. Also, I guided and supported his networking efforts, especially at the outset. He began to regain his confidence and self-esteem as he generated new contacts and more information about the market for his skills. Subsequently, he was hired by a major money center bank, through a combination of networking and referral by an executive search firm.

Change

Change can be more or less difficult for an older client, depending on such factors as the nature and degree of change, as well as whether it is self-initiated, anticipated, or unanticipated. Initially, major transitions, even positive ones, require dealing with unknowns, uncertainties, and ambiguities about the future. In the case of career transitions, they require disengagement from a familiar job and job-related lifestyle, without immediate reengagement. Added to that is an unclear future.

Therefore, people often experience a sense of feeling empty and of being unmoored. They are more prone to self-doubt and feel less control over their lives. In addition, they might have fears about what lies ahead, particularly the potential risks involved.

Counselors can guide older clients in managing change and contribute to their personal growth by:

- Helping them to understand that their feelings and fears are normal, especially at the outset, and to make a distinction between the anticipatory feelings associated with change and the actual change itself.

- Employing helpful techniques, such as encouraging clients to tap into past changes and transitions that they have handled well, and to use themselves as positive role models.
- Assisting clients in clarifying what their future might look like which, in itself, can help to speed up the transition process.

As an example, a client in her early 50s, who was laid off from a data processing job during a large-scale downsizing at a major commercial bank, expressed a clear desire to make a career change into the health care field. After we completed an in-depth assessment and she investigated thoroughly her areas of potential interest, she decided on sonography. However, she stalled at the moment that her decision required action. At this point, I encouraged her to use herself as a positive role model. Through our discussions, she connected with the strengths and traits that had enabled her to conquer many prior obstacles, including coming to the United States from Russia as a single parent with a young child and a minimal knowledge of English. Subsequently, the client began implementing her plans for a career change and is currently completing her internship at a major hospital. She is doing very well and is greatly satisfied with her choice.

Remaining Productive

An ongoing issue for older clients is the desire to remain and to feel productive. This is true whether they are making a job or career change, scaling back from full-time work, or planning to do volunteering. Work gives people a sense that they are valuable to themselves and to others. Therefore, remaining and feeling productive is a high priority.

Counselors need to help clients identify which aspects of their former vocational and avocational activities made them feel productive. Then, as they investigate new opportunities, the counselor can guide them in deciding whether they can replicate in their new paid and/or unpaid work activities those same underlying characteristics that had made them feel productive.

One of my clients, a woman in her middle 50s who had previously been my student in a university course on career and life planning, was a very successful sales manager who had come up through the ranks at a major New York newspaper. However, she had become disenchanted with the changes in the corporate culture, the frequent turnover of bosses, and the increasing stress inherent in her job. Yet, she was not nearly ready to stop working, even though as a long-term employee she was eligible for an attractive severance package.

Our focus was to separate what she liked and did not like about both the job itself and the milieu in which she was working. Then, we developed a proposal for a part-time role based on a number of her "job satisfiers," as well as her assessment of what the organization needed. After negotiations with her boss and his manager (the preparation for which was also included in our counseling meetings), she was able to remain with the newspaper in a newly created part-time position, but with many opportunities for further contribution.

Sense of Identity

Our identity is closely tied to our life roles and activities. Every individual engages in a variety of activities that require multiple roles; and they, in turn, combine to give individuals their sense of identity. Typical roles include worker, family member, friend, volunteer, sports fan, cultural enthusiast, to name just a very few.

When a major role such as that of a worker is either altered, reduced, or ended, it impacts on all other life roles, and, consequently, one's sense of identity. Particularly when work has been at the core of a person's self-definition, a significant change in that role can lead to a loss of identity. In such situations, counselors can help older clients to recognize their other roles, to consider which of them they would like to develop further, and which new roles they might like to add through engaging in different activities. As individuals create a new or modified set of activities for themselves, including a new form of work, they lay the foundation for new roles, which, in turn, lead to a new sense of identity.

A good example is a former client in his early 60s who was eligible for retirement from a large garment manufacturing company. He was being strongly "encouraged" by senior management to leave his controller position. He had already begun seriously considering a move to Florida with his wife who was working part-time as a secretary in a small office. However, his work had always been demanding and fulfilling, and he had not really developed any avocational interests, except for informally helping family and friends with investment and tax advice. Also, he had begun taking courses toward becoming a certified financial planner (CFP).

Over several months, we addressed a number of issues including the role of work in his life, both past and future; possible relocation to Florida; completing his CFP program; and exploring other potential activities. The overall objective was to assist the client in letting go of his old identity, which was tied so tightly to his profession and career, and to help him begin creating an identity that would be linked to a different and broader range of activities. As a result, he decided to move to Florida, where he completed his CFP, began a small financial advisory service, became a board member of his condominium, began learning golf and going deep sea fishing, and resurrected a long dormant interest in bridge.

Some of the issues just discussed usually arise early in the counseling process, but they can surface at any time. Either the client or the counselor may bring them up. However, there are certain situations when a client, for whatever reasons, may neglect to raise them, even though in the counselor's judgment they are seen as obstacles to progress. In such a case, counselors need to bring the issues to the surface in order to help clients resolve them, so that they can move ahead toward their professional and/or personal goals.

NEW WORK REALITIES AND THEIR IMPACT ON OLDER CLIENTS

Several fundamental changes in the workplace have combined to create new realities in the labor market. These changes have had a major impact on older workers. Of particular importance have been the following trends:

• The continuation of widespread corporate downsizing, including by companies making or projecting profits, as well as cutbacks by government, educational, and other traditionally "safe" sectors.
• The transformation of the traditional corporate structure from "vertical" to "horizontal," with fewer levels of employees handling a broader range of tasks, and the diminished likelihood of being rehired by these flatter and leaner organizations.
• The growing dual phenomena of a large, widespread "contingency" workforce at all levels and the outsourcing of total functions. By the 21st century, there will be 133 million people in the workforce, and less than half of them will be in conventional full-time jobs.
• The expectation on the part of the companies that employees take greater responsibility for their own careers, as well as for their financial security and health care.
• The lengthening reach of technology into everyone's work life, calling for workers who can learn and use new technology.
• The growth of small and medium-sized businesses, including franchises. More than 90% of all firms in the United States employ fewer than 500 people.

The results of these fundamental and dramatic changes impact older workers in the following ways:

• Few can count on ever being rehired again by a major corporation. Infrequent exceptions are those with very specialized skills, mostly technological, financial, or scientific. Therefore, older job seekers need to engage in extensive networking and counselors must guide them in the strategies and techniques to increase both the volume and diversity of these activities. This is especially true if an older client has never actually had to network professionally.

• Individuals can no longer depend on long-term employment with one company and need to adjust their expectations accordingly. Counselors can help them to prepare for this major shift in the workplace (which may also require the acceptance of reduced income), by encouraging clients to continue learning and developing professionally in order to remain marketable and to exercise flexibility as a job seeker.

• Job offers that come along may well be temporary ones of short, medium, or long duration. However, temporary jobs do keep individuals involved in the world of work, place them in new environments, help them to maintain and/or develop their skills, lead to new contacts and generate income—all very positive features. Moreover, temporary situations still occasionally lead to full-time positions, although less often than formerly. Certainly, short-term jobs often get extended. Therefore, counselors can help older clients to see the need and value of temporary work, whether it comes through an agency, a consulting opportunity, a subcontracted project, or some other source.

• Going forward, older workers need to take full responsibility for managing their own careers. For many, this calls for a major change in attitude, from a somewhat dependent, "I'll be taken care of" mode of thinking to a much more proactive approach to all aspects of their careers. Counselors can motivate older clients to develop this new mindset and take charge of their work lives, including a continual broadening and upgrading of their skills.

In guiding older adults to develop strategies that deal with these new work realities, counselors need to have clients respond to three critical questions early in the counseling process:

1. What is their financial situation and how does it affect their need to work full-time or part-time?
2. What do they want the role of work to be in their lives? Is it currently central or peripheral? Do they want it to continue as such or change this role in any way?
3. What trade-offs are they willing and able to make, particularly trade-offs involving issues of money, time, commitment, status. For example, will they consider less money for fewer responsibilities? Fewer problems but less power? Fewer hours but lower status? More money but less free time?

The answers will depend on a combination of financial and nonfinancial factors, including the client's personal values, needs, interests, priorities, and goals. Counselors need to help clients clarify these factors. This can be done through a combination of formal and informal assessment instruments and guided discussion.

What work options are available to older adults? Their next step could be a similar or different job in the same field, or a different job in a new field. It could be a full-time, part-time, or temporary position for varying lengths of time, or perhaps a seasonal job. They could be employed by one or more organizations and might even share a job. They might choose to start or buy a business, including a franchise, which could be big, medium, or small. They might do freelance or consulting work. They could decide to work at home, part or all of the time.

Also, an individual's next career move may call for new learning, which could mean obtaining a degree or a certificate, taking continuing education courses, or getting on-the-job training. They could also gain the necessary knowledge and training through a well-chosen volunteer position, which, additionally, can serve as an excellent job-search strategy. Two examples follow.

The first is a former client in her late 50s whose job as an administrative assistant in a large insurance company had been eliminated. She had always been drawn to the medical arena, having wanted to enter nursing years before, and felt that this was an opportunity to make the switch. We agreed that to penetrate a health care setting, she would target a few hospitals and approach them for volunteer work in an administrative–secretarial capacity. She did so and was accepted at a major New York City hospital.

A couple of months later, one of the doctors for whom she handled several administrative tasks, approached her to work as a paid administrative assistant at a clinic he was establishing with several other doctors. Her success was due to a combination of "right place/right time," taking advantage of networking opportunities, and providing herself the chance to demonstrate her skills in her targeted arena. All of these paid off, and rather quickly.

A second example of volunteering as a job-search strategy is a client in his early 60s who had managed his extended family's money and real estate holdings for many years. He had put together a team of financial, legal, and accounting professionals to assist him. After his last elderly relative died, his work dwindled. Although he did not have to continue working, he wanted to do so, and was interested in exploring something new.

He had always worked autonomously in an environment with just a few people. He was used to "calling the shots." Moreover, he wanted to use his experience and knowledge, but in a somewhat different way. We decided that it would be critical to network widely. Along the way, he spoke to someone who was involved in initial public offerings and whose business was growing rapidly.

My client proposed spending 4 hours a day *pro bono* to learn the business better, and offered to bring in his computer to set up certain programs to facilitate support operations. The two men agreed there would be a 3-month "probation" period. At the end of that time, they jointly decided that my client had sufficiently carved out a role for himself and proceeded to negotiate financial arrangements. In this case, the positive results were due to my client's willingness to volunteer in order to build on his background and to transfer some of his skills to a growth area. Also, he created an opportunity for himself to learn in a low-risk situation, and the volunteer situation allowed for a "sneak preview" by both parties.

JOB-SEARCH STRATEGIES

What are some key job-search steps and strategies that counselors can recommend to older clients? A number of them, which have proven helpful, follow. Although most would be appropriate for job seekers of all ages, older workers pay an even higher price if they disregard them. They are:

• Develop and continually expand one's contact network and make it a primary job search strategy.

• Thoroughly explore the traditional job sources, such as newspaper ads, executive recruitment firms, permanent and temporary agencies (particularly those that work with older job seekers), job fairs, alumni college offices, professional and trade associations, and so forth. If possible, go online with the computer. Leave no stone unturned.

• Target small-to-medium-sized companies and go where the growth is. Be a bigger fish in a smaller pond with the potential for making a greater contribution. Consider nonprofit organizations as well.

• Use the library and its career-related resources. Many libraries today have expanded their job information sections. One can learn about all aspects of job search and career exploration, as well as research growth companies, industries, and geographic areas. Moreover, some libraries offer workshops for job seekers and an increasing number have computer facilities to assist them as well.

• Join one or more job-search support groups. There are many groups that meet in churches, synagogues, and community centers. They help to propel a proactive campaign and provide emotional support, along with nuts-and-bolts advice, job leads, and information exchange. Of particular interest to older clients is the organization Forty Plus, with 16 locations nationwide, the American Association of Retired Persons' Works, originating in Washington, DC, but provided at many local chapters, and ABLE, which is Chicago-based, but has more than 40 affiliations in many different states. Mixed support groups for people of all ages can be helpful as well.

• Be aware of and market the transferability of one's skills. A long career might have produced a broad-skill set, which can be recast and repackaged in various combinations. What counts is not what one is, or has been, but what one can do.

• Continue to upgrade one's skills and even retrain to make oneself more marketable. Become computer literate. SeniorNet, headquartered in San Francisco, is a nationwide organization with learning centers for people 55 and older. SeniorNet also has an inexpensive PC online service for members that includes job postings.

• Become part of the contingency workforce, regardless of one's job level or function. It may or may not lead to full-time employment, but could mean long-term temporary employment. If one is a retiree, consider doing part-time, temporary or seasonal work for a former employer. Some companies have established hiring pools for their retirees.

• Do volunteer or *pro bono* work. It keeps individuals in touch with their skills and strengths, helps them to develop new ones in a low or no-risk situation, and occasionally leads to a paying job. Moreover, as illustrated earlier, doing unpaid work can be used as a strategy to penetrate a particular organization or industry. Along similar lines, sometimes individuals can create their own unpaid internship in a targeted company.

• When interviewing, project the three "Es"—experience, energy, and enthusiasm. Do not talk about the "good old days." Instead, face forward and stress the future. Indicate willingness to learn and ability to adapt and work with people of all ages. Overcome age concerns, often euphemistically referred to as "overqualified," by demonstrating nondefensively how one's skills, experience, and knowledge would be of value for many years to the organization's needs and goals.

• Be proud of the knowledge, wisdom, and experience of one's years. Tap into personal resources to propel oneself forward. Do not undervalue one's work, education, training, and skills, because if one does, so too will the world. Maintain a belief that there are organizations out there that need what one has to offer, and act on it.

COUNSELING TECHNIQUES

I have found the counseling techniques recommended in the following list to have a particularly positive effect on the counseling process and/or the counselor–client relationship with older clients.

The techniques are as follows:

• Be aware of one's own counseling philosophy, style, and approach, especially in connection with age-related issues. Be alert to potential obstacles within oneself that might inhibit good counseling of mature adults. Be "age neutral."

- Establish early rapport with the client and take a team or partnership approach.
- Motivate clients to engage in the assessment process by demonstrating its importance at a critical career or life juncture. Indicate how, through internal reflection and discussion, individuals build a valuable "database" on themselves and develop a set of criteria to use at each stage of their job search or career switch. This includes evaluating opportunities, making decisions, and taking action.
- Build the assessment around a "core" consisting of values (vocational and personal), skills and interests that can then be combined with a broad range of other formal and informal assessment instruments, depending on the client and the counseling situation.
- During the assessment phase:

  a. Learn about the client's past career path, job-search abilities, experiences, and decisions as a prognosis of future actions and indicators of possible need for intervention.
  b. When reviewing assessment results, expand the value of the feedback process by having clients participate fully. Include their reactions to the results as an integral part of the process.

- Use the assessment results very pragmatically throughout the various stages of the counseling process so that clients can factor them into their decisions and actions.
- Utilize older adult values such as seriousness, diligence, commitment, and a sense of responsibility to facilitate the counseling process and results.
- Share your rationale for any recommendations with clients. Also, reflect what you are hearing and seeing, and verify your observations with the clients throughout the counseling process.
- Have joint agreement on "next steps" as the clients move along toward well-defined goals and make decisions based on assessment results.
- Reinforce the clients' accomplishments as they proceed and build on them, particularly if they have been feeling somewhat powerless and not in control.
- Remind the clients of what they said early on regarding their interests and goals. Playing back to them their own words and ideas helps to propel them forward.
- Act as a role model regarding life changes and job or career shifts, but decide when, how, and how much self-disclosure is appropriate.
- Have clients use themselves as positive role models based on past successes as they make decisions and take action. Help them to

reframe past experiences from a positive perspective, particularly as they relate to lessons learned.
- When clients get "stuck," ask them for their interpretation and ideas for possible solutions before making your recommendations.
- Project your empathy for their situation, as well as your belief in their capacity for change and improvement of their circumstances. However, acknowledge that it is their responsibility to take the appropriate steps.
- Be cognizant of clients' awareness of time passing in their lives so that your conversations and advice are pragmatic, realistic, and can be acted on in the near term.

CONCLUSION

Counseling older outplacement clients is continually challenging, as well as extremely gratifying. Many older clients bring to the counseling relationship solid values and ethics, combined with a seriousness of intent and an appreciative attitude. Moreover, each client represents a unique combination of life and work experiences, priorities, and goals, all of which call for fresh and creative approaches.

The greatest challenge is a subtle one, but it is critical to successful counseling of older adults. It requires that counselors be able to transmit to clients an optimism about future possibilities and a "can do" attitude about reaching goals. This ability, in turn, needs to stem from a genuine belief on the part of counselors that older adults can continually grow, learn, change, and achieve. Moreover, counselors can help clients bring a sense of their worth, derived from the past, into the future.

Counseling older clients on career-related issues is a rather recent phenomenon. It makes pioneers out of both counselors and clients. There is no script to follow. But together we can write our own scripts, and therein lie the greatest rewards for both.

REFERENCES

Chickering, A. M. (1981). *The modern American college*. San Francisco: Jossey-Bass.
Commonwealth Fund. (1993). *The untapped resource: The final report of the Americans over 55 at work program*. New York: Author.
Erikson, E. (1963). *Childhood and society*. New York: Norton.
Knowles, M. S. (1980). *The modern practice of adult education: From pedagogy to andragogy*. Chicago: Follett.

8 Counseling Minority Clients

Mary Ann Lee
Deloitte & Touche, New York

INTRODUCTION

As we approach the 21st century, counseling minority clients will become a more significant aspect of the career counselor's work. Counseling minority clients requires a very special set of skills. It also requires a unique understanding by the counselor of the special issues that minority clients face. It forces counselors to examine their own ideas and perspectives. This chapter reviews the counseling skills that are needed and then explores the issues related to working with three minority groups: African Americans, Asian Americans, and Latin Americans.

This chapter is intended to be a practical approach to everyday situations faced by career counselors in dealing with minority clients. It is not an exhaustive exploration of the professional literature. It is neither theory nor research based. It is primarily a case study approach highlighting techniques that are effective in counseling minorities.

Why is career counseling for minority clients so important today? If current trends continue, minorities will be entering the workforce in increasingly greater numbers. The issues of race and ethnicity will assume greater importance. By the year 2000, those groups that have traditionally held minority status in the United States will begin to outnumber the population that traces its cultural origins to Europe (Lee & Richardson, 1991). Counseling the minority today prepares one for counseling the majority tomorrow.

This emerging trend of greater numbers of minorities in the workforce will, in all likelihood, be reflected in the populations that seek career counseling. Traditionally, the professionals who have provided career counseling have been White, middle class, and have come from a European cultural background. Their skills and their values will be challenged by minority clients who do not share their cultural orientation.

DEFINITIONS

In this chapter, *minorities* refers to "groups that have been receiving differential and unequal treatment because of collective discrimination. It is a condition of oppression rather than of numerical criteria" (Pederson,

1988, p. viii). The focus is on racial and ethnic minorities, rather than those of gender or sexual preference.

COUNSELOR PERSPECTIVES

The Concept of "Duality"

To a certain extent, all Americans have a bicultural heritage. However, it is only those who come from minority backgrounds that experience a bicultural heritage burdened with a psychosocial history of racism and oppression from the majority culture. When W. E. B. DuBois wrote about the identity of African Americans, he mentioned a sense of "twoness—an American, a Negro; two souls, two thoughts, two unreconciled strivings; two warring ideals in one dark body" (DuBois, 1903/1961, p. 17). The Latin-American acculturation experience (especially the Puerto Rican) has been described as being in two worlds or entremundos. The formation of the Asian-American identity can be explained in terms of a "personal internal identity" (how you see yourself) and a "social external identity" (the view of you by the society at large) according to L. N. Huang (1994). All of these viewpoints suggest that the minority experience is one of duality, where one often has to manage to live between and in and out of two different worlds, that of the majority, dominant, White, middle-class culture in America and that of one's own minority culture.

Minority clients often enter counseling sessions unaware of this sense of duality, of having to moderate between two different cultures. The conflicts that result from being a part of two contradictory cultures can be stressful for minority clients. It is this struggle that counselors must address if they are to help minority clients. In order to empower such clients, counselors must attend to the "personal, cultural and defensive variables that influence the client's coping styles" (Tomine, 1991).

A frequent example of minority clients coping with duality and identity arises with an issue as basic as their "ethnically different" name. This has emerged in my work with clients from all three minority groups. For example, a Latin-American client who was a successful attorney questioned whether his ethnic first name, Enrique, might be hindering his career advancement, especially because he planned to go into politics. Changing his name to Henry was a possible solution. However, Enrique experienced strong ambivalence about this proposed change. He feared rejection from the Latino community for "trading in," as well as a sense of loss and relatedness to his Latino culture if he changed his name. He also understood that, although he wanted the support of the Latino community, he would need the votes of the larger "Anglo" population if he were to win any elections. He believed that having an "Anglicized" name would help to broaden his appeal to more voters. After much introspection, research, and several meetings with other Latino politicians, Enrique decided to legally change his name to Henry. However, he always emphasized his Latino family name, Romano.

Counselors need to address the clients' cultural background and their relationships with the majority culture. Clarification of these issues requires counselors to discuss, explore, and understand the cultural values and sex role expectations of the clients.

Self-Awareness

Self-awareness is important in any counseling situation. However, in multicultural counseling relationships with minority clients, the counselor's self-awareness must go beyond the self to include a broader understanding and appreciation of one's own cultural background. Information on one's cultural background can be found, of course, in various media including reference books, fiction and nonfiction literature, film, theater, and academic classes, to name just a few. Another way to learn about one's family lineage is through discussions with family members and relatives, or active members and/or elder members of one's ethnic community or religious groups.

After counselors have had the opportunity to learn more about their own cultural background, biases, and assumptions, the next step is to learn more about the background of minority clients. As in any other counseling relationship, counselors need to get as much information as possible during the early interviews. No one can be totally knowledgeable about every minority group with whom they will work. A quick method by which counselors can become more aware and sensitive to clients from different cultures is to review "Characteristics of Culture" (included in Harris & Moran, 1987). This volume contains a list that can serve as a handy, quick aid to assist in the observation and assessment of clients during counseling sessions.

Communication

Communication is the process by which we exchange messages and, thus, learn about each other. During career counseling sessions, there are three sets of communication skills that are used: verbal, nonverbal, and listening. Verbal refers to the particular language or dialect spoken. Nonverbal communication includes eye contact, body movements, spatial relationships, touch, perceptions of time, and meanings attributed to objects. Listening (aural) is one of the most critical skills in any helping profession. To listen is to apply one's self, to pay attention, to give heed.

It is my observation that counselors in the United States tend to rely more heavily on verbal skills and are not as skilled with listening and/or nonverbal skills. Most education and counseling courses offer training in verbal skills. Few offer in-depth training in nonverbal or listening skills. As Harris and Moran put it: "Listening is the skill that is first learned, least used and least taught" (Harris & Moran, 1987, p. 38). When counselors are working with minority clients, the nonverbal and listening skills need to be developed and used as intensively as the verbal skills.

Understanding our own preferred communication style is only one side of the equation. To deal with minority clients successfully, we also need to be aware of the preferred communication style of the minority group of our candidates. For example, Asian cultures tend to place major emphasis on listening skills and less emphasis on verbal self-expression, especially for those in subordinate or deferential positions. So, when I work with Asian Americans, I often encourage development of verbal skills.

By way of contrast, many African-American clients have been socialized to verbally express themselves quite freely. In working with certain African-American clients, however, we have devoted more time to the development of listening skills. In general, I have found that nonverbal behaviors differ from group to group in subtle ways. Therefore, it is important to assist minority clients in recognizing the impact of their nonverbal behavior on others in order to avoid misunderstanding or confusion. Payne (1986) is helpful in assessing the communication styles of clients from various minority groups.

Multiculturalism and the Stereotyping Trap

Counselors working with individuals from different racial groups need to guard against the possibility of promoting racism by overgeneralizing and overconcentrating on racial differences. Although generalizing makes it easier to deal with the enormous amount of information on diverse cultural populations, it can often lead to stereotyping of individual clients. Most studies tend to compare minority populations to the White, European-oriented majority. As a result, differences rather than similarities are emphasized. Similarities are often overlooked. As counselors, we need to be sensitive to both differences and similarities in order to fully empower minority clients.

Many of us tend to work with specialized populations. For instance, outplacement counselors tend to work with middle-class, educated professionals from corporate settings. On the other hand, counselors in social service clinics tend to spend most of their time with immigrant clients or those with more limited social, educational, and economic resources. If our population is relatively homogeneous by race, the trap is that we will tend to start treating everyone alike. We may jump to conclusions as to what clients need without doing an adequate assessment. To avoid this trap, use the more comprehensive assessment process described in the next section.

PRACTICAL APPLICATIONS AND SKILLS

Initial Assessment

Getting appropriate information during the initial intake interview is always helpful and necessary in any counseling relationship. During the assessment stage of a counseling relationship with a minority client, it is crucial to have a detailed intake process that includes extensive personal information. Specifically, it is important to have more comprehensive information about sociological, political, educational, and religious background with an emphasis placed on the level of acculturation into American society. The additional information will help clarify the counselor's understanding of the different cultural issues that minority clients bring into the sessions.

Communication Skills

Anytime we work with people of different cultures, there will be issues of language and dialect. Listening is the most important skill in understanding these issues. Listening to the level and type of English spoken offers valuable clues to the counselor about the socioeconomic and educational background of the individual. This helps the counselor to better assess how the client has become acculturated to American society.

In terms of practical application, if we hear that a client has a heavy accent or does not understand English very well, we should raise it diplomatically at the onset of the counseling process. Language differences should be addressed in a sensitive and supportive manner, so that clients feel that their language differences are being acknowledged rather than being ignored or criticized. This will immediately alert both parties to the possible need for adjustments. For example, speaking patterns could be slowed down to enable client and counselor to communicate more comfortably and effectively. This is a two-way process. Not only must we attempt to understand the client but we must also ascertain that the client understands us. This is not a one-shot solution; it should continue throughout the counseling relationship. We should never assume that communication is taking place merely because counselor and client are talking. Communication requires us to take responsibility that our message is being heard and understood.

Although nonverbal communication accounts for 55% of all communication (Harris & Moran, 1987), we tend to take this form of communication for granted. Typically, we only notice nonverbal communication when it is inappropriate or it appears different from our expectations. When we are dealing with clients from other cultures, awareness of this aspect of the communication process must be heightened. Most of our understanding of others is often based on perceptions. Perceptions rely on nonverbal communication. It is crucial that we constantly observe and try to understand the nonverbal communication that occurs during our sessions. It is often difficult to determine whether the nonverbal communication is culturally based or idiosyncratic to the individual. If we cannot determine its basis, we might need more information about the client's cultural background. One way to understand the behavior (gestures or movements), is simply to discuss them when we have developed an adequate degree of comfort and rapport in our counseling relationship. For example, if an Asian American client does not have direct eye contact with us during sessions, it is probably not due to the client's defiance or insecurity. In Asian culture, it is considered rude for a younger person or a person who is not in authority to look directly at an older person or one who is in charge.

The Concepts of Self and Space

In American culture or, more precisely, Northern European-influenced American culture, the concept of *self*, the individual, is all-important. Insight-oriented counseling, which sprang forth from Northern European culture, is a process of talking about yourself in order to better understand yourself. This requires introspection. It also poses a dilemma for minority clients, especially in the Asian cultures, because they do not encourage self-expression and/or active self-expression to a stranger. Therefore, the first step in the counseling process is to become less of a stranger so that the client feels more comfortable. It is very positive that the client has already taken the first step by participating in a counseling session. This client is willing to try counseling. Don't lose this advantage by attempting to rush the process. Early discussions focusing on work or education provide a safe introduction. Sharing our insights and experiences on these same topics facilitates the relationship.

Counseling has traditionally been a process of self-awareness, self-deliberation, and self-exploration. However, the concept of self does not exist in many minority cultures. Instead, the individual's identification is tied to family and to relationships to others, which might be family, tribe, religious group, or community. When we ask clients to make decisions about a career, we may find hesitation or resistance. Clients may not even be able to imagine doing this by themselves. To them, it is really a group decision. Counselors need to be aware that if clients do not want to talk about themselves, or are not comfortable with making decisions, it is not necessarily because of insecurity, indecisiveness, or a lack of intelligence, but may be entirely the influence of culture. When counselors have provided sufficiently safe and supportive environments for counseling sessions, minority clients will be more likely to open up and discuss these issues.

The concept of *space* is another cultural issue in counseling minority clients. In the United States, as in the northern European countries, there is a comfortable "space" of several feet that we keep between ourselves and others who are not close to us (i.e., nonfamily, business associates, etc.). In the Latin and Middle-Eastern cultures, it is acceptable to maintain a closer proximity to outsiders. For example, hugging and kissing business associates is not only acceptable, but may be expected as proper behavior. Therefore, spatial differences must be taken into consideration.

We need to know first what is comfortable for us. Next, we might try keeping the customary distance of several feet for the first few sessions. Unless we notice some discomfort from the client, we could keep the same spatial distance and the same arrangement during future meetings.

However, should we see any nonverbal signs of discomfort during the sessions, we might raise this topic when we feel it is appropriate. One way to address the spatial and seating arrangements might be to ask clients directly if they are comfortable with them. However, if clients are not secure enough to respond directly in the earlier sessions, the counselor needs to bring these questions up again in later sessions. We may find a different response as clients become more comfortable in telling us the truth.

Integrating Other Social Organizations as a Support System

As discussed earlier, the identity of minority clients is closely tied to their family and/or other community or religious groups. It is important to discuss their family roles and group affiliations. After we have a better understanding of how the client relates to these different groups, it is crucial that the significant members from these different social organizations are included in the client's career counseling process. These significant individuals, who might be a grandmother, a minister, or a fortune teller, can offer valuable support for the client during all aspects of counseling. In fact, the success of the entire career counseling experience might depend on the acknowledgment and integration of these key individuals into the process.

COUNSELING AFRICAN-AMERICAN CLIENTS

Sandra B.

Sandra B., a 50-year-old African-American woman, who was a secretary in a metropolitan hospital, came for career counseling because she needed to find a more meaningful career and work that offered more money. Recently divorced, she had total financial responsibility for two teenage daughters. Her greatest concern was being able to finance their college educations. In addition, Sandra had financial responsibility for her 72-year-old mother who had always lived with her and who took care of her daughters.

It appeared that Sandra initiated the divorce, and was relieved that she was now independent. Her husband had been unemployed for at least 10 years of their 17-year marriage. He also had a problem with alcoholism but refused to get treatment. Sandra had never been able to depend on him for any financial or emotional support. The finalization of the divorce also enabled Sandra to reexamine her life, and face the reality of being responsible for her family's financial situation.

Throughout her life, Sandra's mother and the Baptist Church had always been the greatest sources of comfort and support when she needed to deal with a crisis. More recently, her two daughters had also been giving Sandra the positive emotional support she needed. When working with African-American clients, it is important to take into consideration the influence of the extended family, in particular the mother and/or the grandmother, as well as the church, when trying to resolve any career or personal issues.

For the last 4 years, Sandra had been pursuing an associate's degree in liberal arts in the evening at a local community college. She had completed about 60 credits but had no idea what subject she wanted to choose as a major. Although she was motivated to complete the degree, she realized that she also needed to find a more lucrative position before this could be accomplished. She was not clear about what she wanted to do but knew she did not want to be employed as a secretary forever.

Sandra was very verbal and open. She articulated many of her concerns during the initial session. She seemed anxious to resolve all her problems at once and had great difficulty relaxing and listening. It became apparent that she felt extremely burdened with her family and work responsibilities. Because of her age, she felt a great sense of urgency "in getting things done" immediately. Her need for accomplishing her goals became a major asset, as well as a limitation. She had a high degree of motivation to achieve the goals she set. However, Sandra's goals were not clearly defined and her impatience prevented her from clarifying them.

From the onset, it was clear that Sandra needed direction. During the intake, it seemed crucial to clarify the expectations and goals of the career counseling relationship, as well as to end the first session with concrete, practical information for her to review. It was also important to acknowledge her varied concerns and support her use of all available resources to resolve them. With Sandra, as well as with other minority clients, it was necessary to address and understand the personal concerns in addition to the career issues. As in any counseling situation, the line between personal and professional problems is often murky. The two sets of issues are frequently related. Understanding the relation between personal and career issues is especially important in counseling minority clients because their family and other community affiliations are such an integral part of their lives.

Once we developed a comfortable relationship, we also had to address her inability to listen and relax. From our earlier sessions, it became apparent that the anxiety came from her lack of direction and her lack of career information. My role was to work with her on providing career assessment and interpretation along with the research skills and information she needed to make informed career choices. Sandra became much more relaxed once we had the opportunity to explore her interests, skills, values, strengths, and weaknesses. After her career direction became more focused, she seemed much more attentive.

As with other African Americans, Sandra had a very close and strong relationship with her mother and with her church. Therefore, it was important to reaffirm the strength of the relationships with her family, as well as with her minister and other members of the congregation. Because her mother, minister, and many of the women of the church committees were very close to her, I encouraged her to discuss her career decisions with them. They all became a positive part of her career counseling experience.

Because Sandra had a tendency to want to get things done quickly, it became important for her to have not only long-range objectives, but also more immediate ones. The accomplishment of short-term goals gave her the positive reinforcement she needed to feel that she was making progress toward more long-term objectives.

Sandra's eventual decision to become a pharmacist meant that she would have to complete her associate's degree and eventually get a bachelor's degree in pharmacology. This long-range objective also helped to narrow her current job search to organizations or to areas within those organizations that dealt with pharmacology. Her extensive network within her church led her to a position as a laboratory aide in the research department in another large hospital.

Whereas all the tools of traditional career counseling helped in Sandra's situation, it was the recognition, acknowledgment, and referral to her extended family and her church that provided the extra push that made her career counseling a success. Sandra was pleased to be able to concentrate on chemistry at the community college. Although her new position offered her the same salary as her secretarial job, Sandra was very pleased with this opportunity because she knew it was a step in the right direction toward a more distant goal, that of becoming a pharmacist.

COUNSELING ASIAN AMERICAN CLIENTS

John W.

John W., 40 years old, was a vice president of auditing at a major commercial bank for 11 years. He has an MBA in finance and accounting from Columbia University. During his first 6 years at the bank, John had been promoted frequently and was given challenging assignments. However, in the last 4 years, he had only one salary increase and held no hope of advancement beyond his current title. After the bank's merger, he was terminated when the management decided to keep another vice president with the same skills.

John W. is a first generation Asian American with a college degree and bilingual skills. He speaks two dialects of Chinese: Cantonese and Mandarin. John is a Buddhist, married, and has three sons: an 11-year-old with Down syndrome and 14-year-old twins. His wife, who is also first generation Asian American, is employed at the same bank. She is an executive secretary with a degree in accounting and is also bilingual. John's parents are in their mid-70s and live with John. They have been responsible for the care of the three children since birth. The grandparents do not speak any English. The twins attend the local high school and are performing well academically. John and his wife have had difficulty with the 11-year-old with Down syndrome. He is attending an expensive private school that tends to his special needs. John's parents do not feel that this school is necessary because they think their care alone is sufficient for this child's growth. The child's Down syndrome has been a disappointment and an embarrassment for John's parents.

The course of John's career/outplacement counseling was influenced greatly by his Asian cultural background. On the surface, because of his meticulous professional appearance and excellent verbal communication skills, it would have been easy to overlook the cultural barriers to his professional success. He had excellent credentials, experience, and job-search skills but his personal life impacted significantly his motivation and pursuit of career goals.

During the initial interview, I spent a lot of time discussing his family situation and relationships. Because sex-role expectations and cultural values had such a strong influence on his career decisions, it was crucial that he gain a clear understanding of these factors from the onset. John is the oldest son in a family with five children. The family left Hong Kong for the United States when John was 5 years old. Asians value education and family. All the children were expected to excel in school and to find lucrative professional positions after college. John, being the oldest son, had the added burden of having to live with his parents and take care of them. During our sessions, discussions with John were awkward, especially when we talked about his goals. John's indecisiveness was related to his dissatisfaction and lack of interest in corporate politics. He had been very unhappy working in a corporation and was ready to do something else. He was uncertain about the possibilities.

John seemed to want to start his own business but was unclear as to the type of work he could viably pursue. His other concerns were to obtain his family's approval and to be able to support his extended family. Vocational assessment tools like the Strong Interest Inventory (SII) were useful in clarifying what he wanted to do. The SII results made communication about career goals easier by giving us something concrete to discuss. Once it became clearer to John that is was the corporate politics, not the accounting, that he disliked, he was able to begin exploring how to apply his accounting background in other settings. Today, John and his wife share a thriving CPA practice serving the Asian American community.

Working with Asian American clients, it is very important to be concrete and to focus on practical, goal-directed solutions. It is also important to understand and accept the need for family approval of career decisions. Asian clients value and respect the opinions of their families. Because many people would be affected by his decision, John's decision was not just his own, but one that had to be made jointly with his wife and his parents. In addition to the need to arrive at a shared decision, John also had to find an opportunity that would provide enough income to be able to support his extended family. Although his wife's earnings helped, it was assumed that he would bring home the major portion of the family income. A counselor must respect that the input of the family, especially that of an elderly parent or relative, will be a very important aspect of the career decision process for an Asian American client.

Another issue that is noteworthy when working with Asians and Asian Americans is the use of space. This became very apparent during a recent workshop presentation. During a downsizing at a major Asian bank, I had the opportunity to present a 4-day job-search workshop for 25 Chinese-American participants. Some were first-generation and others were more recent immigrants. It was difficult to get everyone to participate in the group discussions. I was well aware that Asian Americans are often uncomfortable speaking up in large groups and I did not expect to have total involvement immediately. I also assumed that the size of the room assigned to us had much to do with the limited group participation. The conference room assigned to us initially was very small and was without windows. It had very little ventilation when the door was closed. I made every effort to find a larger and more comfortable space for the group.

Finally, we were fortunate enough to get a much larger and more comfortable room with sofas and coffee tables. It had three-way exposure and a terrace. To my surprise, the participants appeared even more uncomfortable and became even less participatory in this room. After a whole day in this new space, approximately 10 of the participants complained to me privately. Most of the participants seemed to find the new, larger room to be less comfortable and less conducive for group interaction. They were speaking on behalf of the group and indicated that the larger space was too open and too big and made them very uncomfortable. They also indicated that being in the original smaller conference room with its large conference table in the center gave them a greater sense of security when writing and speaking to the group. After we returned to the original, smaller conference room, the participants seemed much happier and did become more involved in the group discussion.

It also appeared that the closer proximity to others made the Chinese-American participants more comfortable. What I thought was cramped and uncomfortable space was very cozy, safe, and comfortable for them. It is important to recognize cultural differences in determining what "space" is considered appropriate and comfortable. The clients in this group felt sufficiently at ease to discuss the situation with me so that it could be remedied. This might not be the case in an other situation, as many Asian Americans do not feel comfortable directly verbalizing a complaint. Therefore, it is wise to check the use of space and how individuals are situated when working with clients from other cultures, whether in groups or with individuals.

COUNSELING LATIN AMERICAN CLIENTS

Anita G.

Anita G. is a 28-year-old Latin American who was born in Puerto Rico, but came to New York when she was 2 years old. She has been married since graduating from college 7 years ago. With a BA in business and fluency in both English and Spanish, she has always had opportunities in the business community. For the last 5 years, she has been a recruiter for management trainees in sales at a Fortune 500 insurance corporation. Until the birth of her son 3 years ago, Anita had been advancing quite rapidly in her career. Since the birth of her son, Anita has been more limited in her career mobility because she has been unable to travel as extensively as in the past. Conflicts around balancing her career and family life prompted Anita to seek career counseling.

During the intake, Anita indicated that her husband is also of Puerto Rican descent and is bilingual. He has a high school diploma and has been employed as a mechanic. Although he had an opportunity to go to college, he chose instead to work immediately after high school graduation. Both are devout Catholics and very close to their families. Her husband's 67-year-old mother takes care of their son while they are at work.

Her husband had always been supportive of her career. Consequently, it was confusing for Anita that after their son was born, her husband became upset that her work kept her away from home and the family. He became resentful because he wanted Anita to take a more active and involved role in the family. During our discussions, it became clear that Anita was very unhappy that her career advancement was slowing as a result of family responsibilities. In addition, she was unhappy about her husband's lack of understanding and the increased demands on her time.

When working with Latin Americans, counselors need to consider the roles and the relationships within the family. It was the weight of her husband's expectations and the rejection of increased demands from her job that prompted her to seek career counseling. In order to deal with Anita's career and family-life conflict, it was important to get her to talk about her values as well as her roles and expectations as a wife, mother, and a professional woman coming from a Puerto Rican background. It was also crucial to get clarification of her husband's expectations and views on their relationship.

During our first two sessions, Anita was quite verbal and open in discussing her feelings and thoughts. However, during the subsequent three sessions, which her husband attended, Anita became more reticent and cautious. Her spouse took the initiative to open discussions and he spoke more frequently than she. It became obvious to me but not to Anita that her behavior changed when her husband was with her. Although she was given the same supportive counseling environment in which to express herself freely, she continued to defer to her husband. I pointed out this changed behavior to her in our later sessions. Anita told me she was not aware of the changes in her behavior but she did recall feeling uncomfortable.

During the joint sessions, it became apparent that both Anita and her husband were very traditional. They both agreed that Anita should continue her career but felt that she should find work that would allow more time for her family, at least until her son starts kindergarten. They both began to realize that although they had definite sex-role expectations for each other, they were willing to compromise toward a viable solution. Her spouse agreed that he would continue to be more helpful at home if she would work out a schedule that did not require constant travel.

Subsequent sessions with Anita dealt with her career interests, goals, and options. Other career opportunities were assessed and reviewed. She finally decided to research the possibility of being a recruiter for the administrative staff. This would not require any travel, and she could continue to work in the same department in her present company.

Another alternative was to explore her present company's flextime policy, and work out a schedule that would be comfortable for her and her supervisor.

Of the two options, Anita preferred to work a flextime arrangement of 4-day work weeks with longer hours on the days she worked. During our discussions, however, Anita indicated that she was not yet comfortable reviewing this with her supervisor. She felt she did not have the communication skills to negotiate this in a positive manner. It also became clear that she did not feel secure asking her male boss for this special consideration.

Further exploration revealed that, as a Latin American, she felt powerless to ask for this consideration, even though she knew this option was provided by company policy. She thought that her proposed action also made her seem too aggressive. When Anita brought up the issue of being too aggressive, I referred to the sessions with her spouse where I noticed that she seemed more reserved and passive in her reactions and comments than when we were alone. Apparently, she was not aware of this behavior, although she did realize that she felt uncomfortable with herself in these situations.

I supported her by telling her that I, too, come from a culture that fosters, expects, and rewards women for being passive and quiet. Then I asked whether her reaction with men might be related to similar cultural influences. After further introspection, she indicated that everyone in her family had always expected the women to work and do well but not to "outdo" the men and, certainly, never to publicly "show up" their husbands or any other men by being more knowledgeable or even speaking first or more frequently.

This led to a discussion of whether her husband was concerned about her having a BA in business and her holding a professional position. Anita did not seem to think that her spouse was uncomfortable with this. She did, however, avoid any lengthy discussion about her husband's reaction to her career. Instead, she focused on a more immediate concern, that of her ability to ask her supervisor for the flextime she needed to achieve her career goal.

In order to help her achieve her objective, we first had to discuss, identify, and work with the cultural issues that affected her behavior. Then, we proceeded to develop the skills to facilitate her becoming more assertive in discussing her career options. Script writing, role-playing, and video taping the "scenes" all helped to develop Anita's self-confidence and prepare for the meeting with her supervisor. During the preparation, we scripted and rehearsed the remarks she would make to her supervisor and then practiced her responses to his likely questions and comments.

Follow-up meetings with Anita indicated that she did receive a flextime schedule as the recruiter of the administrative staff. Increased awareness of her previously passive behavior has made her more assertive in the work setting but at home she is reconciled to her continued deference to her husband. Recent conversations with Anita indicated that she, her husband, and her mother-in-law are pleased at how she has been able to balance her work and family life.

CONCLUSIONS AND IMPLICATIONS FOR THE FUTURE

Multicultural Effectiveness in Counseling

Can a counselor from one cultural group be effective in counseling clients from another cultural group? From my perspective, the answer is "yes," given the following two requirements. First, the counselor needs to have some exposure to working with individuals from the other group or, at a minimum, have attained some basic knowledge of that group through reading or research. Ideally, this knowledge comes from direct experience in working with clients from that group in a client–counselor relationship. Second, counselors need to be self-aware about their own cultural biases and assumptions and how they impact the relationship in a multicultural counseling situation. Experience without self-awareness is unlikely to result in success.

Perceptions of Value

Although it is easy to be enthusiastic about the need for multicultural counseling, this enthusiasm should be tempered by the reality that career counseling is still primarily utilized and valued by the White, middle class. Minority populations often view counseling, in general, with skepticism. Counseling is neither understood nor valued in some cultures. For other groups, counseling may have earned the reputation as a vehicle for oppression, social control, and maintaining the status quo.

Perceptions by minorities of the value of career counseling will take time to alter. Only through positive experiences of counseling relationships will these perceptions begin to change. Some of the resistance is based on a lack of understanding of the counseling process. As a result, minority clients do not feel comfortable paying for a service they do not understand. For those who do seek counseling, it is important that the expectations and goals of the clients be clarified in the initial sessions. It needs to be made clear what can and cannot be achieved through career counseling. Each additional minority client who concludes that his or her career counseling experience had value helps make the overall perception more positive.

REFERENCES

DuBois, W. E. B. (1961). *The souls of black talk*. New York: Fawcett. (Original work published 1903)

Harris, P. R., & Moran, R. T. (1987). *Managing cultural differences*. Houston, TX: Gulf.

Huang, L. N. (1994). An integrative view of identity formation: A model for Asian Americans. In E. P. Salett & D. R. Koslow (Eds.), *Race, ethnicity and self* (pp. 42–59). Washington, DC: National Multicultural Institute.

Lee, C. C., & Richardson, B. L. (1991). *Multicultural issues in counseling: New approaches to diversity*. Alexandria, VA: American Association for Counseling and Development.

Payne, K. (1986). Effects of cultural assumptions on cross-cultural communication. In O. L. Taylor (Ed.), *Nature of communication disorders in linguistically and culturally diverse populations* (pp. 18–27). San Diego, CA: College-Hill Press.

Pederson, P. (1988). *A handbook for developing multicultural awareness*. Alexandria, VA: American Association for Counseling and Development.

Tomine, S. I. (1991). Counseling Japanese Americans. In C. C. Lee & B. L. Richardson (Eds.), *Multicultural issues in counseling* (pp. 91–105). Alexandria, VA: American Association for Counseling and Development.

$\mathcal{9}$ Counseling Helpless Clients

Sheryl S. Spanier
The Strickland Group, New York

Career consultants and their candidates typically have complementary interests. Consultants working with individuals in transition are motivated by a desire to help; their clients need and want help. Under the best of circumstances, this mutuality leads to new awareness, constructive actions, and satisfying resolutions. The mission of the consultants is to help candidates by teaching them career and life management, job-search strategies, and career advancement techniques. Consultants who provide outplacement and executive coaching help individuals to overcome a trauma or disappointment, gain greater self-awareness, improve work-related skills and relationships, and advance professionally.

The initial phase of outplacement counseling or executive coaching concentrates on assessment of candidate needs and preferences, analysis of work situations, and setting of goals. This part of the work is mainly consultant and/or program-driven. Candidates are provided an opportunity to express their feelings about their situation. Typically, they are then given assignments for completion. They also receive constructive feedback from their consultants. They generally appreciate this attention and information. Consultants usually feel, in return, very excited, empowered, and grateful that their skills and efforts are well received.

Once the groundwork has been laid, consultants encourage candidates to put into practice what has been learned and planned. This requires them to take risks, use initiative, and be willing to be held to scrutiny. Consultants move into the role of coach, confidant, and critic. This stage of the process is a turning point. Most candidates respond with energy and enthusiasm. Others, however, become stuck. In such cases, if consultants continue to apply the standard activity-oriented interventions and candidates respond with inactivity and resistance, the counseling relationship can become a frustrating dance. Clients can become increasingly dependent, demanding, and unable to move forward, and consultants can feel irritated by their inability to contribute toward a satisfying resolution.

I call this the *helpless client syndrome*. It is a set of behaviors that is frustrating to both candidates and counselors. This chapter discusses the syndrome thoroughly. It also focuses on a variety of innovative methods and approaches that are not typically employed with these candidates, but that can be extremely effective, if skillfully used.

107

CHALLENGES OF CORPORATE-SPONSORED COUNSELING

Before turning full attention to a discussion of helpless clients in outplacement or executive coaching, a few words are in order about the special challenges of corporate-sponsored counseling.

Corporate sponsors who make referrals to outplacement and/or executive coaching services often assume that an executive's presenting problem, such as job loss, subpar communication skills, or deficient management or political skills, will remain the focus of the work. The initiator of the counseling assignment is a third person (manager or human resources officer) who might be unaware of potentially complex, underlying issues that have precipitated the referral.

In other counseling modalities, the client seeks out and initiates the treatment. Also, the counselor and client have ample time to work through resistances and obstacles so that the client can take risks. However, in corporate-sponsored career counseling the initial focus and, often, the duration of counseling is dictated by the corporation. Because the work is sponsored by a third party (the executive's organization), the individual may not initially desire the assistance. Also, the consultant might feel obliged to guide the candidate toward a specified outcome. There are tasks dictated by the program that the consultant might be required to implement. Sometimes, therefore, consultants might push resistant clients to act in ways they are unable or unwilling to.

Typically, consultants will address issues of skill development and behavior change, paying less attention to the affect issues that might be interfering with execution. They will, for example, assist candidates in writing a resume, guide them through a video role-play session, give networking assignments, or review weekly progress. Usually, these activities assist candidates to successfully accomplish the goals of the counseling program. However, some individuals who have significant underlying personal issues, unresolved emotional problems, or negative belief systems will not be able to take advantage of the instruction and coaching. At this point, the relationship can break down.

For example, a candidate with whom I worked was referred to outplacement by a major accounting firm. The organization informed me that the executive was an excellent performer with poor political skills who had burned his bridges upward and had no future with the organization. Young, well-educated, and energetic, the candidate appeared ready to launch an active search. However, when his resumé was completed and he had to explain his circumstances to prospective employers, he became immobilized, withdrawn, and inactive. He began to complain of a lack of desire to pursue opportunities and seemed hesitant to take advantage of a supportive network. Continued coaching only exacerbated his frustration. He started to talk about a career change; perhaps to return to his modest origins to take over the family hardware store.

I decided at this point to pull back from our standard program, and to shift to a more in-depth exploration of the executive's history. We discussed some of his beliefs supporting his desire to "go home again." In this context, my candidate talked more freely about his family history. It came to light that this individual had been the child of a divorce and never quite recovered from what he experienced as his father's rejection. After further inquiry, I learned that he had been recruited to his former employer by an older mentor who, reportedly, turned on him as the candidate became more capable and independent. Ultimately, the mentor fired him. By discussing this episode more fully over several counseling sessions, the candidate realized that he was unknowingly associating his job loss and the betrayal by his former mentor with his unresolved feelings about his father. Placing these historical parallels and complex reactions in perspective allowed the executive to explore, once again, appropriate corporate positions. He realized that he was not likely to have a repeat experience in the next position. In addition, his increased self-awareness primed him to be more effective in dealing with authority figures in the future. Had we merely stayed with the prescribed program of job-search training, this candidate could have reestablished himself inappropriately out of fear or misbelief based on unresolved issues from the past, or worse, sunk into more entrenched helplessness.

THE HELPLESS CLIENT SYNDROME

Helplessness often does not emerge until the early stages of a program are completed and participants are asked to put the training into action—to hold themselves to scrutiny, launch a job-search campaign, initiate meetings, and take interpersonal risks.

Candidates demonstrate helplessness in many different ways. Some do it by placing undue demands on counselors, by canceling appointments, being late, or procrastinating. Others do it by acting aggressively toward the support staff, getting distracted by personal agenda, or pursuing career fields or steps that are clearly unrealistic. Sometimes, the unproductive behavior is obvious, especially if the candidate is directly expressing attitudes of pessimism and helplessness. In other instances, the effects are more disguised and indirect. An example would be the candidate who appears on the surface to be conducting a purposeful job search campaign, but on closer scrutiny is really "going through the motions."

Helpless clients present counselors with problems and expect ready solutions. They describe themselves as passive victims of others' actions, have low energy, or lack focus. They may have grandiose or, conversely, excessively modest plans. They are often unprepared for sessions and expect the consultant to provide all of the structure and answers. Or they may spend time in sessions talking about everything but the matter at hand, only to comment at the end of the session that they did not get their needs met. Helpless clients generally see obstacles as outside of their control. They conclude they are too old or too young, or too highly or poorly compensated. Their career path makes their advancement impossible or their network too narrow. They expect others—and especially their consultant—to fix these issues before they, the client, can move forward. These individuals demand more attention, more time, and more resources, and are not taking responsibility for their own actions or changes. Helpless candidates can often be seen rewriting their resumé indefinitely or sending out extensive mass mailings. They complain to their managers that they are getting nothing out of counseling sessions or that they are not getting enough time with their counselor. As their helplessness expands, their internal pressures are increasingly externalized as nonproductive, self-destructive behavior. This further entrenches them.

My theory is that people go through three stages in the job transition process. The first stage is a desire to get out of the immediate situation (e.g., unemployment, difficulty with a boss, conflict with office politics). The second stage is characterized by statements that they "should" do something about their situation; they should network, they should write letters, they should hold their temper or handle the situtation better. In the third stage, the executives turn their energy from moving away from an uncomfortable situation toward a desire to produce significant professional achievements. At this stage, they want to work at something of interest, to pursue a passion for a project or line of work, or desire to impact, professionally, an important issue or organization.

Helpless clients get stuck in the first two stages. Something happens that keeps them from getting to the stage of being impassioned, joyful, and motivated. Consultants can become surprised when the candidate converts from an appreciative recipient of their assistance to a demanding, immobile individual. Once clients become helpless, they start putting all their energy into identifying other services the firm can provide for them, remaining in place physically and emotionally, and protecting themselves from change, exposure, and scrutiny. Their helplessness is, in its own way, very powerful. The helpless clients control consultants, and sometimes the career counseling organization, by their reactions and inaction.

Underlying the helpless, or self-defeating behavior of these candidates is a reservoir of feelings, which if left undetected and unexplored, will undermine the entire counseling process. When clients become dependent in the ways just described, they place others in positions of unrealistic responsibility and consequent ineffectiveness because the clients' demands become overwhelming and disempowering. Feeling unsupported, these clients become increasingly anxious, more demanding, and spend increasing amounts of energy draining others in their service. Energy that would be most useful in moving ahead is diverted to staying in place. Ironically, helpless clients get the opposite of what they need most. Rather than being cared for, they get rejected. In these cases, staying with "the program" can exacerbate helplessness. More "therapeutic" techniques can become appropriate to help them move forward.

COUNSELING TECHNIQUES FOR WORKING WITH HELPLESS CANDIDATES

Helpless clients present an opportunity for consultants to expand their skills and to be creative in their work. There are several methods that can be applied effectively to these individuals. Consultants working with clients who get stuck can benefit from taking a break from career search or career improvement tasks. Then they can bring to the attention of helpless candidates the behaviors that are getting in the way, reflect on the impact of attitudes and feelings, and use their own reactions as a mirror for the clients to examine motivations and choices. Breakthroughs can occur when consultants begin to address some underlying issues, feelings, or belief systems that are obstructing progress.

However, caution and good judgment must always be exercised. Outplacement and career management professionals must always be mindful of the level of their counseling skill and training in order to avoid exceeding those levels. Boundaries need to be respected. Our inquiries and interventions into more personal matters must follow from a well-considered rationale that is linked to the client's career issues. Outplacement and executive coaching are not therapy, even though they may be highly therapeutic to individuals experiencing a major life stressor.

The Consultant as Instrument

Beyond focusing on the needs and attitudes of their clients, career consultants can attend with greater awareness to their own reactions and concerns. Consultants can recognize helplessness by looking inward. This spotlight will provide a wealth of information that assists in the work. A typical first sign of client helplessness is that we, as consultants, feel we are working harder than the client. We consistently provide all the ideas, suggestions, and alternatives only to have them rejected by the candidate. Or, when it comes time to do corporate feedback on the client's progress, we are confounded by the lack of movement or activity to report. Our enthusiasm and efforts are worn down by the helpless candidate's doubts and defeats and we can come to doubt our skills and the value of our work. We begin to feel defeated along with these candidates.

Somehow, helpless clients transfer responsibility for change and growth onto counselors who may think about them, talk about them with colleagues and family, become preoccupied with ways to help them; in short, to give them even more attention and energy. Eventually counselors can become angry and resentful about helpless clients. We might come to dread our sessions with them or feel bored or distracted during sessions. We try harder only to be rebuffed or undermined by passive, rejecting, or complaining behaviors. These reactions are a message that the helpless client is sending to the counselor. Recognizing the message and attending to the causes of helplessness will allow the work to move forward.

Counselors are in a unique position to observe and compassionately bring these insights to the clients' attention. For example, a consultant can comment that the client never takes notes, seems disinterested in sessions, and writes letters expecting the reader to follow-up. Then, consultants can wonder aloud with the client whether this is usual behavior for the client. In response, helpless clients might share a belief that they have no control over the circumstances of their lives or that they must be perfect in everything they do. Sometimes, candidates might indicate that others are responsible for their circumstances or that they feel humiliation and inertia regarding their present situation.

When we use ourselves as a source of information, counseling sessions can become fertile opportunities to explore how candidates express their unresolved issues in unproductive ways. One executive I worked with had tremendous difficulty networking. He complained that no one ever gave him adequate information and that he believed that his age and seniority were intimidating to contacts. In one particularly frustrating session, while we were discussing a letter he wrote, he responded to my suggestions for improvement by looking down in apparent disgust. Experiencing his reaction as more rejecting that appreciative, I commented on his facial expression and body language and asked him what he was thinking. He stated that he was angry at himself for not having thought of the right way to write the letter without my help.

I shared my reaction to his apparent annoyance at my advice, stating that when he looked unappreciative, I felt somewhat rejected and less willing to continue to help him. He seemed surprised that his behavior had this impact. Taking time to seriously consider my reaction, he noted that he was upset that I gave him advice because he believed that he should have all the answers himself. His insightful response turned the corner for his search. He realized that he must be behaving in a similar way with those he networked with, causing them to feel that their assistance was not appreciated or even rejected. Thus, they were not going to be very forthcoming or responsive to his questions or requests.

Combining Psychological and Practical Approaches

When career counseling is done well, it operates on both the pragmatic and psychological levels. Working on these two levels allows consultants to understand and work with the underlying issues that might interfere with the ability of some executives to receive and act on the advice, training, and support offered.

The use of questions, rather than statements or dicta, can be the quickest and most productive path in assisting a client to move forward, and to work on both the psychological and pragmatic levels. The questions that follow are aimed at tapping both pragmatic (regular type) and psychological levels (italics). They are offered as examples of ways to gather information and raise the level of candidate awareness of underlying feelings and beliefs:

Deepening Questions

At early stages in the process:

How is this experience impacting you right now?
How does this experience make you feel about yourself?

What is the impact on significant others?
How are your friends and family reacting to and treating you?

What are your major concerns as you face this transition?
What are your fantasies? How confident are you that you will make it?

What ideas or plans do you have about what you might do next?
Sometimes people have strong reactions to this experience or have concerns about what others might think. What is your hunch about what the important people in your life might be saying?

How have you made career decisions and plans to date?
How do you see yourself happily re-established?

When would you ideally see yourself re-established?
How do you see us working together?

At advanced stages in the process:

Ideally, what would you like to do professionally and personally?
You have been looking for quite a while. As you look inward, what do you think about your emotional reserves and resources?

How do you spend your time?
How are you feeling most days? How do you feel Mondays and weekends?

How many hours a week do you devote to your search? How do you spend that time (ads, networking, recruiters, reading/researching, interviewing)? *When you are getting ready to take action, or when you are alone, what do you say to yourself? What are your inner dialogues?*

How do you think I can be most helpful to you at this point?
What do you expect me or the outplacement service to do for you now?

What do you plan to do as a next step in your search?
Do you think you will make it and how?

Whether phrased pragmatically or psychologically, questions like these enable clients to uncover underlying issues. Consultants can engender a sense of esteem in clients by encouraging self-exploration and disclosure, although not imposing interpretations and beliefs onto the individuals. They become partners in discovery.

Once clients and counselors can collaborate in a trusting and supportive environment, learning and growth can occur. The counselor's job can simply be to highlight or identify the limiting behaviors, thought processes, or attitudes through which feelings are expressed. Often, this is the first time the executive has heard about these issues. Questions can be a primary source of information and an excellent tool to explore and explicate the clues and causes of career derailment. When consultants address observations as questions, candidates can maintain control and self-esteem, and can see themselves as the source of results. Resistance to advice, defensiveness, and dependency can be minimized.

Action Time-Out

There is an understandable tendency for consultants to want to move candidates along in the counseling program by making challenging assignments and coaching on self-development techniques or search strategies. Yet, these efforts can meet with resistance or frustration in the face of helpless clients. Thomas Moore (1992) in his book, *Care for the Soul*, distinguished between "curing" and "caring." He posited that working hard to change a trait or feeling is often counterproductive to a desired sense of integrity and wholeness. Rather, embracing and experiencing the full thrust of life's caring or uncomfortable reactions can lead to a fuller experience and resolution of internal conflicts. These ideas might apply here. Helpless candidates will often respond to an opportunity to learn ways to accept themselves. Consultants can assist them in this effort by fully accepting and acknowledging them as people, regardless of whether they accomplish their program "assignments." Creating a therapeutic alliance in which trust and support are experienced, regardless of progress, often frees up candidates to explore conflicts that are obstructing them.

I experienced such an outcome while working with a female client who was grappling with a combination of work and personal concerns. She was employed in a very competitive environment where she wanted to succeed professionally and, at the same time, she wanted to care for her two very young children. In addition to her career and life conflicts, she had gained a lot of weight, felt out of control, and was struggling at both home and work. She was short-tempered and abrupt with subordinates, was on edge with her colleagues, and seemed unable to attend to details at work. Once home, she would cry at the slightest provocation. She took little joy in her children or husband's overtures for affection.

The coaching assignment was to assist her in becoming a more assertive manager. She was very defensive about admitting to her negative impact on others and highly resistant to taking responsibility for change. At one point in our work, she noticed my family pictures in the office and we started to share childrearing anecdotes. This informal discussion raised some feelings she had about child-care issues. We explored her concerns about motherhood and her feelings of guilt and fear about delicately balancing work and home demands. She reported feeling trapped in a life that was not of her own choosing because of commitments, an unemployed husband, and financial pressures. Several sessions were spent in emotional outpouring by her. My role was to listen and be supportive. I offered no advice or suggestion about what she should or might do. I remained supportive, receptive, and relaxed about the progress of our program. Finally, after three sessions that were more emotional than practical, we were able to move back and focus once again on the work issues. This executive just needed an opportunity to unload, she explained. She needed to talk out her conflicts with someone who did not have a plan or an agenda for her. She wanted to be heard and understood—not pushed forward. Awareness that her conflict was not shameful, or even resolvable, enabled her to accept her situation and focus on what she could do to control her professional life and accept the compromises she needed to make.

In some cases, when a client starts to express serious underlying psychological issues, a referral to additional sources of assistance is appropriate. When the causes of a career disruption are more complex, long-standing, or entrenched, career consultants who push on with a standard "nuts and bolts" program or involve themselves in extensive work on personality or affective issues can do a candidate a great disservice. Such cases would include people who are involved in substance abuse or addictive behavior, who have long-standing personality problems based in childhood experiences, or who are suffering from severe psychological difficulties.

I found myself eliciting underlying personal issues with a senior executive I worked with on a recent executive coaching assignment. He was referred for assistance because he had difficulty creating a loyal bond with his staff. He lived alone and never socialized with colleagues in the company. He was described as cold, rejecting, and demanding. He was in jeopardy of losing his position because he could not retain employees despite his great technical success. He believed that people should do their jobs without a lot of fanfare or praise. He rejected the idea that he might communicate to his employees other than by e-mail and occasional critical corrections of ineffective work, usually displayed in a tirade. Repeated exercises in communication techniques and team building were ineffective. Efforts at addressing developmental issues, which grew out of some formal assessments, were resisted with logic and rationalizations. As we explored his point of view, I asked him what would happen if he got close to his staff. He looked quite disturbed at this possibility, and commented that it was best not to bond with people because they always left anyway. I was struck by this response, but was unable to get this candidate to open up further about his management theories.

Finally, we redirected ourselves to an exploration of his beliefs about how people are motivated. Respecting his need to keep his personal life private, I asked him about his experiences in school as a way to understand his philosophy about how people are motivated and learn. As this point, he told me that he had been a student in seven elementary schools. As it turned out, this executive grew up in a number of foster homes after his mother died in childbirth. He was afraid to get close to anyone for fear of loss, and demonstrated this in the way he managed. In this case, I recommended that he seek therapy to work on his relationship beliefs and I continued to help him to address management and communication style issues. He began to see that his approach to others was grounded in survival behavior that might have worked successfully in the past but worked against him in the present. As he started to open up, showing warmth and trust, others responded positively. He developed more collegial relationships and eventually created team events and an open-door policy with his staff. The crowning achievement was the day his staff surprised him with a bouquet of flowers for his birthday. The very successful outcome from our combined work was evident.

An action time-out permits candidates to move inward in order to move forward. When consultants provide an environment that is conducive to self-exploration and self-disclosure, candidates can feel secure and supported in talking about ideas and feelings that could cause shame, sadness, or anger, and interfere with progress.

To be effective in providing this therapeutic environment, consultants need to be aware of appropriate boundaries between career counseling and therapy. Taking an action time-out to explore underlying issues can be very effective if kept to a clear purpose. It is critical to draw a line with candidates in career counseling with regard to the purpose of the work at hand.

ANTIDOTE TO HELPLESSNESS

Helplessness, which creates dissonance in the counseling room, can be addressed on the affective level to allow clients to gain courage, develop new behaviors, and move forward. When clients are assisted in bringing out the hurt inside in a validating way, self-esteem and a sense of personal power can be reestablished.

The ability of counselors to teach the techniques of career management can best be applied in an atmosphere of acceptance and support. In working with candidates who become helpless, training and preparation on the pragmatic level are ineffective while underlying self-defeating attitudes, beliefs, and feelings fester. When counselors ignore the feelings that underlie a helpless attitude, they cooperate with clients in ignoring them in themselves.

To succeed, consultants need an abiding optimism and a belief in the individual's desire to succeed. Consultants who believe that their clients are helpless or who enjoy the power of being the sole "expert" and who adhere inflexibly to a prescribed program despite the candidate's response will often engender helplessness. Counselors who consider clients capable of solving their problems in their own time and in their own way can help stuck individuals to break through dependence and despondency. Taking time out to uncover what is going on underneath the helpless behavior will often create the medium in which effective work can begin, and can actually shorten the counseling process. Unearthing and then validating previously unexpressed issues releases motivational power and energy, not only for the client but also for the counselor. Once released, the power of emotions that had undermined progress can be applied to change, risk taking, and growth. Eliciting feelings and sharing observations and reactions are counseling techniques, which border on clinical methods. Career counselors who are interested in applying some of these methods would benefit from some clinical training that would expose them to effective ways of eliciting and responding to the feelings of their clients in appropriate ways.

Above all, the counseling process should help clients feel respected. Our job as consultants is to give our all to executives in transition and trauma. We demonstrate empathy, warmth, and genuineness—the three essentials of the counseling relationship. In addition, our deepened understanding of the impact of clients' underlying attitudes, thoughts, and feelings on the counseling process helps us to help them.

Feelings of helplessness will dissipate when the unexpressed issues behind them are revealed in a nonjudgmental atmosphere of trust, interest, and respect. The experience of being accepted and understood will often be the most important factor for candidates who have become entrenched by their feelings. A caring and receptive attitude is vital to working with all people—and critical in assisting helpless candidates. Our candidates can flourish when they believe that we are willing to involve ourselves in their concerns in a curative as well as a corrective way.

REFERENCE

Moore, T. (1992). *Care of the soul*. New York: HarperCollins.

10 Counseling Lawyers

Gil Allison
Brecker & Merryman, Inc., New York

In the past two decades, hundreds of thousands of employees from large corporations in a variety of different industries have had their jobs eliminated. Today, few corporations can provide the secure employment they once did. However, publicly held corporations are not the only type of organizations whose employment practices and patterns have changed in recent years. Large, privately held service industry partnerships, such as law firms and accounting firms, have been affected as well.

Historically, partnerships of this nature conjured up images of comfortable clubs of successful and self-confident professionals who operated somewhat "above the fray" of the commercial world they serviced. Being a partner meant having a job for life and a very comfortable level of income. Partnerships saw themselves as talented individuals who worked better under self-rule than as mere cogs in a corporate machine.

However, in the past few years, many of the practices, privileges, and loyalties that made partnerships different from corporations have been disappearing. Many junior associates, and even some partners, have been asked to leave their firms, much like their corporate brethren.

This chapter discusses the special circumstances surrounding job loss among members of partnerships, and the counseling challenges posed by this phenomenon. The focus is on attorneys from large law firms, although the lessons learned are transferable to candidates from other partnership structures as well. The chapter draws on my first-hand experiences working as a consultant to outplaced attorneys. In order to highlight some of the major issues, it presents material gathered directly from interviews with outplaced attorneys.

THE TRADITIONAL SEPARATION PROCESS

Historically, in most professional service firms, there was a clearly delineated career path. Successful individuals progressed from junior associate to senior associate, and then a certain percentage were elevated to partnership. If an individual was not likely to become a partner, it was sufficient to employ rather subtle, indirect suggestions to inform him or her that it was time to move on. This was consistent with the culture and tradition of the large law firms. Also, the absence of financial pressures on the organization made it unnecessary for the individual to depart quickly. The departure could take place at a more leisurely pace. Also, the firm would often try to offer assistance by placing the departing lawyer at one of its clients. As one lawyer stated:

> It took me a while to adjust to the "failure" of not making partner ... however, I had seen the individuals before me eventually move on to clients ... some taking a year or two ... (no one ever had a specific date at which time they had to leave) ... but they always left with a sense of having their dignity intact ... and many times through the assistance of the firm. (Corporate Associate, 1983)

Today, many attorneys who have been outplaced realize that they know very little about planning their careers and especially about conducting effective job-search campaigns. They realize that they are not well prepared when their career game plans do not unfold as anticipated.

The individuals employed at large law firms had expected to follow a plan. They thought they were clear about what had to be done to achieve their goals. First, they had to be successful students earning high grades at the most prestigious undergraduate programs and then the best law schools. That opened the door to summer associate positions at the "best firms" and eventually to offers to join the firms following graduation. Then, following 7 to 10 years as associates, they would, ideally, be selected to become partners. In other words, the best grades at the best schools led to the best firms. Successful stints as associates led to partnerships. The route was clear and well-marked. They were very ill prepared for job loss and a serious disruption of the plan.

> After it was over (the job search) I realized just how ill prepared I had been to think through what was to be my next career step, let alone manage a job search ... what was worse was the people trying to help me (the partners) had never made any sort of career move other than to interview off of campus to join the firm I was leaving. It really was the blind leading the blind, but you couldn't figure that out till it was over. (Litigation Associate, 1984)

It is also worth examining the business conditions that have impacted the changing employment patterns in law firms. Historically, the financial stability and prosperous conditions enjoyed by the large law firms allowed for the perpetuation of the "up or out" system described earlier. This was the case up through and including much of the 1980s, which was a particularly prosperous period. Firm profits rose sharply and firms grew quickly. The demand for the best talent increased accordingly.

> We knew in January that we would be making a profit at year end ... business was good, very good, we had loyal institutional clients. (Managing Partner, Major New York City Law Firm, 1989)

Even if associates were asked to leave the firm, there were ample opportunities elsewhere. Junior associates could leave and, within a short period, have multiple job offers. There seemed to be a true sense of entitlement. The firms thought the high demand for legal services would continue and the associates felt there would always be many career opportunities. Neither turned out to be correct. What developed in the 1990s was an economic downturn for the corporate clients that was eventually felt by the law firms. Corporate clients brought more work to their in-house legal departments, began to scrutinize bills more closely, and demanded more cost-efficient services. Competition from other law firms also increased. Firms started to lose control of the pricing of their services, which for some meant their "collegial" organization needed to be run more and more like a business. All of these changes caused legal personnel committees to look at how the management, or the lack thereof, of the traditional up or out system needed to be changed. Associates were asked to leave earlier and more often and they found themselves scrambling to adjust to the new realities. They were not well prepared for these changes.

> I had been told that there was no chance that I would be considered for partner ... so I started looking at that point and my method was pretty much the same as everything else I had done at the firm, which was when you needed something you called up and ordered it. Like if I needed a translator I called up and ordered one, if I needed a taxi I called up and ordered one, and so I needed a job and I called up a headhunter and ordered one and I was sure that would take care of the matter. (Litigation Associate, 1989)

ACTING AS THE ATTORNEY'S ADVOCATE

One of the most important steps in all counseling relationships is the establishment of trust between counselor and client. This is no less true in working with attorneys. There are some special challenges in establishing the relationship. One of them is for the counselor to demonstrate knowledge about the law firm environment. Otherwise, the client might not engage at all in the process.

> I chose *not* to work with the outplacement counselor I first met because he kept on referring to my *firm* as my company . . . he clearly didn't know anything about the law. (Junior Associate, 1990)

The counselor must quickly gain trust and establish rapport. Speaking the language of the lawyers is important. It will not be totally sufficient to establish trust. However, not speaking their language will be a more than sufficient reason to lose trust. The Glossary will serve as a beginning guide to understand more of the legal lexicon. Other ways for counselors to become more familiar with the milieu include reading trade publications, speaking to "lawyer friends," and attending programs addressing legal employment issues such as those sponsored by local bar associations.

In the early stages, counselors can quickly establish that they know something about the profession by asking candidates about such topics as their practice areas and the type of matters on which they have worked.

LIVING WITH AMBIGUITIES
AND TRANSITIONS

Another of the challenges in counseling outplaced attorneys is that the terms of their departure from the firm are not always made clear. This often results in uncertainty and confusion that hinders candidates in moving forward. The special nature of partnerships often contributes to the confusion.

> They told me I have to leave the firm and you would help me with my job search . . . I can't stay . . . I have to get back to the firm . . . I have so much *work* to do. (Associate, 1991)

> One of the partners told me I had 3 months to look for a job . . . later, another partner told me not to worry about that . . . I'll probably get plenty of time. (Associate, 1991)

> When I told them I had an offer I was going to accept, they asked me if I wanted to stay. (Associate, 1991)

Central to the concept of a partnership is the notion of self-rule and joint decision making. This can lead to mixed messages and double binds where different partners deliver contradictory information to departing lawyers. In working with an associate, the counselor should be prepared to think through the very real situations described earlier. The associate "caught" by such ambiguity will be looking for guidance from the partners. Because the partners are the very source of the ambiguity, one possible strategy is for the counselor to help the candidate to negotiate clearly about the terms of the separation process, including the role of outplacement, as early as possible. Some associates will reject this as "not possible," but for others, this can be accomplished with the appropriate support. For the latter group, this will serve as a significant step in clarifying how they want their search to move forward. This can also be the start of taking more active control of their job search in a very constructive manner.

Another opportunity for counselors to assist associates in dealing with ambiguity is in the management of the "Reason for Leaving" statement. The way in which candidates frame their departure from the firm to curious search firms or hiring partners of prospective firms is very important. Associates will often get different messages from different partners about the basis for their departure. This can cause them to lose sight of the truth, especially in the emotion of the moment.

> One partner told me he felt my work was not up to the level of other individuals in my class and, therefore, it was time to look elsewhere. Two weeks into the search I was told by another partner that someone "had it in for me" and my work was really o.k. (Mid-level Associate, 1993)

Even when not confronted by such clearly contradictory information, associates often find it difficult to incorporate their own honest description of what happened into an effective "Reason for Leaving" statement.

> For the past 10 months I was looking for a job and actually got an offer, but felt it would be more of what I disliked about my current circumstances. So, I turned it down . . . I got the feeling that they (current firm) knew I was dissatisfied and might even have known I was looking. . . . When I was told it was time to look outside the firm because I wasn't going to make partner, it didn't seem to be a surprise to them when I hinted that my search was already underway . . . so what will my "Reason for Leaving Statement" be? What choice do I have? . . . I was fired! (Senior Associate, 1994)

In this kind of situation, counselors want to assist candidates in accomplishing the following:

1. Emphasize, to the extent possible, that the candidate made the choice to leave the firm before being asked to do so.
2. Assist the candidate in crafting a statement to be submitted to the current firm.
3. Support the candidate in solidifying the statement as early as possible in the search to gain support of it from future references.

In current conditions, fewer individuals are making partner in medium and large firms. Even junior associates are asked to leave largely for economic reasons. Consequently, the formulation of a "Reason for Leaving" statement must be faced by many attorneys. It is an opportunity for candidates to concretely take control of the search right from the outset.

ADDITIONAL POSSIBILITIES FOR ADVOCACY

The active generation of leads by counselors is a service that produces good results when dealing with a well-defined and circumscribed field like law. In general, most counselors will pass along job leads to candidates with whom they are working as they hear of them. Outplacement firms can provide a distinctive benefit to lawyer candidates by institutionalizing this kind of effort. Organizing lead generation around a candidate's specific targets as well as their more generalized practice areas has proven to be an effective way to shorten job searches. A secondary result from this kind of effort is that the outplacement firm develops a reputation in the marketplace as a source of quality candidates. This then results in additional leads finding their way to the firm.

Job-related research is another area in which counselors can make a significant contribution to the success of outplaced lawyers. Two reference volumes stand out as being especially helpful. The first is *Martindale Hubble*. It is a comprehensive listing of lawyers in the United States and can be used for networking purposes to research individuals who practice in law firms. *Martindale* on CD-ROM can produce an excellent list of potential contacts comprised of individuals from the candidate's class at law school. Second, the *Directory of Corporate Counsel*, also on CD-ROM, focuses on information from in-house law departments. Counselors should be familiar with both of these reference volumes. A good reference library will also provide numerous other directories useful for lawyers in connection with a job search, including professional publications such as the *New York Law Journal* where employment ads can be found.

Finally, the use of job-search groups can be of benefit to lawyers. These groups can be especially effective when combined with individual counseling.

Lawyers can benefit from participation in job-search groups in the following ways:

1. The groups provide a sense of community. The lawyers recognize they are not alone in their circumstances.
2. They provide specific introductions to organizations and individuals.
3. They provide specific suggestions about leads to open positions.
4. Groups are a vehicle to gain multiple suggestions on issues that arise in the job search.
5. Groups are a way to develop long-term networking relationships.

The conventional wisdom among counselors is that lawyers do not do well in group formats. Based on my experience, there is little evidence to support this premise.

Legal Search Firms

Contingency search firms (those earning a fee only if placement occurs) that specialize in the placement of lawyers can be very useful in a candidate's job search. In general, they are most helpful to junior to midlevel candidates; those 1 to 5 years out of law school. However, such search firms can also be of service to a candidate at any level in a "hot" practice area or a partner with a "book of business" who wants to move from one firm to another. A book of business refers to those transportable clients who will, in all likelihood, follow the partner to a new firm.

There are some basic principles for counselors to keep in mind when coaching candidates about how to enlist the aid of legal search firms. They are:

1. Network first.
2. Control introductions.
3. Know how to talk about the business you have.

Network First.   In a competitive environment, both corporations and firms of all sizes are looking at cost controls. Consequently, if there is a significant fee attached to the hiring of a given individual, it can make a big difference in how attractive the candidate is to a prospective employer.

Keeping this in mind, it is very important for candidates to have started their networking before engaging the help of contingency search firms. Candidates should have a feeling for the "reach" of their own contacts. This will enable them to determine whether they can network their own way into a given organization or whether they will need a search firm to introduce them into the organization. The former means of entry can certainly be to the candidate's advantage.

Control Introductions.   It is appropriate for candidates to be working simultaneously with two or three contingency search firms for the simple reason that one firm does not have knowledge of all openings. The selection of firms should be based on several considerations. They include prior positive experience with a particular recruiter in the firm, recommendations of others who have had direct experience with a specific recruiter in the firm, and the candidates' own evaluation after their initial face-to-face meetings with a search consultant from the firm. It should also be noted that with some practice areas, such as Tax or Trusts and Estates, there will be certain firms who specialize.

Once a relationship has been established, the candidate must manage it to ensure that there is no "crossing of paths" between the candidate's networking efforts and the efforts of this and other search firms.

To avoid crossing paths, it is crucial that candidates keep accurate records of where they have networked. Also, they should reach an agreement with each search firm that no presentation of the candidate be initiated without prior permission from the candidate.

An extensive list of legal search firms, the *Legal Recruiters Directory*, is published by *The American Lawyer* each year. It is a good starting point for candidates to survey the field and get oriented to the large number of firms from which to select.

Know How to Talk About Business That You Have. Generally speaking, individuals who have been outplaced do not have a large "book of business." A case can be made that no one really has business, but only individual relationships. Nevertheless, lawyers are regularly asked, as part of the job-search process, whether they can bring any business with them to a new firm. A danger exists if candidates make this a "yes" or "no" response. What usually happens when a "rainmaker" joins a firm is that introductions are made, discussions take place about the new firm's capabilities, and how the recently hired attorney fits into the new organization. All these talks are related to the ways in which the needs of the clients can be serviced by the new firm as well as, or better than, they were by the old firm.

The major opportunity for the candidate is to emphasize the doors they can open. Specifically, they want to focus on the introductions that could not otherwise be made without their contact list. Ironically, as the network of a candidate grows during the job-search process, the number of potential relevant introductions increases.

Coaching a candidate to explore possibilities in this "grey" area allows candidates, at a minimum, to think more broadly about their networks. It enables them to see that they can view the individuals with whom they interact on a daily basis as potential business generation contacts (Allison, 1995).

PARTNERS

This section addresses some of the special considerations that arise when partners depart from a law firm. It addresses some of the underlying assumptions that many partners hold dear. These assumptions often create a more difficult separation process for the departing individuals, and hence demand more skills and knowledge from counselors.

Assumptions Held by Partners

As indicated earlier in the chapter, there have recently been a number of fundamental changes in the legal marketplace. These changes have caused firms to look more closely at how they conduct their business and how they evaluate the performance of their partners. It can be argued that the underlying assumptions under which partners have operated in the past are no longer on solid ground. The assumptions are as follows:

1. The large firm provides a job for life.
2. I am what I do.
3. There are limits on good career moves.
4. Partners do not ask for help.
5. Someone else generates the business.

Assumption 1: Job for Life.   With some departing partners, the counselor will have to assist the individual (and very often the spouse) in working through intense feelings of betrayal.

> They really can't get away with this ... the partnership agreement doesn't permit it ... they will have to put it to a vote to really push me out and they would *never* do it! (Partner, 1994)

Yes they will! Clearly, there are no longer jobs for a lifetime.

Assumption 2: I Am What I Do.   Counselors need to be aware that in dealing with individuals who have made a 25-year commitment to a profession, such as law, their personal identity is likely to be very entwined with their work. It can be difficult for some partners to even think of themselves in a different law firm, let alone consider transferring their skills to different types of work.

> I've been a partner at this firm for 23 years ... my father retired from the firm ... you don't seem to understand, I like doing what I do, a lot ... I'm not so sure I could see myself doing very much of anything else. (Partner, 1994)

Assumption 3: There are Limits on Good Career Moves.
Some long-term partners will try very hard to explore suitable alternatives. The issue is in the word *suitable*. They often reject what appear to the outside observer to be reasonable career alternatives. The partners quickly reject these options because they are lacking in prestige, equivalent compensation, or any number of elements that they feel are absolutely necessary in a new position.

> Please understand, there are only three or four firms that I would consider joining ... if I went in-house it would only be for the *top* job ... and there are only a few corporations who could pay me what I'm worth. (Partner, 1993)

The combination of Assumptions 2 and 3 can be a prescription for a long, frustrating job search. Counselors must intervene and assist the candidates in reframing their views of reality. This will allow them to appreciate the multiple opportunities that might exist for individuals who are so highly skilled and who have been so professionally successful.

Assumption 4: Partners Do Not Ask For Help.
To be successful in a thriving law firm, partners must believe, among other things, that they can independently tackle and solve all problems with which they are presented. They are trained to be experts in a particular field and have accumulated large amounts of evidence that attest to their problem solving abilities.

> If you give me enough time, I'll come up with a solution. (Partner, 1995)

That is what they "get paid for" and if they need to ask for much help, it may be viewed as an inadequacy.

This attitude can be an obstacle to fully exploring the marketplace, especially through contacts. Individuals can too easily view networking conversations as "asking for help," "begging for a job," or, at a minimum, making themselves vulnerable to the perception that they need a lot of help.

The counselor has an opportunity to refocus the partners on the possible benefits of exploring the marketplace, especially for someone as accomplished as they are. Also counselors can assist in helping to reframe the partners' point of view as to what elegant networking really is—research—something they are expert at.

Assumption 5: Someone Else Generates Business.
It can be argued that today's partners must meet higher expectations than ever before. These include the boosting of firm revenues and the building of their own client base.

> If I move to another firm, I'll face the same thing ... if I don't generate business, I'm in trouble. (Partner, 1995)

Here, counselors have a real opportunity. In teaching a partner to successfully network for a new position, they are simultaneously teaching "rainmaking" skills to the individual who wants to develop in this area. Most partners find new positions through building relationships in the marketplace. Rainmaking and seeking a new position through contacts call on the same kind of networking skills. So, even as counselors assist the partners in gaining some short-term career management skills, they are also helping the partners develop some more long-range career management skills. Learning to improve their networking, for both job-search and business-development purposes, will help the partners in advancing their careers.

CONCLUSION

The employment practices and patterns of law firms have changed in recent years. Many associates, and even some partners, have been asked to leave their firms. Consequently, the demand for outplacement consulting for individuals leaving firms has grown and will continue to grow as we approach the year 2000.

These developments present both challenges and opportunities for career management professionals. There are many ways in which career professionals can assist outplaced attorneys in managing the separation process and conducting effective job-search campaigns. Some of the counseling challenges are generic to all clients, although other aspects require specialized knowledge of lawyers. There are also opportunities for firm-sponsored "upstream coaching," where lawyers still at the firm are assisted in managing their careers in a way that benefits both themselves and the law firm.

Counseling individuals from professional service firms, especially lawyers, is an opportunity for career management practitioners to expand their practices and to enhance their counseling skills. It presents excellent opportunities for professional growth.

APPENDIX

A partial list of terms helpful in understanding professional service firms, especially law firms.

Associate: A lawyer who is not a partner.

Administrative Partner: An individual who oversees the firm's administrative duties. Might still actively practice in addition to administrative responsibilities.

Billable Hours: Recorded, client-compensated time. Typically, lawyers in major urban firms are expected to bill 2,000 to 2,500 hours per year.

Book of Business:	Business that will walk out the door with the lawyer. Also referred to as *portables*.
Director of Legal Personnel:	Midlevel administrator. Equivalent to human resources official in a corporation.
Date Certain:	End point of financial support for departing individual.
Executive Committee:	Usually "runs" the firm. Also called *management committee*.
In-House:	Legal staff position in a corporate organization. In public accounting, called *private sector*.
Lateral:	Experienced attorney who moves from one firm to another at a comparable level.
Law Review:	Similar to "Dean's List." Important factor in getting hired in large firms. Usually means individual is in top 10% of law school class.
Managing Partner:	Usually runs the firm on a day-to-day basis.
Nominated for Partner:	The process of actually being sponsored by current partner(s).
Of Counsel:	Affiliated with the firm, but not a true "member."
Partner:	Used to be tenured position at the end of the rainbow. Typically, takes from 5 to 8 years in law firms and up to 13 years in public accounting firms to achieve.
Partner Track:	A position that, given time and demonstrated legal and business generation skills, provides an individual with the opportunity to become a partner.
Passed Up for Partner:	Usually the signal to start a job search.
Rainmaker:	Business developer.

Summer Program:	Summer jobs in law firms for law students. Can lead to job offer on graduation from law school.
Senior Attorney:	Relatively new job category. Can be a permanent position as nonpartner.
Up or Out:	The generally accepted practice that you either make partner or leave the firm.

REFERENCE

Allison, G. (1995). *How rainmakers develop: Clues from lawyers in transition*. New York: Brecker & Merryman.

11 Professional Standards in Outplacement Counseling

James J. Gallagher
Founding Chairperson, The Outplacement Institute

If any topic is guaranteed to bring forth the multiple personalities within the outplacement field, it is the subject of professional standards. After nearly three decades of existence, outplacement still suffers divisions among its practitioners about many philosophical issues important to the definition and survival of the field.

For instance, we argue whether the marketing or the delivery of services drives the field and whether psychological services are the ruination or the core of the business. Furthermore, we debate who is to blame that our golden calf has become a commodity, and what to do about the fee reductions that follow.

Just for good measure, we disagree about whether outplacement practitioners are consultants or counselors. We shake heads in unison that it is awful we do not get the respect we used to. Everyone asks whether our business will be okay if we change that terrible name, *outplacement*, which nobody ever liked anyway, to *career management*?

On top of that, there is disagreement over the definition of outplacement itself, largely between the shrinking number of full-time outplacement practitioners employed in firms and the growing band of roving, independent practitioners hired on contract only when various firms need them. Is outplacement only corporate-sponsored services or just another form of career counseling that can be paid for by individuals? The independent, solo consultants frequently do individual retail work to stay alive; the firms defend their corporate-only ramparts.

Pure outplacement contracts are third-party agreements. So, is outplacement the service that is so competitively sold to the human resources officers who pay for it, or the service that is so diligently delivered to employees who have lost their jobs? Most recently, is outplacement distinct from career management? (By the way, when is somebody going to define what career management is and is not, anyhow?)

HISTORY OF ESTABLISHING CREDENTIALS

The Outplacement Institute ventured into this muddy playing field in early 1994. With a shining vision, it aimed at "building professionalism of outplacement practitioners and achieving recognition for that professionalism." The means employed to meet these aims, credentialing, proved threatening to nearly everyone at first. Practitioners wondered what the criteria would be and whether they would pass muster.

As the definition and procedures of credentialing earned a time-consuming but essential consensus, Institute credentials became widely and warmly endorsed throughout the field. Before the end of the first-year "grandfathering" period, more than 300 practitioners applied for member or fellow status. During 1995, the Institute issued certificates to 92 fellows and 134 members. A truly international group, they came from nine separate countries. They represented 21 states of the United States and four provinces of Canada.

The consensus on credentialing grew out of a 4-year process of education, collaboration, and commitment within the International Association of Career Management Professionals (IACMP; then under its original name International Association of Outplacement Professionals). The vision of "improving the breed" and workable ideas about how to do so found champions in the IACMP founding president, Winifred S. (Winnie) Downes and her successor, Joan Strewler.

The need for outplacement credentials has long been discussed by practitioners who were dissatisfied with the overly general and widespread use of the term *quality* to sell outplacement services. Like beauty in the eye of the beholder, quality assumed no specific measurements, and was claimed by practitioners both good and bad. The ambiguous term, *quality*, provided no guidance to either sponsors or consumers of outplacement services.

If anything, such glib usage attracted media critics whose business-press exposés fostered a growing cynicism about the integrity of the field. During outplacement's greatest years of growth in the recessions of the 1980s and 1990s, the media delighted in referring to outplacement consultants as "corporate undertakers," and dredged out selected case studies to prove that outplacement did not deliver the timely new jobs or the other services it promised. Talking among themselves at industry conferences, outplacement insiders admitted quietly that the criticisms were not entirely unfounded.

Standards for professionalism and credentials attesting to such standards became a figurative holy grail among practitioners. Most agreed on the wisdom of having standards that would inhibit the questionable practices of others. Only a few could envision standards that would objectively evaluate the variety of people in the field in nearly a dozen different countries. So, the case for outplacement credentials needed to be made first around the benefits they would provide both within and outside the field. Through discussion and agreements reached in hours of meetings and corridor talk during the early IACMP meetings, some consensus developed. Credentials were deemed valuable and needed.

For customers and candidates, credentials provide criteria for evaluating outplacement providers in this age of new consumerism. In addition, they educate users about what outplacement providers can be expected to deliver.

For outplacement practitioners, credentials provide a wide array of benefits:

- Identification of outplacement as a distinct profession with competencies of its own.
- Development of analytical thinking about the profession and consequent articulation of principles designed to improve its practices.
- Benchmarks for professional growth and encouragement for practitioners to exceed them.
- Perhaps most significant for their acceptance, standards would provide credentialed practitioners with a marketing edge in a competitive business.

The ambiguity of the term *professionalism* proved to be the first hurdle for the IACMP Professional Development Committee, a group of some 20 members, who volunteered at an annual meeting in 1991 to advance the effort. If professionalism was to be certified, it first needed to be defined. As an example of how not to proceed, the committee members were reminded of the muddled debate on pornography in the U.S. Congress. Its highlight was the memorable statement by one lawmaker: "I don't know how to describe it, but I know it when I see it."

Professionalism is an equally slippery concept. The discourse focused on two salient attributes of professionals in other fields:

- *Competency*, comprising specialized knowledge, skills and a period of experience at practicing them, and
- *Attitude*, embracing a mode of relating to clients usually described in the profession's code of ethics.

It helped to analyze the characteristics of other socially recognized professionals to determine what the outplacement practitioners could be measured against. The models were plentiful including the legal, accounting, engineering, architectural and, of course, the medical fields.

Concurrent with the work of the Professional Development Committee, another IACMP group developed a code of ethics for professionals. Observance of the code was included in the certification process. Each applicant was required to attest to recent review and compliance with the code.

As for the remaining competency component, the certification process needed to provide satisfactory and widely accepted answers to a number of intellectually rigorous questions. Formulating the answers proved to be a lengthy educational process for both the developers of credentials and the constituency for whom they apply. Practitioners needed to envision a process that would treat everyone fairly and equitably and apply to the complexities and differences of practices from firm to firm and from country to country. The hurdles of certification also needed to be low enough to scale, but high enough to be respected.

POLITICAL CONSIDERATIONS AND THEIR IMPACT ON CREDENTIALING

A large threat was looming that ultimately focused everyone's attention. Sooner or later, it was clear that somebody would get around to developing credentials for outplacement practitioners. In the United States, for example, government money, primarily through the U.S. Department of Labor, began supporting job-search services in a number of sites throughout the country. The U.S. Federal Reemployment Act of 1994 was to have funded more than 300 "one-stop job centers" across the country.

If past experience provided a norm, federal money would be awarded to people and groups that could prove they had passed some kind of evaluation, such as college and social service agency accreditation, which usually includes individual certification. Despite the best efforts of a lobbying coalition of outplacement firms, the Act might have closed out the private-sector outplacement firms from participating in the federal windfall, and literally eliminated the outplacement business as it existed in the United States.

Fate intervened in the form of the surprise Republican sweep of the U.S. Congressional elections that fateful November of 1994. The Reemployment Act—considered a "shoo-in" before the election—never made the agenda of the new Congress.

If that was a close call for the outplacement industry in the United States, in other countries, the issue had already been lost. The United Kingdom's personnel association, for instance, had developed standards for outplacement, much to the chagrin of local practitioners who had no input into the criteria. Readily accepted by sponsoring corporations, the standards proved to be unhappy tunes for the outplacement firms to dance to.

The urgency for self-evaluation became real, voiced in terms like, "If we don't get our act together inside outplacement, somebody else will impose standards on us that we might not be able to live with." Such politically realistic awareness provided the climate in which people were willing to talk about credentials.

COMPARISONS TO OTHER FIELDS

The planning group inside IACMP started to address the basic questions:

- How do we define the knowledge specific to outplacement?
- How do we measure the achievement of such knowledge?
- What skills are necessary for outplacement practice?
- How do we measure such skills?
- What levels of knowledge, skills, and experience are needed for certification?
- How can practitioners acquire the required levels if they do not already possess them? Will there be study requirements and opportunities?
- Who will make the judgments and what qualifies the judges?
- How can the process be fair to all applicants and still maintain standards that are respected in the field?
- How can the integrity of the process be assured?
- How do we accomplish a credentialing program that is self-funded?

Early in the committee work, Dr. Bonnie Maitlen's (personal communication, February 15, 1992) study of other credentialing processes raised the question of whether separate certification for outplacement professionals was even necessary. After all, the National Board of Certified Counselors (NBCC), for instance, already provided testing for a National Certified Career Counselor certificate to individuals who qualified for it.

The planning group examined the NBCC structure and requirements and concluded that outplacement is, indeed, distinct on two bases:

1. Outplacement is essentially a corporate and organization-sponsored service, even though its recipients are individuals. It is not enough for an outplacement practitioner to be just a counselor. Outplacement counselors also need to be knowledgeable about business and industry. So, the NBCC programs do not go far enough in this respect.

2. Conversely, the NBCC programs go too far in requiring degrees in counseling psychology for applicants, and crediting continuing education only in the counseling field. Such standards might be appropriate for the more academic, scholarly, and social service agency constituency of NBCC. However, this was not the constituency of IACMP. Research I presented at Association of Outplacement Consulting Firms International (AOCFI) conferences in the late 1980s showed that licensed psychologists and trained counselors made up only a modest percentage of the outplacement professionals who practice and serve the adult employees of corporate organizations. Although many outplacement practitioners have studied social sciences, most carry degrees from other fields.

ESTABLISHING COMPETENCIES

With the differences between outplacement professionals and other career counselors thus clarified, the next step was to develop a list of competencies that are common to outplacement practitioners. Five were identified and drafted, circulated to the IACMP membership for comments, revised, and ultimately adopted by the IACMP Board. With the major exception of Category 1, "Consulting with Corporate/Organizational Clients," the remaining competencies could be judged to be common to other career consultants who work primarily with adults.

However, even as it relates to the other four competency areas, outplacement consultants do the work of assessment, job-search training, career consulting, and consulting with candidates from a distinctive point of view. Their approaches emphasize business and professional issues, not psychological ones, and typically follow the problem-solving and issues-management models learned by candidates on the jobs they occupied before termination.

The final version of the five outplacement competencies delineates specific examples of what is required under each of the following categories:

1. Consulting with corporate/organizational clients.
2. Consulting with candidates:

   a. on an individual basis.
   b. on a group basis.

3. Assessment.
4. Job-search training.
5. Career consulting.

(A complete listing of the IACMP Competencies Standards is given in the appendix.)

Once the competencies were defined, they provided the basis for devising a syllabus of instruction in outplacement. The Professional Development Committee then campaigned among IACMP chapters and regional and international program planners. These are the organization's providers of professional development programs. The outplacement competencies now function as a structure on which local meetings and conference programs are built.

For example, a local IACMP chapter will schedule a yearly cycle of meeting presentations around the five competencies. Both speakers and attendees earn professional development credits toward Institute certification. Reports in the monthly IACMP newsletter circulate speaker topics to other chapters. Coverage of the five competencies during the year earns a chapter credits in the IACMP Chapter Recognition Award competition. Similarly, annual conferences list presentations according to the competency treated by the subject, and attendees and presenters similarly earn professional development credits.

EVALUATING COMPETENCIES

Before all this could be set in place, however, a major stumbling block loomed in the question of how to measure competencies, skills, and experience. Conventional credentialing programs employ written tests, often based on detailed study programs that involve written materials and live instruction. These proved impossible for the scantily funded Outplacement Institute. (It was grateful for a seed-money loan of $5,000 from the sponsoring IACMP for working capital, but development of an adequate test would absorb at least ten times that amount.)

Requiring formal course credits was impractical, because there have been only a few courses about outplacement taught anywhere. The Outplacement Institute borrowed a feasible option from the model of "universities without walls." Such programs award degrees on the basis of portfolios for life experience. At such colleges and universities, applicants submit organized documentation that analyzes and illustrates the knowledge, skills, and experience they have gleaned from particular experiences in their lives. Candidates relate their informal learning to the structured learning they might have received in a catalogued college course. If presented skillfully and judged adequate, their life experiences receive equivalent credit in the subject matter of the formal course.

The portfolio method of presenting life experience-based learning provided The Outplacement Institute with an answer. Documentation of life and professional experience, plus participation in outplacement-related presentations and programs would earn certification. (As a point of historical accuracy, for the first year of the Institute, its study program requirement was lifted for practitioners who qualified otherwise for "grandfathering.")

Portfolios, however, cannot provide the objectivity of a validated and consistent paper-and-pencil measure. Still, the portfolio must be evaluated fairly and expertly. An initial group of judges, called "sponsors" by the Institute, was needed as charter fellows to guide applicants through the process and approve portfolios. As additional applicants earned fellow status, they also became eligible to review new member and new fellow portfolios.

The same consensus-building process employed for getting the outplacement competencies accepted worked again. Through the organization newsletter, IACMP members were asked to submit nominees who met published criteria for the charter fellow job.

Nominations were "vetted" by the IACMP Board and balanced according to geographical locations of large groups of members across the world.
The shorthand criterion for nominees was that they be "bulletproof," that
is, individuals of such stature and recognition in the field to be trusted
and respected by all. The international group of 13 charter fellows fulfilled
all requirements.

The initial 1994 guidelines assumed that publication or public presentations on outplacement-related subjects was an adequate means of
demonstrating knowledge in the field. An Institute feedback session at
the IACMP conference several months later provided an excellent idea
that had been overlooked originally.

There are two categories of practitioners in the real world of outplacement. The first includes those who publish and present and thus demonstrate their contributions to the development of knowledge in the field.
A substantially larger group, likewise significant to the field, delivers
services reliably and competently but does not publish or present. The
Institute developed a second tract to certify the latter group. It required
not articles or speeches, but case studies that identify and demonstrate
command of the principles of practice. Those who qualified for the latter
track are referred to as members.

So many candidates wrote instructive case studies as part of their
applications for member status, that the Institute published a case book
in 1995 entitled *Excellence in Outplacement Practice*. It contains more than
100 cases. These are sorted by the competencies they illustrate and
indexed by candidate occupations, and by the principles and issues they
illustrate. A third index lists contact data for authors. The case book,
designed for use by experienced practitioners as well as in training new
ones, is available directly from The Outplacement Institute.

Other improvements made during 1994 at the behest of member
feedback include new provisions for resolution of portfolio disputes (there
have been none as of this writing, but the policy is reassuring to constituents), and a legally required policy for accepting applications from non-
IACMP members.

GROWTH OF OUTPLACEMENT INSTITUTE

With the striking success of the Institute in its first year, support for
credentialing took a great leap ahead early in 1995. The trade association
in the field, the AOCFI, joined with IACMP in cosponsoring the Institute,
and added a matching $5,000 seed-money loan to assist with the Insti-
tute's growing administrative costs.

With the AOCFI participation in the Institute, another 13 charter
fellows from five countries were added to represent the interests of
outplacement managers. A new credential category, *fellow manager*, was

added with special requirements suited to individuals who supervise outplacement delivery, but who may not deliver outplacement services themselves.

Organized early in 1994 shortly after the Institute was announced, the task force that worked out the cosponsorship evolved into a governing board of 10 members representing both sponsors equally. Through the efforts of the board, the Institute is slated to become separately incorporated and an independent body to conform with recommendations by the National Organization for Competency Assurance, a credentialing agency.

As a "work in progress," the Outplacement Institute will continue to change as the needs of the industry and its constituents change. There is a groundswell of interest in new and allied areas of practice, such as executive coaching and career management. As these become part of the outplacement practitioner's expertise, The Outplacement Institute might become a vehicle for definition, identification, measurement, and evaluation of the knowledge, skills, and experience needed in such new practice areas.

For the present, one thing is certain. Credentialing of outplacement practitioners is in the hands of outplacement professionals themselves, rather than others who might know less about the practice and be less respectful of its integrity and values. After decades of talking about the need for quality in the field, standards of professional practice are finally in place, and hundreds of practitioners are subscribing to them.

APPENDIX: THE IACMP COMPETENCIES STANDARDS FOR OUTPLACEMENTPROFESSIONALS

Competencies are derived from an individual practitioner's combination of knowledge, skills (i.e., applied knowledge) and experience. Because of variations in the ways outplacement professionals practice (i.e., as members of firms or companies or as independents), not all standards apply equally to all outplacement practitioners. For certification, however, all outplacement practitioners will need to demonstrate some level of competency in all five core areas.

The five core competencies within the practice of outplacement professionals are:

Category 1: Consulting with Corporate/Organizational Clients

Including but not limited to:

- Managing corporate relationships.

- Interpreting business/industry trends and issues.
- Guiding client organizations and people through transition processes.
- Preparing managers to handle termination meetings.
- Managing career centers.
- Reporting status and results to sponsors.
- Negotiating reference guidelines and "Reason for Leaving" statements.
- Consulting on and providing services to deal with "survivor" issues.
- Maintaining confidentiality within legal requirements.
- Working within ethical standards of the profession.

Category 2: Consulting With Candidates

Including but not limited to:

On an Individual Basis

- Managing the consultant–candidate relationship.
- Handling special situations such as "stuck" candidates and candidate dependencies.
- Problem solving with candidates.
- Consulting on termination trauma and stress.
- Motivating candidates through job transition.
- Identifying candidate "blocks" and referring to other appropriate assistance.
- Identifying support systems and training candidates to use them effectively.
- Maintaining confidentiality within legal requirements.
- Closing the job search and preparing candidates for future assignments.
- Working within ethical standards of the profession.

On a Group Basis

- Organizing and administering group programs.
- Presenting complex data to groups.
- Maintaining appropriate authority and control.
- Adapting "individual" issues and procedures (see Category 2) to groups.
- Presenting programs on specific subjects related to outplacement, for example, preretirement, survivorship, career transitions, self-employment.

Category 3: Assessment

Including but not limited to:

- Intake procedures and effectiveness.
- Analysis and/or assessment of candidate experiences.
- Interpreting and/or reporting and applying results of standardized measurements.
- Identifying critical skills and accomplishments.
- Identifying values that apply to work.

Category 4: Job-Search Training

Including but not limited to:

- Strategy and planning job campaign.
- Research methods.
- Networking and other search techniques.
- Developing resumes and other campaign tools.
- Developing interviewing skills and protocols.
- Teaching salary negotiation.
- Evaluating and/or negotiating job offers.
- Understanding business and/or economic trends.
- Developing job opportunities.
- Utilizing other resources for support and/or assistance.
- Job market data interpretation.
- Developing and/or utilizing specific employer data.

Category 5: Career Consulting

Including but not limited to:

- Developing individual specific career plans with defined goals.
- Life and/or work planning.
- Career change and/or options consulting.
- Career decision making.
- Identifying personal and/or environmental issues that impact career decisions.
- Identifying and/or exploring self-employment options.
- Mastery and/or use of career resource information.
- Interpreting corporate cultures and structures.
- Developing educational plans to support career goals.

III

INNOVATIVE APPROACHES IN OUTPLACEMENT AND CAREER MANAGEMENT

12 Special Challenges in Leading Groups

Peter Prichard
Seagate Associates, New Jersey

As the outplacement industry moves through the last decade of the 20th century into the next millennium, it is buffeted by many factors. Not the least of these factors is the need, as a maturing industry with intense competition and pressure on profits, to find new and effective ways to move individuals quickly, successfully, and profitably through the career transition process. Firms and individual practitioners that do this are likely to survive and prosper.

One of the strategies that has been used to make the outplacement process more profitable and effective is the use of groups. Groups have been used for years to train individuals in job-search techniques and to help them be more effective in their job searches. The aim of this chapter is to provide the practitioner with a clear understanding of:

- Why certain groups have been embraced by the outplacement professional and others have not.
- Who is providing the service and who is being served.
- How groups can be facilitated effectively.
- What the prognosis is for the use of groups in the future and where the practitioner can turn for more information on this subject.

A HISTORY OF JOB-SEARCH GROUPS

The Azrin Model

Nathan Azrin is credited by many as being the initiator of the use of groups to help job seekers. He organized the first Job Finding Club in the early 1970s. Azrin (1982) described the Job Club process:

> In Job Clubs, small groups of approximately eight members meet daily to find jobs, assisted by a counselor. They make phone calls, write letters,

exchange job leads, study want ads and the phone book, write resumés for themselves, obtain letters of recommendation, rehearse interviews, give each other rides and moral support, and do the myriad things for each other that will help in obtaining work. When club members get jobs, they notify the others—often by phone, but sometimes in person, and describe how they got it. Then they turn over their lists of job leads and the process continues ...

There are two premises to the Job Club approach: You have to be an almost a total invalid before you are completely unhirable; and you have to stop being a stranger to the people who can give you the work you really want at the rate of pay you really deserve" (pp. 2–3).

Azrin followed up his initial work with three studies of the results of the Job Club approach. In his first sample of "average" people:

> After three months, two out of five of the control group were still unemployed. At the same time, 93% of the Job Clubbers had found work; the few who hadn't, had dropped out of the Job Club. On average, the Job Clubbers got jobs in one quarter the time it took the first group, and more than six times as many got professional or management jobs. The Job Clubbers average salary was a third higher than the non-members. (Azrin, 1975, pp. 24–25)

> A second test was conducted with people who had severe problems ... 95% of the Job Clubbers got jobs inside of six months, most within ten days. Almost three out of four of the non-clubbers failed to find work, and, again, the Job Clubbers' average salary was well above the non-clubbers'. (Azrin, 1979, p. 150)

> A third test, with a thousand welfare recipients in five cities, from Harlem to Washington state, had about the same result. At follow-up, about twice as many of the Job Clubbers had obtained a job compared with those not using the Job Club. (Azrin, 1980, p. 137)

The success of Azrin's efforts lead to the development of the National Office of Program Development under one of his coworkers, Robert Philip. This organization was chartered to promote the Job Club program nationally. By 1982, Job Clubs had been established in 18 states and had successfully assisted thousands of individuals to find new jobs. Most of their efforts until that time were with welfare recipients.

College and University Job Clubs

Colleges and universities have also used the Job Club concept since the 1970s as a very successful means for helping students and alumni find jobs. I cofacilitated a program with Kitty Arnold of Indiana University at the American College Personnel Association national convention in 1983 titled, "Job Clubs Revisited: 'With a Little Help from My Friends.'"

In that program, we presented information on how Job Clubbers had helped a significant number of college students and alumni at a variety of colleges and universities. An excellent article on this topic is "Job Club," by Ruth Parsell and Gretchen Thompson (1979).

Teams for the General Public

A number of professionals have used teams and groups to help members of the general public find jobs and move toward other goals. Barbara Sher's Success Teams are probably the best known. Sher and Gottlieb (1989) provided a very thorough description of how to develop success teams; "a small group of people whose only goal is to help every member of the team get what he or she wants" (p. X).

Use of Groups in the Outplacement Industry

As was mentioned earlier, the outplacement industry has used groups for years to assist job seekers. Most of these groups have been in one of the following four formats:

1. *Comprehensive 1- to 5-day job-search workshops.* These workshops are designed to provide job seekers on all levels with the basic information needed to do a job search. All provide information on how to write a resumé and the techniques needed to identify jobs and interview for them. The length of the group and the number of individuals in attendance impacts how much information is covered.

Other factors that are considered when these programs are offered include:

• The comprehensiveness of the outplacement program. These groups are usually offered either as stand-alones for terminated employees or as part of an outplacement firm's basic training held in conjunction with the typical one-to-one counseling.
• The salary and level of the terminated employees. Traditionally, group outplacement programs like this were the sole outplacement services offered to those at lower levels in the organization. More and more employers are now offering group workshops as the sole service to more senior individuals. Even the most senior executives are being put into 2- to 5-day job-search workshops as part of their initial training in a program that also includes individual counseling and the use of an office and secretarial support.

• The geographic location of the individuals being terminated. Employers will often opt for a group outplacement program when the location being impacted is sufficiently remote to make it impractical to send a counselor to do one-on-one job-search training and follow-up.
• The philosophy of the employer and the money that they want to spend. Many employers are not disposed to spend a lot of money on people they are letting go, even though, at the same time, they realize that it makes sense to offer some kind of support. These employers will often offer a one-time group workshop as the sole outplacement service for terminated employees.

2. *Topical/didactic workshops.* Firms have offered topical workshops in their offices for many years. These are designed to assist candidates to understand more fully a particular aspect of the career transition process. These workshops traditionally last from 1 hour to half a day, many being offered in a "brown bag" lunch format. Topics such as "Advanced Networking," "Re-energizing Your Search," "Managing the Stresses of the Job Search," "Identifying Employers Who are Hiring," and numerous others are offered regularly.

Some firms have these didactic offerings as part of their basic training in job-search techniques. Candidates choose those they need from a menu. Other firms only offer these didactic offerings to candidates who have been prepared in job-search techniques and are fully engaged in their job search.

3. *Workshops for special populations.* Groups, usually lasting one to two meetings, are offered when there is sufficient interest to justify the time and money. Topics such as "Entrepreneurial Options," "The Role of Age in the Career Transition Process," and "Job Search Realities for Women/Minorities/Accountants/Career Changers/Dual Career Couples" are typical. Again, these groups are more didactic and informational than ...
4. *Ongoing job-search team.* The outplacement industry began in the 1980s to offer groups based on Azrin's model as well as other models. These groups are a mix of job-search techniques, group process, and the psychology of behavioral change. This type of team is described later in the chapter.

THE EMPLOYMENT MARKET OF THE 1990S

A Demand for More Groups

During the 1990s, there has been a significant increase in the use of groups in the outplacement industry, especially at more senior levels of employees. This trend is expected to continue. There are a number of factors that have contributed to the increase.

From the Employer Buying the Outplacement Service

• Employers are much more sophisticated about the consulting services they are buying for their employees. They are less likely to be sold on the need for a full program than they were when they first began to purchase the services in the 1970s and 1980s.

• Employers are under significant pressure to cut costs. One of the ways they are doing this is through closer scrutiny of the fees they pay for consulting. In situations where they have not seen the quality results that an outplacement firm or practitioner promised, they are less likely to pay what they paid previously for a service that was unsatisfactory.

• Downsizing has become part of traditional management practice. The large number of employees that companies are terminating requires employers to look at options that will provide services to the largest number of people for the best possible price.

From the Outplacement Provider

• Outplacement firms have set up entire divisions to handle large-scale group projects. They have been extolling the benefits of groups in order to get the large-scale downsizing business. The same employers who are hearing these benefits are also coming back and demanding that these group programs be offered to more senior level employees who normally would only get individual outplacement.

• Pressures to increase market share have pushed a number of firms to market their group services for more senior managers and executives.

• Some firms have structured their marketing around the personalities of counselors they have on staff who are particularly gifted at group facilitation. Others have marketed the benefits of group participation for introverts and others who might not network well in a competitive market.

• Many firms and practitioners see that team and group activities shorten the job searches of candidates who take part. They are offering more of these activities because shortened searches and the ability to impact more candidates per counselor have a positive impact on profitability.

Both employers and outplacement providers realize that a competitive labor market that is pushing increasing numbers of individuals into career and geographic changes requires the use of as many resources as possible to assist with the transitions. Groups and teams are increasingly seen as one of the important resources.

THE PEAK PERFORMANCE
TRANSITION TEAM MODEL

A relatively new approach to the use of groups in the outplacement field
is the ongoing job-search team. Built on the work of Azrin, Sher, and
others, it brings a group of job seekers together for a specified period of
time to do their job search as a unit or team. I have been leading these
types of teams since the late 1970s, beginning in a college environment
and transferring in 1984 to the outplacement arena.

What follows is information about the model I have developed that
has helped more than 5,000 job seekers. Having trained more than 100
career and outplacement counselors in this model, I have had the chance
to observe how they have adapted it to meet their style, the culture in
which they work, and the population with whom they interact. These
successful adaptions have reaffirmed my belief that there is no one right
model for the delivery of an ongoing program for job seekers.

Purpose and Goals

The primary purpose of this approach is to help job seekers do a more
effective search than they would if they were doing it by themselves or
solely with the help of an individual counselor. I agree very strongly with
Barbara Sher's (personal communication, January 26, 1995) statement
that "isolation is the dream killer." For most people, doing the job search
in a team will increase their effectiveness because they will:

- Receive referrals from fellow job seekers that will eventually lead
  them to their job.
- Attempt job-search behaviors they would not have tried because
  they saw that they were working for one of their peers.
- Be pushed by members of the group who saw that they were not
  doing well and confronted them with that information in a way that
  got them "unstuck."

Attracting and Selecting Members

Members come to the teams through either referrals from other counselors
or associates of the facilitator, through individuals who have taken part
in the team and found it helpful, or through advertising of an orientation
session in which the team program is explained.

Job-search teams that are offered by individual practitioners through
their own outplacement or career management company might consist of
a mix of members from the public who pay to join.

Teams that are offered through an outplacement firm need to take the following factors into consideration:

• It is better if team members are genuinely interested in joining the team rather than being coerced into joining. Individuals who are not interested in being there will be a hindrance to the development of team spirit and an atmosphere of mutual support.

• Teams that are a mix of functions (marketing, accounting, sales, human resources, law) are more effective than a team that is made up of only one type of function. Lawyers have a different world view than sales representatives who have a different way of looking at the job search than data processing professionals. The sharing of these different ideas leads to a more active and educational exchange.

• Teams that are a mix of sexes are also more effective for the same reason.

• It is preferable, for networking purposes, to have individuals who work for different employers as team members. This is not a requirement, however, because I have led successful teams who work for the same employer for years.

• The one area where heterogeneity is not better than homogeneity is job level. I have found over the years, at least in job-search teams, that a wide disparity in income levels and/or title has a negative effect on the success of the team. The job-search questions that a $40,000 manager will ask and be interested in discussing are quite different from those of a company president making $400,000.

• The orientation session is a very important part of job-search teams. These sessions usually last 30 to 60 minutes and are an attempt to attract appropriate job seekers. Individuals are provided with information on the purpose, structure, and pros and cons of the team approach.

It is critical that potential team members understand the realities of what they are getting into so they will be more likely to stay for the duration of the group and support the efforts of their fellow job seekers. They need to know that they are expected to be on time for all meetings, to be attentive to and respectful of fellow team members, and to come prepared to discuss how to move ahead in as constructive a manner as possible, rather than dwelling on the past or the negatives of their situation. Regular attendance is stressed during the orientation. Candidates are told that teams that do not have a commitment by their members for regular attendance are teams that are often not as successful.

I usually explain that the types of individuals who do not do well in these teams are those who are self-centered and who have a need to be the constant center of attention; those who are unable to look ahead or to think positively about any aspect of their situation; and those who are unwilling to listen to and assist others. I would rather discourage some from enrolling than to have them show up and monopolize the group for their own gain.

The Structure of the Teams

Peak Performance Transition Teams run for 8 to 10 weeks. Anything less than 8 weeks does not allow enough time for the group to jell and for there to be significant sharing of ideas and leads. An optimal size is between 8 and 10 participants. A group with 6 members who come regularly is acceptable, and I have reluctantly gone to as many as 12. Anything more than 12 is too unwieldy.

Peak Performance Transition Teams meet at the same time every week for 2 hours. They are facilitated by an experienced outplacement consultant. The participants also have access to an individual counselor. These teams can also work well without the availability of an individual counselor, although they then spend more time on the "how-tos" of job search than is necessary in the teams where there is a separate counselor who is working with each team member.

The Activities of the Teams

There are four activities that form the basis of the weekly group meetings.

Discussion Time.   Time is spent each week reviewing issues, questions, and developments in each group member's job search. This discussion might take 5 minutes or the whole period, depending on the group dynamics. Group members are encouraged to discuss their situations. Members are told in the orientation that they will usually learn as much from their peers as they will from the facilitator.

Groups that are going well are characterized by a significant amount of problem solving, brainstorming, and generation of referrals for each other to organizations of interest. I am constantly going to the flip chart and saying such things as, "OK, Bill is interested in making a significant career switch into the entertainment industry. Ideally, he would like to move to California and work for George Lucas whose studio is outside of San Francisco. Who has ideas of people he might talk to or resources he might use to get closer to his entertainment industry goal?"

In this particular situation the group came up with 12 referrals. One was to Pele, the international soccer star, another was to a Guru, in northern California, who has Stephanie Powers and other entertainment industry celebrities as members of his ashram. Five were to individuals who work at television stations in New York City, and the rest were to entertainment lawyers, actresses, and agents.

Didactic Presentations.   Didactic presentations are delivered by the facilitator or one of the group members around topics of interest that have been raised by the team. These are usually topics that either take preparation or require team members to think about them prior to the presentation. The general discussions often cover these topics in a more impromptu manner.

Setting Weekly Goals.   This is an important aspect of the Peak Performance Team model. This is usually done in the second session, after team members have gained a certain level of rapport and trust. A chart is created that identifies the current activity level of each job seeker in four job-search activities. They are then asked to identify where they want their activity to be in each of the categories at the end of the 8 weeks. The chart captures information on the following four job-search techniques:

• Number of unsolicited phone calls, visits to personnel departments, or target letters sent. This category covers any direct approach that is made to a company that has not solicited a query and where there is no referral contact.
• Number of job or networking meetings.
• Number of phone calls and/or face-to-face meetings with employment agencies or executive recruiters. Face-to-face meetings with new or existing contacts is more important here, although individuals doing a long distance job-search, or who have strong existing relationships with recruiters do not have the same need or ability to set face-to-face meetings. A distinction is usually made on the chart between face-to-face meetings and phone conversations.
• Number of want ads answered.

The chart looks like this:

Name	Want Ads	Executive Recruiter Meetings	Networking Meetings	Direct Unsolicited Contacts
Bill	Current			
	Desired			
Janet	Current			

The beauty of having a chart like this is that the facilitator and the team members have a snapshot of each individual's current activity level and a point of discussion in terms of future goals. I have had teams whose current activity level was high and whose goals were basically to maintain that level. The work with them is going to be quite different than with a team whose activity level is nonexistent and needs a lot of basic work on how to utilize each of the techniques.

There are three primary benefits to doing this chart early in the process:

1. Members who have made a commitment to the team are often more likely to act in a way that meets the goal than if they were doing the goal setting on their own.
2. Members hear what is working for their peers and adjust their strategy or ask questions to clarify the factors that led to the success of their fellow team members. This is the point where a savvy, active job seeker can pull up the expectations and activity level of the team.
3. The facilitator can quickly identify important issues and design interventions to deal with them, based on the figures on the board.

Most team members over the years have liked the idea of setting goals, because they have managed by objective in their former employers and like applying a business procedure to a counseling process. They also like that the facilitator can provide more substantive answers to questions regarding their job-search progress by looking at their current and projected activity levels.

A key question at this juncture is how the facilitator plans to use this data for the remaining team sessions. There are two primary ways to go with this. The first is to identify activities to which each member is committed in the intervals between sessions that allow them to move toward their goals. For example, if a member is currently not networking because he or she is uncomfortable about calling a friend to request a meeting where he or she can get some advice, the assignments might center around the team's helping this person to make that first successful call.

In another example, a participant might have low goals because of uncertainty regarding what he or she wants to do. This makes goal setting about activities problematic. The work between sessions with that individual might focus on identifying goals that motivate the team member to action. In a third example, a member might have low goals, and is so disorganized that the idea of being productive at all is lost in disorganization. An activity with this member might be to set up a work schedule that allows him or her to feel more in control.

Peak Performance Training. In this phase of the teams, we move away from job-search techniques and into a variety of exercises designed to help team members maintain a positive self-image and desired level of productive activity.

Richard Nelson Bolles summarized my feelings regarding why this motivation/barrier breaking work is often more important than the job-search strategy aspects of the Peak Performance teams.

I have learned (oh, how I have learned) that you can tell a job-hunter all the right strategies, the job-hunter can absolutely memorize those strategies, and yet ... and yet ... they don't budge an inch. And when you later ask them what's wrong, they will say, with sort of a puzzled frown, "Well ... I don't really know. I guess I'm stuck. I don't know what to do next." Apparently knowing-what-to-do does not automatically free up the person to do it." (Bolles, 1984, p. 1)

This is the part of the team that becomes less "hard" external strategy and more "soft" internal barrier breaking. The amount of this that is done will be determined by the skill level of the facilitator, the openness of the team members, and the predisposition of those who run the operation within which the teams are being offered to allow these activities. These activities have fallen into four general categories:

1. Developing the ability to relax, lessen feelings of stress and focus completely on the task at hand.
2. Developing the ability to identify and visualize goals and move toward them utilizing positive statements that help maintain an ongoing sense of optimism.
3. Developing the ability to deal effectively with personal and job-search setbacks by learning a system for lessening the effect of negative occurrences on individual performance. This work is based on cognitive psychology and neurolinguistic programming. A good general introduction is *Unlimited Power* (Robbins, 1989).
4. Developing the ability to approach the job search with energy and a sense of well-being, based on simple principles of nutrition and exercise.

This model provides a wide array of options regarding the expressed purpose of helping individuals do a more effective job search as a member of the team than they would if they were not a member of a team. Some counselors have taken one part of this model and built their job-search teams around it.

One counselor spent minimal time on job-search techniques, because there were other services in his environment that addressed them well. He designed an 8-week course focusing strictly on goal setting, values clarification, and meditation. He felt that if individuals are centered and clear on their goals, opportunities will begin to happen for them—a belief I share.

Others have done away with the goal charts, focusing more on team-building exercises and how the individuals can help one another between sessions to meet goals set on a weekly basis. Still others have focused completely on the charts, using those statistics as the focal point for all discussion.

The point is that a team model has infinite variations, as long as individuals are willing to listen to and assist themselves and others. The remainder of this chapter provides additional information regarding successfully organizing and facilitating ongoing job-search teams.

Group Facilitation of the Teams

There are a couple of key facilitation techniques that are important to consider at this point in the team's development. The first is the importance of not passing judgment on an individual's unambitious goals on the chart. If the reaction to low output or low activity goals is a "put down," the individuals might not return. As a supportive team environment develops, individuals with low goals will often ask the team for help and raise their expectations.

The second facilitation technique is tapping the positive influence of group members. A frequent pattern is that team members want to help each other more than they want to help themselves. Once an issue has been identified that is keeping someone from moving effectively toward their goals, it is important to ask the team members what they might suggest as a strategy for moving ahead. They can then help that individual with the issue between sessions, so that by the next session the person has seen some improvement and has gained momentum.

Going back to the three barriers that were mentioned earlier, what follows are some ways that teams have helped with them.

There are dozens of situations where team members have mentioned that they are afraid of calling people for networking purposes. My intervention will often follow three stages. "OK, Bill, I know you are probably not the only person in the team who has that as an issue. Do you want to work on it?" (It is important to get their commitment to work on it before you expend good energy trying to help those who are not prepared to help themselves.)

If they say no, I might probe further, or say, "OK, when you are ready let us know. Does anyone else have that as an issue?" Often the more verbal or self-assured will volunteer to deal with it, allowing the shyer individuals to learn what to do by observation.

If the person says yes, I'll say, "Great. OK, Bill, tell us all the negative thoughts or expectations that go through your head when you think of making a call. We want to get them all on the flip chart so that we can deal with them." I really encourage them to get at any issues, even if they sound silly. "OK, Bill, is that all of them, because we need them all in order to be able to move ahead?" Among the main reasons that typically surface are the following: embarrassment, not knowing what to say, not knowing the contact's expectations, not wanting to have to owe the contact.

There have been a number of instances where an individual has listed the issues, and upon doing so has said, "This is ridiculous, these are not a big deal, I can do this. I am going to make some calls." When that doesn't happen I will say, "OK, team, any suggestions for Bill?" There will invariably be some suggestions, and, if not, I will prime the pump with my own suggestions. Once we have brainstormed and charted a number of suggestions, I will then say, "Bill, of all that have been suggested, what ideas seem the most likely to help you?" Once we can get him to commit to an action, I will try to convert it to a modest goal that can be successfully achieved by the next meeting.

An exciting phenomenon that will often happen during this brainstorming is someone will say, "Bill, I'm great on the phone. Why don't I help you this week overcome your concerns. You can listen to me and then we'll get you to make that successful call." It is rare for that kind of invitation to be turned down. I then, obviously, make a note to myself to ask them how it went during our next meeting.

I usually follow the same procedure—identify the issue, brainstorm suggestions, identify action steps regarding the issue that will be done between team meetings—with the problem of someone being disorganized. Again, I have had many people volunteer to help someone else get organized. The facilitator has to be careful here, because everyone has a different style of organizing. A system of daily time sheets and colored folders might work well for an analytical accountant and might not work well for a creative copywriter. The facilitator needs to monitor the team's good intentions during this discussion.

Members whose issue is lack of clarity about goals, will often not get as much help from the team, because setting personal goals is a more individual issue. It is my firm belief that having a mission that motivates is key to effective career transition.

All career and outplacement counselors have their favorite goal-setting exercises. The best book I have found on goal setting is called *I Could Do Anything If I Only Knew What It Was* (Sher, 1994). It contains dozens of exercises plus a framework for understanding the different kinds of barriers to identifying one's goals.

One of her many goal setting exercises works beautifully in a team environment. It takes a whole chapter titled "Resistance, or What's Stopping You Anyway?" This powerful exercise contains seven steps:

1. Meaningful work. Write down as much as you can about what that means.
2. The job from heaven. Give yourself free rein to design the perfect job.
3. The job from hell. Again, free rein to put in all the negatives.
4. Job rewrite. Rewrite the job from hell as its opposite.
5. The self-correcting scenario. Team up with a buddy who takes the two descriptions, presents his or her interpretation of your perfect career movie, which you listen to and improve.

6. The temporary permanent commitment. You must promise to do this perfectly designed career scenario for 1 hour. You roll up your sleeves, do away with all the "what-ifs" and begin in earnest to make it happen.

7. Listen to your voice. Your resistance will surface now, and once you have identified the key to movement, you can deal with it in your team."

The remainder of Sher's book provides ideas for dealing with each of the different types of resistance.

In Peak Performance Transition Teams, this exercise has helped to identify resistances that the team can then overcome in the ensuing weeks.

Strengths and Weaknesses of the Peak Performance Team Model

The strengths of the model are fairly obvious. Individuals share leads, provide suggestions and support, and spur each other on to meet increasingly higher goals. The momentum that builds can often pull along quieter, less competent job seekers, bringing them to a level of involvement that they never imagined.

There are, however, a number of weaknesses or problems with the model:

• It presupposes the availability of another counselor to help the individual with personal issues that are inappropriate to be brought up in a nontherapy team such as this, or that, if brought up, would slow the team down.

If this separate counselor is not available, the teams typically become much more technique oriented because members need to understand how to network before they can determine whether they have a problem with it. They also become much more prone to slow down if populated with troubled individuals whose personal issues are better dealt with in the traditional one-on-one counseling model.

The environments where this has worked most effectively are larger outplacement centers where there are other supports or resources available to help with personal issues and job-search techniques.

• It requires an experienced facilitator who is skillful at managing dominating and angry clients. Many counselors who are very effective in one-on-one counseling are less effective facilitating ongoing job-search teams. It is my strong belief that leaderless teams in a job-search setting are less effective than those that are facilitated by an experienced skillful consultant, because it is very easy for a dominant job seeker to provide wrong or misleading information.

There is a lot of anger and frustration that surfaces from unemployed people in job search, particularly from those who have been downsized from their former employer. It is for these reasons that these teams are much more susceptible to the domination of a strong and angry, or misinformed job seeker, than teams that come together to meet personal goals in a structured environment with an experienced career counselor.

• It is hard to judge if a team is going to come together. There are teams that do not jell because of issues of chemistry or circumstance.

• Team members must be able and willing to confront difficult issues, both in themselves and in others. A team member might really be "up," and come into a team meeting where the first 40 minutes are spent helping three fellow team members who are "down." Members need to be informed of this reality during the orientation and again during the opening session.

• It is hard to quantify the success of these teams. Those counselors who work in settings where resources are restricted unless a measurable result is shown, might not be able to demonstrate conclusive proof about the success of job-search teams. The only way to prove, conclusively, that job-search teams shorten job searches, would be to have evenly matched candidates, some of whom participate in teams and others of whom do not. This type of rigorous experimental design control is unlikely in an outplacement setting. These considerations aside, there is already a great deal of anecdotal experience that strongly points to the many benefits of job-search team participation. These include referrals and job leads from fellow team members, increased levels of job-search activity, and improved morale.

QUALITIES OF SUCCESSFUL FACILITIATORS FOR ONGOING JOB-SEARCH TEAMS

These types of groups are a challenge to facilitate. The members are out of work and dealing with a competitive job market. All the members are at different levels of frustration, each with their own ideas about how the team might help. What follows are the key qualities of successful facilitators of these challenging teams:

• The flexibility to adopt a number of roles in the team; from expert to teacher to listener to cheerleader to facilitator. Individuals whose style is to function primarily from the expert role do not normally make good facilitators, because they do not let the group members draw from the strengths of one another and solve many of their own problems and issues.

• The ability to be spontaneous and adapt to the needs of the group at any particular moment. Strong facilitators trust their "gut" instincts about when to be involved and when to back off. The excitement of being a group facilitator is knowing that every session will bring different issues and challenges that one will have to respond to in an unplanned and instinctual way. The decision, that one makes in a group setting, that is right for one individual might be the wrong decision for the majority of group members. Excellent one-on-one career counselors or trainers do not necessarily make excellent ongoing group facilitators.

• The ability to tune out all other activities and approach the team with enthusiasm and a centered and focused approach to the team's activities.

• An understanding of group process and the stages and dynamics that make up a successful group. The book *Facilitation Skills for Team Leaders* (Hackett & Martin, 1993) is a good overview of team facilitation in a business environment.

• The ability to motivate and deal effectively with a diverse group of individuals possessing a wide range of personality traits and attitudes toward the facilitator and the job-search process.

• The credibility to deal effectively with all the strategic and motivational aspects of the job-search and career transition process.

Handling Difficult Team Members

One of the challenges and frustrations of leading ongoing teams is dealing with difficult team members. Hackett and Martin (1993) provided some very helpful ideas.

These are four of the most frequently encountered types of troublesome team members that hamper group growth. Additional facilitator tips to modify their behaviors are included.

The Mummy.   This person will not freely participate in discussions. The motivation might be indifference, an inferiority complex, confusion about the issues or process, or a feeling of superiority.

Facilitator antidotes:

• Be patient.
• Use a warm-up exercise; give the Mummy a major role.
• Ask direct questions to the person on topics on which you know he or she has expertise.
• Ask the Mummy if he needs any further clarification about group topics or expectations.

The Windbag.   This individual comments too frequently and tends to dominate discussions. He or she also tends to be the first to speak on each issue.

Facilitator antidotes:

- Establish procedures to limit the Windbag's discussion; for example, "Each of you has a nickel and that represents only 5 minutes of remarks on this issue."
- Target questions to other members by name.
- Use nonverbal signals; no direct eye contact, focus on another part of the meeting room.

The Rambler.   This individual will often get off track in his or her remarks and uses low-probability exceptions or far-fetched examples to make a point.
Facilitator antidotes:

- Preface the Rambler's remarks with, "Bill, because of time constraints, give me your short version—20 words or less."
- When the Rambler pauses, say, "Thanks Bill, but we do need to get back to the agenda."
- Consider making this individual a recorder, thus neutralizing his or her remarks.

The Homesteader.   A person who takes an initial position and is highly reluctant to budge or consider other viable alternatives.
Facilitator antidotes:

- Overwhelm with facts.
- Enlist support of team members.
- Give the Homesteader a graceful way out with an alternative.

These types surface in job-search teams all the time. Two other types of difficult team members can be added to the list.

The Past Dweller.   A person who is constantly referring to his or her old employer or to situations that worked in "the good old days." Comments like, "I'll never find another company like ... " or, "We really knew how to work together back at ... " are frequently voiced.
Facilitator antidotes:

• Force the Past Dweller to look to the future with his or her comment, "Bill, how would that comment relate to your objectives for your current job search?"
• Ask other team members to respond to the most recent past-oriented comment, "Does anyone have any thoughts on Bill's recent comment?"
• Ask for specificity. "Bill, give me some specifics on what was particularly positive about that situation." Once that has been done, ask the Past Dweller how it can be applied to his or her current situation.

The Fence Sitter.   This individual has difficulty making any kind of decision, thus staying paralyzed and stuck.
Facilitator antidotes:

• Point out that not making a decision is, in fact, making a decision, one that is leaving the Fence Sitter stuck. Identify an easier decision that the Fence Sitter can act on by the next meeting, and ask for a volunteer to help with the implementation in the week before the next meeting.
• Have the group brainstorm all the pros and cons regarding a decision that is pending. Push the Fence Sitter to defend why he or she will not go with one or the other, hoping that this exercise will push him or her to see enough merit in one option to act on it. Have the Fence Sitter agree to call one of the other group members with a progress report midway through the week between meetings.
• Ask the team to take 10 minutes and list in writing any benefits they are getting from not doing something in their job search that they know they should be doing. Have the group members read these to their peers. This exercise, although embarrassing, sometimes generates insight or admissions that spur action. It is done with the whole group so that the Fence Sitter does not feel singled out.

Additional Issues That Surface in Ongoing Job-Search Teams

There are four other issues that sometimes surface and need the attention of the facilitator.

Uneven Attendance.   It is extremely important to stress at the orientation, and again in the first session, that regular attendance is a key factor in a team's success.
If a team has uneven attendance during the first two or three sessions, it is important for the facilitator to bring this to the attention of the members, asking them point-blank if there is a commitment to the team and the process. I have had to cancel two or three teams over the years because, for whatever reason, they were not willing to attend consistently and do the minimum amount of work required. Usually when the mirror is held up to them, they respond by pushing each other to attend more regularly.

Overreliance on the Facilitator.   It is natural and advisable for the facilitator to take an active role during the first and second sessions while the team is forming. The team members need to see that the facilitator has a knowledge base about the job-search process from which they will be able to learn.

Teams that do not want to draw on their own resources, will often turn to the facilitator to provide insights for them. The less experienced facilitator might be flattered by this and bask in the limelight. The sessions can then become more content-driven than is desirable. More experienced facilitators will sometimes be lured into the role of teacher as well. The appeal typically comes from wanting to be seen as the expert or because of a discomfort with dealing with the "softer" group process issues.

It is quite simple to break from this role. Any time a question is pointed toward the facilitator, he or she simply says, "That's a good question; what does the team think?" or, "I've been doing a lot of the talking lately, let's hear from some of you." Another approach that works is for the facilitator to shine a light on what has been happening; "You know, I have to admit I've rather enjoyed pontificating this last session and a half, and I know that is not good. It is much better if you also draw from each other, because we have a talented group here. I'm going to step out of the limelight. What do all of you think about Phyllis' question?"

A Focus on Job-Search Strategies and Not on Barriers to Action.

It is human nature to want to take the easy way out, as Bolles mentioned earlier in this chapter. The facilitator can use some of the same techniques mentioned in the previous example to point out to the team that the conversation seems "safe," or "theoretical," or "abstract" and not related to what "they" are really doing for themselves.

Comments such as, "We've spent a lot of time talking about techniques; I'd like to shift the focus to what is happening with those techniques as they relate to your particular searches. Let's go around and talk specifically about how active your searches are ..." or "OK, this team probably has the techniques pretty well covered; I'd like to ask each of you what is not working in your search, so that we can begin to notch our way to peak performance levels."

A Stuck Team.

Occasionally, even the best teams get stuck. A strong member might have landed a job and left the team, another member might be grappling with a personal situation, such as a death in the family, which is disturbing the other team members, or possibly the facilitator is distracted in a way that is counterproductive.

The best strategy I have found to deal with this is simply to shine a light on the issue and use the pressure to find out what is really going on. "You know, I have noticed that we don't seem to be cooking the way we were in the last few sessions. What's going on?" This kind of a query puts pressure on the team to deal honestly with their stuckness. It will not work, however, if the facilitator is not then willing to remain quiet and let an uncomfortable silence push the team to substantive statements about their lack of movement. Silence is one of the most powerful and under-

utilized counseling techniques available to the individual or group outplacement counselor. I cannot remember a time when the comment
mentioned earlier, followed by silence, has not elicited a response that
was helpful to the group in dealing with their issues.

THE USE OF TEAMS IN THE FUTURE

The competitive pressures in the outplacement business and the continuing complexities of the labor market will combine to push outplacement
firms to cut costs as we move toward the new millennium. A primary way
to do this is by shortening the searches of as many candidates as possible.
The use of groups or teams is a primary way of accomplishing this
objective. It is for this reason that groups and teams, of all types, will be
utilized more frequently as we move forward. Career planning and
outplacement professionals who have the ability to deliver topical job-
search groups, as well as ongoing job-search teams, will have positioned
themselves well for the outplacement and career planning marketplace of
the future.

REFERENCES

Azrin, N. H. (1975). Job Find Club: A group assisted program for obtaining employment.
Behavior Research and Therapy, 13, 17–27.
Azrin, N. H. (1979). The job club method for the job handicapped: A competitive outcome
study. *Rehabilitation Counseling Bulletin, 23*, 144–155.
Azrin, N. H. (1980). Comparative evaluation of the job club program with welfare recipients.
Journal of Vocational Behavior, 16, 133–145.
Azrin, N. H. (1982). *Finding a job*. Berkeley, CA: Ten Speed Press.
Bolles, R. N. (Ed.). (1984). *What to do when you are feeling absolutely stuck in your job hunt or
career change: Newsletter about life/work planning*. National Career Development Project,
Walnut Creek, CA.
Hackett, D., & Martin, C. (1993). *Facilitation skills for team leaders*. Menlo Park, CA: Crisp
Publications.
Parsell, R., & Thompson, G. (1979). Job club. *The Journal of College Placement, 39*, 63–65.
Robbins, T. (1989). *Unlimited power*. New York: Fawcett Columbine.
Sher, B. (1994). *I could do anything if I only knew what it was*. New York: Delacorte.
Sher, B., & Gottlieb, A. (1989). *Teamworks!* New York: Warner Books.

13 Personal Business Ventures: A Proposal

Robert J. Lee
Center for Creative Leadership
Greensboro, North Carolina

This chapter deals with the topic of outplacement counseling for individuals who are not going to get traditional jobs. A general model is proposed for how we might become better at handling this important task.

For many years, outplacement firms have been working with a few individuals who seriously want to go into some form of self-employment (e.g., as entrepreneur or consultant). The professionals in outplacement firms have been relatively effective in helping candidates select themselves into or out of this choice, often more by reality testing than any other method, and then providing relevant resources for the few who want to make a go of it.

Typically, candidates likely to succeed as traditional entrepreneurs have needed the least help. They tend to be decisive, resourceful, self-reliant, often passionate, stubborn, and self-managing. In fact, these individuals probably should not be called candidates. They make their own futures. Traditionally, they represented not more than about 5% of the population of outplacement clients. The others were "counseled" away from this option and found work elsewhere.

These days we have a rapidly growing population of individuals who seek the same kinds of consulting or entrepreneurial careers, but who are rather different as people. They are not the storybook kind of assertive, risk-taking, achieving, decisive, resourceful, passionate, and self-managing people of our American mythology about entrepreneurs. Perhaps, because they know they do not fit the stereotype, or for whatever other reasons, they are not the ones who quickly get into new ventures. They hang around, overanalyze, wait for ideas and support, look to their counselors for answers, and dabble with various consulting projects. They do not plunge ahead with a sense of passion. They do not take risks. They also cannot get traditional corporate jobs elsewhere because of all the downsizing taking place in the large organizations in which they were previously employed. This imbalance leads to serious personal, career, and economic

167

problems for the clients, and to serious professional and economic problems for the outplacement firms.

I do not believe we know enough about how to help these people. We need new models for understanding their career options, their personal needs, and our service requirements. This chapter is a start toward that goal.

THE SIZE OF THE TASK

We are confronting a large and growing task. To put things into perspective, here's "The 20% Scenario" (rough numbers):

• More than 20% of the unemployed in the United States are white-collar employees, even though they represent less than 15% of the overall workforce.

• More than 20% of the unemployed are becoming "long term," more than 6 months out of work. This is the highest percentage since World War II.

• The percentage of all candidates following a self-employment route has been climbing, and now reaches the 20% range in many outplacement offices. They are joining the many millions of Americans who are self-employed or working as temporaries (including 125,000 professionals), part-timers, contract workers, or consultants.

• Twenty percent of the new businesses evaluated by Dun & Bradstreet have only one or two employees in them. These people are better educated and more sophisticated about business than ever before. Still, only about 20% are surviving the 5-year point.

• In the early to mid-1970s, 20% of America's workers worked for the Fortune 500. Today it is below 10%. These were, and are, our candidates.

Our task is to help these individuals feel more positive and upbeat about the adventure they will soon start. They need to go into their new business lives with a sense of power and confidence if they are to maximize their chances of success. This is a very large task for society and for each of our clients. It is also a major task for those of us in the outplacement field who will be their coaches, encouragers, reality checkers, co-celebrators, escorts, and so many other things.

What follows is some thinking on this matter in the form of a Proposal. It is not a full-blown solution to this major problem, but should serve a useful purpose in stimulating discussion. The proposal covers these areas:

• Responsibility.
• Taxonomy.

- Diagnostics.
- Delivery: includes (a) shifting in real time, (b) career identity, (c) empowerment, (d) reinforcements, (e) decisions, and (f) effectiveness evaluation.

This discussion is followed by some comments on what consultants should know about change in adults. The chapter concludes with a discussion of practice implications for outplacement firms' consultants, and implications for management and career development.

A PROPOSAL

Progress in this area will require movement in these four areas:

1. We need to accept *responsibility* for helping a broad range of people, especially those who are 45 or older, to make the most of their situations through personal business ventures (PBVs).
2. We need a *taxonomy* for describing PBVs that clarifies the varieties that exist, going beyond the stereotype of the traditional entrepreneur.
3. We need a good set of *diagnostics* and profiles for this activity. Perhaps, almost everyone can move into a PBV, but they will need differing kinds of supports.
4. We need a *delivery model* for implementing these insights with client populations who need to start PBVs.

Responsibility

How Much of the Responsibility Should Rest With the Outplacement Firm or Practitioner? Who Else Should Carry Some of the Burden?   Our responsibility as outplacement practitioners has shifted from "keeping them out if they don't belong in it," which was how we saw things 5 to 10 years ago, to "helping them make the most of what they have." We now try to deal, constructively, with the relevant transition supports they need, rather than telling them how hard it is for midlevel, midcareer, middle-aged people to strike out on their own. They already know how hard it is!

What we are doing in our outplacement firms works better than it once did, but probably not well enough. A more complete and effective service would likely also require development of the client's technical and business skills, and support from financial and social services. The ideal solution to the whole problem would require the assistance of individuals from banks, various levels of government, large businesses, colleges, and schools of all kinds, and the client's family. In the long term it will also require the expertise of researchers in psychology, economics and other fields who, hopefully, will figure out what makes for success in various entrepreneurial circumstances.

One of the ways some outplacement firms are reflecting this shift in responsibility is by moving toward a reemployment focus. This means connecting more closely with services that actually find open jobs for the clients: job listings, search firms, and permanent and temporary employment agencies. Shifts in expectations are occurring within corporations and in the individuals themselves. Even if they need counseling, they surely need a new source of income as quickly as possible. So, let's get serious!

While all these shifts are happening, there is likely to be a gap between expectations and achievements. Both, the client and the human resources contact at the sponsoring organization, can harbor hopes that are not easily realizable. Sometimes, an outplacement firm will make matters worse by overpromising. It is important that we be honest with ourselves and with our various clients, even if that means making a few people unhappy at the start of our services. The alternative is to make these same people unhappy during and after the services.

A related matter has to do with what is a reasonable fee for this very difficult kind of service. That topic goes beyond the scope of this chapter, but clearly relates to what is expected and provided by various parties to the relationship.

Taxonomy

We Need a Taxonomy for Describing PBVs. What do we call all this? We have no really usable taxonomy. PBVs is proposed as an all-inclusive label for the wide array of activities an individual can do outside of employment in an organization. The definition contains three important elements. It is personal—yours alone to make and to have. It is business—pragmatic, pays the rent, and is based on adding value. It is venturesome—risky, uncertain, and exciting. If an individual sets forth to do PBVs forever, or if that is what happens, then we say that the individual in pursuing a personal business career (PBC).

Labeling all of these things as PBVs is a convenience, but it still does not clarify the options, nor how individuals can choose among them. However, the traditional labels do not serve us well either. Entrepreneuring does not fit what most of the individuals do. It implies risk and adventure at levels inappropriate for these candidates, and is not descriptive of their activities. Consulting also does not usually describe what is happening. Their work usually does not resemble what goes on in consulting forms. Self-employed is an oxymoron. Can a person hire him or herself? Some of the specific labels that are relevant from time to time are: business purchase, business start-up, contracting or subcontracting, franchise ownership, freelancing, home-based business, interim, job shop, outsourcing, part-time, studio work, serving as rep or agent, telecommuting, temporary, vendor.

The rationale behind these ways of doing business is usually the same. They can generate a reasonably stable and adequate level of income when an individual does not have a steady paycheck coming in. However, these are not equivalent roles, and some will be more appropriate for certain candidates at certain times, in various industries or economic situations. As counselors, we need to discuss these options with our clients. It would be very helpful to have an agreed-on set of terms for that discussion.

Beyond serving as a primary income vehicle, Howard Figler (1994) suggested some other potentially legitimate rationales for pursuing what I am calling PBVs:

- Multiple employers and buyers may be necessary in today's marketplace.
- Part-time business can support individuals when they are between jobs.
- Part-time business can supplement an individual's regular income.
- They can be a source of income that an individual is building for retirement.
- Business ideas can be cultivated to see how they feel.

A number of writers and theorists are speculating that the future business world will have a lot of solo people in it. Information technology, we hear, enables people to think of themselves as self-contained small businesses. This theme recently has been discussed in *Fortune* several times, once in an article by the most prominent advocate of this trend, Bill Bridges (1994), and also by Walter Keuchel (1994). The task still remains: How shall we describe and label these roles for our clients?

Diagnostics

We Need a Good Set of Diagnostics and Profiles for PBV Activities. Perhaps almost everyone can move into a PBV or a PBC, but they will need different kinds of supports. How should we determine who needs what?

There are many stereotypes, images, and partial models, but there is no systematic process for reviewing an individual's career and identifying the assets and limitations that need to be considered or dealt with in contemplating a PBV. I have worked with many of the available psychometrics, but there really is not one that successfully focuses on this set of issues. (My regrets here to the individuals who feel they have found "the system" or "the tests" that accomplish this important task.) The items to which the diagnosis needs to be applied are listed in the next section.

Delivery

We Need a Delivery Model for Helping People Who Need to Start PBVs.

I suggest six major elements of an appropriate system for delivering help to PBV clients. There are six areas in which we as consultants need to have competence and need to be able to provide help: shifting in real time, career identity, empowerment, reinforcements, decisions, and effectiveness evaluation.

Shifting in Real Time. In today's corporate world it is common for human resources executives and senior line managers to recognize the need for employees to take more control, initiative, and responsibility for their own lives. Thousands of companies are taking steps so that employees will feel more in control and will be more proactive. The managers also know that this kind of attitudinal shift can take several years to occur. We in the outplacement business have to help people achieve this same shift in several weeks! Among the external factors that promote this shift more rapidly are the stimulus of unemployment and the prospect of financial hardship that stare our clients in the face. Those still employed face these factors as possibilities, not as realities.

Typically, employees do not want to leave Judith Bardwick's (1986) "comfort zone of entitlement." She correctly noted that they need to feel both frightened of where they are, and confident they can get somewhere else, which will be a better place. Perhaps it is our job to try to give them that confidence. Maybe we need new ways to coordinate our efforts with the people who control the client's severance, bridging pay, retraining funds, and other economic elements, so that they can serve as incentives and rewards, not just legally mandated payments. Beyond the financial considerations, perhaps we need to dig into each client's world far enough to find out what the client needs from us, and from others, in the way of confidence.

There are two kinds of skills needed in connection with making a shift in real time. One has to do with shifting. This involves moving from where you are to where you would like to be, or at least where you might be better off. The other kind of skill concerns the new kind of work that needs to be done.

In the shifting category are self-management skills. These include the following: problem solving, experimenting, building support, maintaining confidence, facing challenges, establishing control, regulating negative moods, managing ambiguity, and devising methods for recontracting. Included in the new work-world skills are the following: sales, computer literacy, networking and alliancing, budgeting, and financial controls. The more of these skills individuals possess, the greater the likelihood they will be prepared to pursue PBVs.

A related issue of importance to outplacement firms has to do with confrontation and timing. When do we confront candidates who are not even attempting to shift in real time? Typically, these candidates are looking for a traditional job, or are overanalyzing all the PBV options. When do we have the discussion with them about no longer looking for jobs that apparently do not exist, and encourage their efforts on making a PBV happen? After all, it is their life, not ours. Do we have the right to tell these individuals what kind of career they cannot have? If we do not have that conversation, we all might pay a heavy price.

Career Identity. We know that what makes a difference for many people is the way they anchor their identities. So, how can we best help people shift from their existing job or employer identity to a more generalizable profession or industry identity? If the client's identity is firmly planted in the form of, "I do this work for that company," then we have a situation where one can truly remain stuck. Clients need to let go of that identity and move toward one that says, "I do this kind of work, for employers in this general industry."

Caela Farren (1994) had some excellent career planning materials in this area. She saw this as a generalization and a continuity issue. Clients need to be able to articulate effective answers to the following questions: what can I do, and for whom, given who I am, and what have I been working for? Clients need to generalize their sense of identity away from a narrow employer-linked locus and shift it toward a broader profession and/or industry focus. At the same time, they will still need to maintain a certain amount of continuity in their career identity. Otherwise, they run the risk of feeling lost and at sea.

Empowerment. In Judith Bardwick's (1986) terms, empowerment meant something like seeing what is important and not being perceptually frozen. Then, it involves using clear data, sorting out values and priorities, making decisions and then doing it. It requires initiative, risk taking, resources, support, and an action plan. All this leads to getting unstuck. Nicely phrased, but more difficult to do than to say.

Similarly, Mihaly Czikszentmihalyi (1990) in *Flow* identified the conditions necessary to turn a predicament into a productive event. They include having a clear goal, determining a good match between task and skills, receiving frequent feedback, maintaining focus, and establishing control over your actions.

So, how do we get the PBV candidates to experience this kind of empowerment? How do we get them to flow out of their comfort zones and into a PBV that will succeed? These are some of the major challenges we face as outplacement counselors.

Reinforcements.   What many organizations are trying very hard to get their employees to do is exactly what successful PBV individuals will need to do as well. This includes having personal pride in the quality of their work and being committed to their PBV organization. It also means adapting to customer needs. Further, it means running a low-cost operation and having pay tied to performance. These actions will lead to greater likelihood of business success. Unfortunately, it may be a while before the free market economy rewards the PBVer in a meaningful way. A PBV can take time before it is relatively successful. The outplacement firm may have to provide some of the early reinforcements to keep the right behavior going, because there is no longer a corporate structure to do so.

Decisions.   Outplacement practitioners will need a way to help clients make a decision in favor of or against a particular form of PBV, and to understand clearly the reasons for it. We will need a "decision model" that considers technical skills, of course, and also the commitments and supports available. Then we will also need to understand the P, B, and V factors. What makes it personal for the client? Is it a good business to be in? Is this a venture the client can afford to take? Then, there is the importance of the madness and passion elements. It helps for these two things to be there (as Zorba said at the end of his film) because PBVs are not the easiest way to make a living! Someone needs to put all these things into a rational model.

Effectiveness Evaluation.   What are our measures of effectiveness and success for PBVs? Who should do the measuring? Who should see the results? As these questions suggest, it is not always easy to evaluate the effectiveness of PBVs. One of the particularly tricky issues for outplacement consultants is to ascertain the duration for which services should be provided to candidates starting a PBV. How do we determine when a PBV is up and running? Do we end services when candidates purchase their business cards? Secure their first paying client? Complete a successful 3-month business cycle? There are no hard and fast answers.

This, then, is the proposal. At a minimum it is designed to stir professionals in the outplacement field to look more carefully at how we extend our services to people who seek the PBV path. The next section suggests some of the many implications that follow from the proposal outlined earlier.

IMPLICATIONS FOR CONSULTANTS:
WHAT THEY SHOULD KNOW ABOUT
HOW ADULTS CHANGE

The larger topic of "adult change" underlies the radical occupational changes we are discussing. Although a very large topic, here are some important elements that are especially important when outplacement consultants work with PBV clients.

How Can We Talk More Clearly About Making the Change?

How do we work with metaphors of change so that the candidate's own identity shifts usefully? How do we assess how much of a shift is involved, or is possible?

According to Marshak (1993), who wrote on the topic of images of change, you can listen to which metaphor a person is using, and this helps enormously in understanding how they see their requirements for making a change in life. Moving to a PBV is not a matter of "fixing" something (making it right). Nor is it a matter of "developing" it (making it better) or "transitioning" (moving to the next step). We are talking about "transformational" changes, becoming something else. That is not how most of our clients talk when we first meet them.

How to Deal With Resistance to Making the Change

People hold on to nonworking views of the world too long for many reasons. According to Barker (1993), some of them are:

- It takes a lot of energy to change them.
- It is uncomfortable to do so.
- Any one change has many other implications.
- The new way of doing things is not clear yet.
- The old logics are used to try to explain the new data.
- There is a nasty middle ground during a transition.
- More successful people have the most to lose.
- The change violates existing power, prestige, and preparation.
- The old investment becomes almost worthless.
- A lot of pain is needed to be motivated. This is why "outsiders" tend to be the ones who change most easily—the young, restless, immigrant, marginal people with the least to lose.

Barker's points were made in another context, but seem to apply here. And he is not alone. The library is full of material on overcoming resistances. It seems important that the consultants at outplacement firms have more skills for dealing with the resistances of their clients. We will know this has happened when we have fewer sessions on "Dealing with the Difficult Client" at our annual meetings. We can practice these resistance-management skills and still be on the safe side of the line that divides outplacement work from clinical counseling.

How to Maintain a Sense of Continuity

An internal sense of goals and ideals is formed as we grow up. We incorporate the things and people we feel are good or valuable, and goals are set around these images. These goals tend to last a very long time, and they provide a way of maintaining a sense of equilibrium and meaning across time. Without the stabilizing influence of these goals, life transitions will not occur effectively.

As opposed to the literature on change, there is a lot less literature on how to keep people whole during these changes. How can we help them find new uses for existing skills and experiences in new contexts? Externally, how can they find business trends that will prove profitable and productive? Internally, how should they deal with their myths, values, and sense-making scripts? How can we help our clients recognize their life stories in their new work settings (Rosenwald & Ochberg, 1992)?

Codependencies

We spend a lifetime building and solidifying *relationships*. We use this term to describe how we depend on other people and they, in turn, depend on us. This is a healthy process, and leads to such good outcomes as identity, support, commitment, and predictability.

Unfortunately, some relationships are more accurately described as a codependency, with its negative overtones. In his book, *Healing The Wounds*, David Noer (1993) used the term *codependency* when describing the former employment contract, the one that implied that employees who perform well enough and fit into the culture can count on a job until they retire or choose to leave. This organizational codependency is analogous to the concept originated in the treatment of alcoholism, and since expanded to other addictive relationships.

When the term was first used in 1979, codependence was meant to describe people who deny their feelings, alter their identity, and invest a great amount of energy in the attempt to control someone, and in doing so make themselves into permanent victims. The codependent's sense of value and identity becomes inordinately based on pleasing and/or controlling someone else (e.g., spouse, boss).

Living free of any form of codependence is a lifetime effort. Noer encouraged each individual to have a goal to live life as an adventurer, not as a victim. However, this is an ideal, not the usual state. At midlife, there may be some well-developed relationships that have stagnated at a codependent level. What started out to be ordinary social interdependence slipped into corporate codependence. Then, when employment termination occurs, the outplacement consultant is presented with an unhappy situation, especially if that individual must pursue a PBV.

IMPLICATIONS FOR MANAGEMENT DEVELOPMENT AND CAREER PLANNING

From an outplacement perspective, we see a lot of people who have not received the kind of development they need to compete effectively in the external labor market. This may be due to overall lack of resources, including time and money, that have been invested in the individual. Quite often, however, the training is there, but it is not the right kind.

Here is my hypothesis: Especially when it is done well, in-house development in some corporate cultures may lead to results that are contrary to the skills needed by someone who may have to go out on his or her own. This also applies when outplaced individuals seek jobs in other large but progressive organizations. Often, those organizations are looking for the same kinds of talent that is necessary for success in PBVs. I will go even further. The individuals who received those developmental experiences in their traditional organizations probably were not even getting the best training for success in their former companies!

In some ways, the PBV route is the most severe test of an individual's competence at effectiveness without the full-time support of a nurturing system. If the competencies are not there, the former employer may have shortchanged itself over the years, and now the individual is certainly at a disadvantage. Why does this happen? In-house development often focuses on such things as:

- A flexible set of skills that can be used in various parts of the company, as needed, rather than a narrow specialty.
- A thorough knowledge of this particular organization, an ability to get things done in the system and to make the system work better.

The skills one is likely to need when transitioning to another organization, or to an external role serving multiple organizations are different. They include:

- A specialty that the individuals can do better than most others. The individuals can create a reputation for being good at the specialty so that they can solve a felt-need problem (i.e., so they'll hire you or even call you).
- Good knowledge of practices in many other organizations, and relationships with the people in them.

Finding a better balance between these two approaches to career and management development should become a priority. It should also be a joint responsibility between individual and employer. Perhaps, if we help create adventurous, autonomous, and competent employees we will not need to have them find their own PBVs as often. However, if they go off on their own, they will be better prepared.

This chapter offers a proposal for approaching the major task of providing relevant counseling to outplaced individuals who are not likely to find traditional jobs. Although acknowledging the significant strides we have taken, it also outlines the author's view of the work that remains. We end on the hopeful note that organizations may need to develop their employees for new roles in a way that would make forced departures less necessary, less difficult, and less frequent. That would be good business for all of us.

ACKNOWLEDGMENTS

Portions of this material were presented at the 1994 annual meeting of the IACMP and at the Academy of Management, both in Dallas, and at the September 1994 meeting of the New York Human Resource Planners Society. The author is now president of the Center for Creative Leadership, Greensboro, NC.

REFERENCES

Bardwick, J. (1986). *The plateauing trap*. New York: AMACOM.
Barker, J. (1993). *Discovering the future*. Des Moines: Excellence in Training Corporation.
Bridges, W. (1994, September 19). The end of the job, *Fortune, 130*, 62–74.
Csikszentmihalyi, M. (1990). *Flow: The psychology of optimal experience*. New York: Harper & Row.
Farren, C. (1994). *Leading career indicators*. Scranton, PA: Career Systems.
Figler, H. (1994, March). *Why everyone must be an entrepreneur in today's job market*. Paper presented at the Puget Sound Career Development Association, Seattle, WA.
Keuchel, W. (1994, April 4). A manager's career in the new economy. *Fortune, 129*, 68–74.
Marshak, R. (1993, Summer). Managing the metaphors of change, *Organizational Dynamics, 22*, 44–56.
Noer, D. (1993). *Healing the wounds*. San Francisco: Jossey-Bass.
Rosenwald, G., & Ochberg, R. (Eds.). (1992). *Storied lives: The cultural politics of self-understanding*. New Haven, CT: Yale University Press.

14 New Models for Career Centers

Joan Strewler
Career Dynamics, Inc., Bloomington, MN

Career centers grew out of the need to provide outplacement support for the individuals whose jobs were eliminated by the large-scale corporate downsizings and facility closings in the late 1980s. These career centers became the candidates' "office" for conducting their job searches. The centers also provided a host of services and programs leading to more proactive job campaigns.

At their best, these facilities are the nerve center of job campaign activity for tens, hundreds, or thousands of employees. Competent administrative personnel provide quality support in a business office environment. Diligent campaigners spend hours utilizing reference materials and telephones. Job leads are posted on boards so that candidates can quickly pursue them.

At their worst, career centers are depressing environments with overcrowded cubicles. Candidates communicate their helplessness and hopelessness both verbally and nonverbally. The job lead board, if it exists, has stale or inappropriate leads. The administrative support staff are overworked, resulting in lengthy turnaround times for campaign correspondence.

Traditionally, career centers focused on providing services for employees of a single corporation within a prescribed geographical location. They were run by the employees of the company or were contracted to outsourced providers. The single company career center remains the prevalent model.

In the late 1980s and early 1990s, a few multicorporate career centers were born. These are permanent career centers utilized by multiple corporations, thus creating a critical mass of users. Multicorporate centers have several advantages including more extensive programming, ongoing job development activity, increased cross-corporate networking opportunities, and cost-effectiveness due to the economies of scale.

Multicorporate career centers have not replaced the corporate-specific centers. Only a few freestanding, multicorporate career centers are found

179

in cities like Minneapolis, Minnesota, and Rochester, New York. However, these centers hold promise for the future.

In this chapter, I review the evolution of career centers. I highlight the importance of ongoing cooperation and team work among the service providers, sponsoring company management, and candidates using the center. I also address the emerging partnerships between public and private organizations in delivering vital job-search services to the workforce. One of the complex plant closings on which I have consulted extensively is used to illustrate the structure and operation of an effective career center. Successful practices, especially those that involve teaming paradigms, are discussed. Such practices will be very important in adapting career centers to meet the demands and challenges of the next decade.

CORPORATE-SPECIFIC CAREER CENTERS

Corporate-specific career centers are designed to handle a group of laid-off employees for a defined time period. The purpose of the center is to provide an office environment and clerical support for employees in job transition. The candidates' efforts are supported through job lead development, support groups, computer labs, and reference libraries. A Honeywell study in 1993 showed that career center users took 2 to 4 months less time to find other positions than those who did not use a career center (V. Assads, personal communication, October 11, 1993).

The career center is typically located either at the employer's site or off site, but almost always in close proximity to the corporate client. The work stations and administrative personnel are determined based on a ratio of expected users. These ratios vary from 2:1 to 10:1 (employees per workstations) depending on the project requirements.

Staffing for corporate-specific career centers includes administrative staff, job lead developers, and outplacement consultants. For larger projects, a career center director might also be on site to provide project management and/or center management expertise.

Administrative services typically include typing of campaign correspondence, resumes, and references. Some centers also provide administrative support for mass mailings, business plans, and other self-marketing materials.

Professional services include both group and individual counseling. Group training includes 1-, 2-, or 3-day outplacement workshops, mini-workshops on outplacement topics, and various support groups. Individual services involve sessions with an outplacement consultant based on specific candidate needs. Group and individual services are delivered at the career center. Some corporate clients require typical tracking of statistics such as placement rate, transition time, and presalary and postsalary comparison.

MULTICORPORATE CAREER CENTERS

Corporate-specific career centers initially grew in response to massive downsizings and plant closings. However, as companies stabilize their employment levels and re-engineer their processes, the number of job eliminations often decreases. Companies determine that they can no longer sustain the critical mass for a dedicated career center, yet still have occasional outplaced candidates. This trend has spawned the concept of a multicorporate career center catering to several employers within a geographical area.

Multicorporate career centers are permanent facilities for nonexecutive candidates. They benefit from a critical mass of users, allowing more extensive programming and networking opportunities. Corporations can refer single individuals to the center, and still provide them with services more typically offered employees during large downsizings. Corporations in the community help support the ongoing job development efforts by posting their job openings at the center.

The structure and operation of a multicorporate career center is much like that of a corporate-specific center, except for the permanent nature of the operation. It requires permanent staffing, long-term facility leases, and ongoing programming. Over time, services and systems become more sophisticated allowing for better service delivery.

CAREER CENTER STAFFING
AND TEAMING STRATEGIES

Multicorporate career centers are typically staffed with a center director. The role of the director is to manage the overall operation of the center while developing both programs and staff. The center director is responsible for developing a positive working environment for the candidates. Customer service needs become a top priority.

In addition to the center director, some centers also employ job developers. These individuals are responsible for ordering and maintaining the reference library, databases, periodicals, and developing and posting job listings. Job developers may also train and coach the users in research techniques, thus enhancing their ability to utilize the center's resources.

A core administrative staff provides word processing for resumes, references, and other campaign correspondence. With the help of the center director, they develop clear guidelines for submitting, proofing, and finalizing word processing requests. Administrative staff also serve as receptionists and message takers.

Multicorporate career centers occasionally provide special services, especially if they are catering to individuals who remain on their jobs while beginning their use of the center. For example, block scheduling of consultants as well as second-shift and third-shift scheduling might be required to meet the needs of plant employees. Specialists might be needed. For example, a personal adjustment counselor (PAC) might be needed for workers who have personal issues that interfere with their transitions. This frees the outplacement consultants to focus on job campaign planning and implementation.

IMPLEMENTING A SUCCESSFUL PLANT CLOSING THROUGH A CAREER CENTER

Career centers have a very important role to play in situations where a plant is closing. The establishment and maintenance of an effective career center can greatly assist both the organization and its employees in responding to the complex challenges of a plant closing. Among the major issues to be addressed are the nature, quality, and delivery of the center's services. Experience has shown that a high level of teamwork and cooperation between management and its employees is vital in running an effective center in connection with a plant closing.

During a plant or facility closing, the career center serves as the hub for outplacement activity. Group and individual outplacement consulting, reference materials, and workstations make up the core of the center. The career center becomes the "island of safety" to which all employees can turn during their transition.

Service delivery needs to be based at the career center. Adequate facilities are critical. The space needs to be close and convenient to the plant or facility. The career center should have an inviting environment that can be achieved through offering free refreshments or other "draws." All shifts will need access to the center. This requires careful planning.

The atmosphere created at the career center should be different from the plant. A positive atmosphere needs to be created to promote the "moving forward" theme of the center. A "moving forward board" can provide visible impact by showing successful transitions of employees. The successfully transitioned employee's picture, new position, and other information can be included on the board. Also, a "successful separation graph" can serve as another visual cue of the number of employees who have successfully found new jobs each month. This number can be compared to monthly separation goals, but this should not be introduced until after the midpoint of the project because separation goals may be demotivating if introduced too early in the process.

Organization of a Career Center in Plant Closings

The outplacement team must partner with the plant or facility management team to successfully integrate the services into the organization. The career center needs to be in close geographic proximity to the workforce. If this geographic advantage is not provided, the center may fail to attract users, which defeats its purpose for existence. The staff at this type of career center includes a transition manager who develops and manages the career center and its services. Transition managers function most efficiently if they become part of the plant management team. Daily meetings with the plant manager should become a priority in managing the plant closing. Some of the key responsibilities of the transition manager include the following:

- Participate as part of the plant management team.
- Facilitate the transition team.
- Manage operations of the career center.
- Schedule training.
- Train, schedule, and supervise consultants.
- Coordinate with public sector service providers.
- Develop and manage job lead development function.
- Update career center postings and information board.
- Participate, at the direction of plant manager, in media relations.
- Publish monthly calendar of events.
- Publish monthly newsletter for transitioning employees.
- Track statistical results of project.
- Report on project progress to plant manager.

Creative Services Can Make a Difference

Creative programming at the career center can ensure a higher rate of utilization. A center-opening celebration may help launch a successful operation by reinforcing the positive spirit of the center. Allowing employees to use the career center and participate in its programming on company time will increase its effectiveness. To support this "down time," a new contract needs to be established with the employees. Employees commit to cover each others' work to insure production goals are met. Allowing the workers to plan for individual participation in programming, based on daily production requirements, will offer a sense of control, as well as a team focus on both their production and transition goals.

In plant and facility closings where large numbers of employees need to be transitioned, outplacement consultants are challenged by the mechanics of delivering group programs. One suggestion in meeting this challenge is to organize employees into Zapp teams. Zapp teams are cross-functional teams of up to 15 employees that go through the transition and outplacement training together. Since they are cross-functional, their composition prevents leaving specific work teams understaffed during training times. As they move through several training sessions together, they develop an identity and comfort with one another. In some cases, they can evolve into job clubs or peak performance teams. However, this approach will only be effective if all the team members have a common goal of job placement. Those whose goal is returning to school or retirement need to be clustered in support groups with other employees having the same goal.

Many creative services can be offered at the career center during a plant closing. Some suggested services include the following:

- Unemployment information session.
- VA information session.
- Vocational rehabilitation information session.
- Career fairs.
- Educational fairs.
- Job fairs.
- On-site employer visits (informational or job interviews).
- Individual financial planning.
- Guest speakers (topics of interest).

With multiple groups and special services being offered, a monthly calendar of events is vitally important as a communication tool. Additionally, a monthly newsletter allows for new information and/or programs to be communicated.

The center's services will change depending on the sequence and pacing of the plant closing. It is well documented that individuals impacted by a plant closing experience a cycle of different emotions. Typically, these emotions emerge as follows:

Denial ⟺ Depression ⟺ Anger ⟺ Fear ⟺ Acceptance

These phases need to be identified, and will require appropriate services and support to match each phase. Newsletter articles can help to address these changes and provide helpful tips to deal effectively with the specific stressors that emerge during each phase. Monthly project reporting will be helpful to both the plant manager and the outplacement firm. Statistics should be tracked and included in this report (e.g., placement rate, transition time, presalary and postsalary comparison, etc.). A final project report is important to summarize the results and outline the lessons learned.

Teaming With Employees to Produce Successful Transitions

Consistent and early involvement of employees in plant closings is essential. We know that service needs and the "plant mood" change over time. It is critical that there are communication mechanisms established to convey these changes to management. Communication plans during closings are typically focused on bringing information down from management to the workers, but often fail to consider ways of communicating workers needs back up to the management team.

An effective tool is the establishment of a worker-based transition team. The purpose of this group is to lead the transition, communicate broadly to all interested parties, monitor the organization's mood, and provide input on service needs and schedules. The transition team needs to be established as an advisory group the first week after notification of the plant closing. It is critical that it be representative of all employees, taking into account such considerations as diversity, union membership, and various shifts. The transition team needs to be viewed as a credible and influential body that will help navigate through the "white waters" of the transition.

The transition team should assist in the early grouping and scheduling of employees for transition training. The transition team's weekly meetings at the center need ground rules for smooth operation (e.g., providing positive feedback on the transition prior to mentioning negative feedback). This serves as a preventive technique to avoid these meetings evolving into "gripe sessions." An effective transition team will manage the rumor mill, assist with crisis management, and can serve as a credible forum for media contacts.

Training of Both Management and Employees is Key to a Successful Transition

Group training options are numerous. The backbone of the group services should be a comprehensive outplacement workshop. This can be delivered in a daily training format or broken into modules to better meet scheduling requirements. In addition to the outplacement training, other group programs that can be beneficial include the following:

- Supervisors' training.
- Transition management.
- Couples in job transition (for affected couples).
- Financial planning I (cash flow analysis).
- Financial planning II (tax issues).

- Entrepreneurial workshop I (self-employment options, does it "fit").
- Entrepreneurial workshop II (writing a business plan, identifying resources).
- Later life and career planning (pre-retirement planning).
- Assessment interpretation.
- Career exploration.
- Exploring relocation.
- Returning to school.
- Job development workshop.
- Research workshop.
- Cold-calling techniques workshop.

PRIVATE–PUBLIC PARTNERSHIP

In recent years, substantial amounts of public funding have been made available for displaced employees. However, the use of public funds for outplacement services is often complicated for both the outplacement provider as well as the corporate client. Organizations looking to tap public funds on behalf of their displaced employees will need to determine the relative advantages and disadvantages of utilizing public funds. They will also need to discuss how to integrate these services with private sector outplacement efforts.

The outplacement industry has supported a position of utilizing public money to supplement, not supplant, private sector services to dislocated workers. Although this may make sense on a conceptual level, the implementation is problematic.

The public sector has specific requirements for service delivery to dislocated workers. The dislocated worker programs can vary from state to state. However, most often the process is time consuming. It can take 1 to 2 months from first contact to the start of service delivery. Meanwhile, the dislocated workers are left without transitional services, unless the private sector provider begins with earlier intervention services.

Features of publicly funded dislocated worker programs typically include orientation and enrollment, assessment and counseling, adult continuing education, occupational training, job-search workshops, placement services, and support services. The flow chart in Fig. 14.1 describes the typical sequences of services.

Because there is obvious duplication in the services offered by the private and public sectors, a discussion needs to occur during the project planning phase regarding what sector will be providing what services. The greatest overlap of services falls under the readjustment services—career counseling, assessment, labor market information, job clubs, job develop-

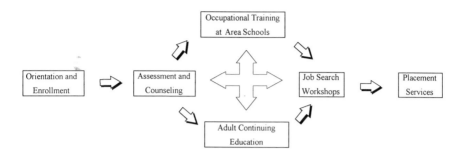

FIG. 14.1.   Dislocated worker programs service model.

ment assistance, and pre-layoff assistance. The retraining and support services (e.g., mileage, child care, etc.) are typically offered only from the public sector. However, to qualify for retraining or support services, a dislocated worker must complete orientation and enrollment and assessment and counseling that may have already been provided by the private sector.

Due to the time-consuming steps involved in applying for dislocated worker grants, the public sector services often come on board after the private sector's initiation of service. Because the government grant money will continue until placement, the public sector may be delivering services after the private services have been terminated (assuming the private sector is contracted for time limited services). Therefore, planning needs to occur around the transition of work between the private and public sectors.

One recent project on which I consulted demonstrated the ways in which public and private sector services can be coordinated. On this project, the private–public partnership included preplanning service delivery, co-locating consultants in the career center, and shared client files. This front-end project planning was essential in minimizing duplication of services. Coordination of services at this level required project leaders from the private and public sectors to meet on a regular basis to make sure that services were coordinated, and that both sectors' administrative and service delivery needs were met.

Specifically, to facilitate the introduction of the public sector services, intake information required previously by the private sector provider was shared with the public service provider. This resulted in a briefer orientation and enrollment for the public services. The assessment results from the outplacement provider were utilized by the public sector provider. This enabled them to meet the Minnesota state requirements for testing reading/math grade levels as part of the Individual Service Strategy form.

Some retraining programs were brought on-site as part of this project. A computer lab was built at the plant, which allowed greater accessibility to both training and hands-on practice. The computer training was utilized not only to increase employability, but also to reinforce the employees' self-concept regarding their ability to learn. Adult Continuing Education and English as a Second Language (ESL) classes were offered at both the plant location and an alternative community location. It was important to offer a community alternative for those employees who wanted to maintain confidentiality while seeking services.

Because public–private partnerships are new, consultants from both sectors might feel threatened with the idea of collaborative services. Historically, the outplacement industry has considered the public sector services to be tailored for blue-collar employees and to generally lack the sophistication found in the outplacement industry.

However, a number of high-quality programs have been introduced by public sector providers during the past year. The Department of Labor is eager for the dislocated worker programs to expand both the number of dislocated workers they serve as well as to expand their service provision to all levels of employees. With recent cutbacks in the use of certified associates by the outplacement industry, some of these individuals have found employment in the public sector programs. Therefore, the quality of the public sector counselors has recently improved. The Department of Labor has also made customer service a top priority for the state dislocated worker programs.

Our corporate clients are looking for financial relief in providing outplacement services to their employees. Increasingly, they expect outplacement consultants to be informed about public sector services and to assist them in securing and implementing these services.

The advantages of a close private–public partnership are the comprehensiveness of services and, when they are coordinated, the near-seamless service provision for the dislocated worker. The corporate client obviously gains from utilizing the best services offered from both the private and public sectors.

If it is a goal to integrate public sector services as part of the outplacement process; it is suggested that the career center space be planned for the co-location of the public sector services. This will promote a "seamless service" between the private and public service providers. The facility should include training rooms, private consulting offices, workstations, administrative support area, reference library, and a "break" room. Additional space might include offices for education classes (e.g., basic skills, ESL, etc.), and computer training lab.

FUTURE CHALLENGES

The career center can be an effective tool in assisting employees in job transition. Although both corporate sponsors and displaced workers themselves want to see individuals making successful transitions to new jobs, each faction has a different emphasis. Management's emphasis is to minimize disruption to work flow and to avoid public relations debacles. The displaced employees have to be guided through their emotional losses and anger, and helped in developing and implementing their job transitions. Effective career centers can meet both corporate and candidate needs by assisting employees in making smooth transitions to new employment.

Our corporate clients are already demanding high quality, cost-effective career center services. This trend will continue to challenge the outplacement industry, and will require the development of more sophisticated, but cost-effective, programs and delivery systems. Group delivery models are increasingly used as a partial solution to this challenge. However, other solutions are needed.

Technology will become critical for developing and delivering better center services to both the corporate client and candidates. Job campaigns will become increasingly dependent on technology. The use of databases, interactive software, video teleconferencing, and networks (e.g., Internet) will become commonplace. All candidates will be expecting laptops as part of the career center services.

Corporate clients will also expect greater efficiency through technology from career centers. They might ultimately require networking capabilities with their vendors for ease of referral, communication, reporting, and billing. As they select providers, they will more closely scrutinize the technological resources available to facilitate candidate transitions.

Demand for leading-edge services and programs will require greater investment in program development. Candidates have already increased their sophistication to the point that they expect more from career centers. Programs and services that reduce transition time will be identified and favored. Proof of success will be expected from corporate clients and candidates alike.

Results! Accountability for positive outcomes will take on a new meaning. Through sophisticated programming, supported by state-of-the art technology, results should become easier to achieve. However, the challenge of the future will also revolve around managing the rising costs of center program and staff development. Additionally, the necessity of increased technology investments will need to be balanced against operating a cost-effective center.

One solution may be increased strategic partnerships among corporations, public sector providers, technology vendors, and other private sector providers in an effort to meet the increasing demand for sophisticated services and still lowering costs. New models and systems are needed to increase efficiency while ensuring quality.

Certainly, the private–public partnership remains one of the biggest challenges for the outplacement industry during the 1990s. Developing a stronger partnership with the public sector will become increasingly important. Maximizing service delivery to our corporate clients by guiding them through successful private–public partnerships has already become imperative. Educating policymakers, with the ultimate goal of influencing legislation promoting the private–public partnership, is already occurring. It needs to be expanded in the future.

In this chapter, the many issues associated with the successful use of career centers have been reviewed. Career centers will be increasingly utilized in the future to assist both, organizations and individuals, with their career transition efforts. The success of these centers will be judged on their measurable results. Our clients will expect us to maximize the benefits of innovative and sophisticated career centers.

15 Confronting Change and the New Technologies: A Guide for the Practitioner

Mark J. Carsman
Career Management Consultant, New York

Give a man a fish, and he eats that day. Teach a man how to fish, and he eats for the rest of his life.

This sensible sounding maxim has long been offered and accepted by career management professionals, particularly those dealing with job-search matters, as a metaphor for what they do for their clients.

As a metaphor, it implies that the goal of consultants is to make their clients competent and self-sufficient, not only regarding current needs, but for future needs as well. With respect to job search, such an orientation dictates that consultants prepare clients to look for a job both now and in the future. It further implies that it is not the consultant's goal or responsibility to provide the job, just the core knowledge and tools that a client needs to gain a desired job.

Given such an approach, it becomes the responsibility of consultants to learn the defined and largely static body of knowledge to an expert degree, and then devise or adopt methods of instruction to convey effectively that body of knowledge and skills to their clients. In longer term relationships, consultants motivate clients to apply the newly acquired skills and knowledge. The consultant's role in this context is that of teacher and coach, not agent or provider.

This approach has worked well in outplacement consulting for many years. A body of generally agreed upon knowledge and commonsense wisdom regarding job search has been compiled and conveyed in what have become standardized forms of communication and training: manuals, seminars, interactive role-plays and, in some cases, audio or video material. Changes in content and instruction approaches, when they occurred, have been infrequent and small. After all, "fishing was fishing," so to speak, and what could ever be new about that?

191

Like most generalizations, the fishing metaphor has limitations. It tacitly assumes that individuals have a long-term orientation to their lives. It also assumes that things never change. However:

- What if the client does not want to learn how to fish?
- What if the client is a vegetarian and wants to sustain him or herself with other forms of protein?
- What if the client is shortsighted, or just very hungry, and so wants someone to assist in helping him or her eat immediately, with no regard to how he or she will eat next week or next year?
- What if fish that were once abundant have been overfished or have migrated, moving from shallow to deep water?
- What if the fish have become smarter or more choosy and no longer take the same bait?
- What if all the fishers were told to fish in the same spot? Or, what if all other fishers are using the same techniques, thereby confusing or scaring the fish away?

Much is changing in the world of career management professionals and their clients. Much of that change is coming from dramatic developments in the business world and in the proliferation of affordable computer and telecommunications products and services. This chapter examines the way in which technology has already impacted outplacement counseling. Furthermore, it challenges career management professionals to become more knowledgeable about technology so that they can assist their clients even more effectively.

THE CHANGING LANDSCAPE

Before 1980

The Client Population.   In the earliest days of outplacement consulting, job loss was a singular event for those individuals who were provided with outplacement support. Taken as a group, candidates were senior-level employees. In general, they were sophisticated in the ways of the business world, yet naive about job search. Most were higher level "career employees" or "lifers" whose "career for life" with a given company was cut short. For this group especially, unemployment was a new and genuinely stigmatizing experience. Many did not possess the personal experience or resources to make a smooth transition on their own. This group needed and greatly benefited from expert advice and teaching regarding how to conduct a job search while involuntarily unemployed. Given the stigma associated with job loss in this period, individuals also

needed and benefited greatly from the personal support and encouragement provided by consultants. Often derided by critics of outplacement
as mere "hand holding," this support made a great difference to those who
received it. Candidates received and required a physical office as an
important component of outplacement assistance. The office was important both for its pragmatic value and for the face saving and morale
boosting it provided. In this period, it was rare to encounter anything
other than an "Executive" program, meaning that most candidates were
executives and one program of services was suitable to all. One price and
one size fit all.

The Technology.   The technology that was needed to operate an
outplacement service prior to 1980 was quite minimal: telephones, a
telephone answering device or service for the firm ("executive offices"), a
copier machine, a "library" that included some company directories,
reference books, and typewriters. Some firms also owned and used an
audiotape recorder for practice interviews. At its barest minimum, the
staff consisted of a secretary-typist and a consultant, neither of whom
needed to have any technological proficiencies.

Quite often, outplacement consulting firms who were leaders, or
otherwise had deeper pockets, bought VCRs and video cameras and began
to use them for role-playing with candidates. This technology had been
available before the 1970s, but only in an expensive "industrial" format
found in large corporate training departments. Typically, this was a
product that neither consultants nor candidates owned at home nor had
experience in using.

During this period, corporate clients and their candidates expected
outplacement consulting firms to be useful in getting their calls answered
and messages taken (by hand) and resumés and letters typed and copied.
Although the use of a VCR in interview training might have been an
impressive distinction for some firms, technology per se was largely
irrelevant to both parties, so long as the results were achieved; namely a
swift and gracious placement.

1980 to 1990

The Client Population.   As this decade developed, business began to cast off employees continuously and in large numbers. The words
downsizing and, much later on, *re-engineering* became a part of the language
of the average citizen. Whereas the majority of individuals in the work
force probably never attained the idealized "job for life" represented by
the images inherent in companies like IBM, Equitable Life, and Bethle-
hem Steel, such a goal was still viewed as attainable and desirable by
most.

Job loss at all levels and in all industries was becoming more "normal." It became a fact of life that could happen to anyone. Accordingly, the stigma associated with job loss was beginning to dissipate, even among the old-line executive recruiting firms who had generally resisted presenting the unemployed to their clients. However, as a result of their "old-fashioned" value system regarding job loss, candidates often felt more stigmatized than they actually were.

Outplacement was being sold successfully to companies as a service for all levels of employees. Once the province of the senior executive, one could now find secretaries, blue-collar workers, and others being provided outplacement assistance.

Despite the explosion in unemployment and permanent changes to industries such as banking, the 1980s were, nevertheless, largely prosperous years. With the important exception of truly dislocated workers, it was not too hard to find another job within 6 months of losing one.

During this period, the task of outplacement consultants remained largely to help people regain their composure and recover an optimistic stance. They helped candidates to reassess their goals, to package and prepare themselves to get another job like the one they had before, or perhaps an even better one. As in the prior time period, this involved preparing a conventional resumé and proceeding toward the goals using conventional job-search methods. Fishing was still fishing, so to speak, although more people than ever were now doing it.

As the volume of individuals in outplacement grew and their average income and educational levels dropped, outplacement firms began to feel the need to deal with more people in less time and for lower fees. As a result, shorter programs became more prevalent along with the use of group formats. In addition, the offering of different "programs" became commonplace, with differing levels of service or support being provided. Senior executive programs continued to provide private offices for many, but the trend was toward reduced levels of support. For the majority, "office" meant the use of a cubicle in a shared space.

The Technology.   The revolution in consumer electronics during this period brought many changes to the business of outplacement consulting. New electronic and telecommunications products were being invented, revamped, or simplified for average users. At the same time, these products became consistently less expensive for businesses and consumers.

Perhaps the most significant aspect of this period, from a technological perspective, was the democratization of technology. Increasingly, candidates either already had or could afford to buy the technological products and services that were once available only from organizations like their former employers or outplacement firms. The outplacement firm's value and uniqueness to them, in this area, began to erode. That trend continues to the present.

VCR, camera, and camcorder products were now priced within the reach of all outplacement consulting firms and even some independent practitioners. By 1980, a portable camcorder could be purchased for less than $1,000, eventually for much less than that, if one shopped carefully. It was not uncommon for candidates to own and operate these products at home. They were less likely to be predisposed toward a firm for having this equipment and, for the same reason, might be negatively impressed by a firm that owned less sophisticated equipment than they or their neighbor owned. They could do it at home if they chose.

In addition, the advent of the IBM personal computer (PC) changed the face of business and society in many ways. In these early days, some outplacement consulting firms began to use these computers as a tool in the management and operation of the financial and operational aspects of their business, such as accounting, billing, and marketing. In addition, many firms whose outplacement programs included the typing of resumés and letters for candidates, which was not uncommon for the "full" programs of this period, began to supplant typist-operated typewriters with word processor-operated PCs.

Personal computers were expensive at the start of this period, often costing $5,000 for a model no one would begin to find useful today. In 1981, I recall my employer adding a hard disk to a computer. For $2,700 he acquired a 20 MB disk. Today, $2,700 buys a PC that is very close to the top of the line in performance from many leading manufacturers. At the time, no one but well-heeled hobbyists and professionals who needed a computer were buying them for home use.

Despite their high cost, the new PCs and the new sophisticated word processing software were cost-effective. They produced camera-ready resumes in-house, that were often duplicated in the office using new model copiers. This often reduced or eliminated completely the use of more expensive typesetting and printing services. Counselors, for the most part, initially viewed the PC as just another kind of typewriter, an extension of the typist, and of little personal interest or value.

In theory, the use of PCs for resumés and letters allowed candidates to tailor their communications to the specific recipient, which had always been advocated by most career consultants. Ironically, this labor-saving device often put greater financial and time burdens on the firm's staff, because candidates would often want to make more changes to PC-based documents (or multiple versions) than they would with those that are typeset and printed. Candidates could often spend an inordinate amount of time in developing multiple variations of documents, as well as working on the same documents seemingly without end. In some firms, counselors were given the unenviable burden of trying to satisfy a candidate's needs while controlling the volume of material produced, given its negative impact on profitability.

Paralleling the rise of the desktop computer was the growth in information technology. Online information services began to proliferate, albeit to sophisticated and affluent users such as large businesses and academic researchers (who, as members of not-for-profit organizations, often operated under lower fee structures). Examples of such service included Nexis/Lexis, BRS, and Dialog Information Services, each of which offered access to hundreds of databases. Much of this was, and is, information taken from other media such as newspapers and periodicals. Its instant recall is especially useful in a job search for targeting companies and preparing for specific interviews. Such a service replaced numerous hours spent in libraries for candidates who wanted to research companies. It also provides useful information to candidates who would not have the competence, patience, or fortitude to do the digging themselves. When used well, online research can speed targeting and improve all aspects of interviewing and is a true value-added service to job seekers. Even when not used effectively or at all, it became increasingly necessary for firms to offer these information services, because the outplacement business was becoming intensely competitive.

Access to these services was, and is, very expensive, and is not typically added to the sponsor's fee. In addition to having a computer, the outplacement firm or consultant also needed a modem to communicate using a phone line, usually a "dedicated" line, which became yet another overhead expense item. In the early part of this period, modems too slow even to be manufactured in 1995 were priced at more than $600.

These services were usually billed by the minute, with additional charges levied for reading or printing discrete items. Charges of $2 per minute were not uncommon. Typical research questions could be answered for $25 to $200. Given the steep prices, using these services required speed, accuracy, and search skills. It made economic sense to restrict their use to either a professional business researcher or someone who has taken vendor-supplied training and already achieved a level of proficiency. These services were usually reserved for "full" program candidates, given the overhead involved.

Although most counselors have not been asked to learn to use online technology, it has nevertheless placed additional burdens on them. They have to know when the use of an expensive database search is justified both from an administrative perspective ("Is it in the candidate's program?") and from a counseling perspective ("Is this the information they *really* need?"). Counselors need to know how to use this information and how to teach their clients to use it as well. During this period, online information technology was not commonly available to candidates at home or through their own resources, although some local libraries provided limited free services of this type.

Candidates were often becoming more sophisticated in using the PC for word processing and for administrative matters than the typical outplacement counselor. Many candidates, particularly those who were technically or financially oriented in their professions, had already integrated the PC to into their professional and personal lives. They were familiar, if not competent, with word processing software and spreadsheets such as Lotus 1-2-3. They wanted to use these tools in planning and conducting their job-search and expected that an outplacement firm would help them with equipment and advice in this area.

1990 and Beyond

The Client Population.   During this period, the job-search environment has continued to change. Whereas life-long employment remains a goal for most workers, there is a lower expectation of achieving it in a single company. Indeed, many have come to believe that the only constant in business is change. Individuals, increasingly, believe that they may have many jobs and even several different careers.

Job loss at all levels and in all professions has become normal, with relatively little stigma attached to it, even among executive recruiters and their clients. The need for a face-saving office has diminished greatly except, perhaps, at the most senior levels. Indeed, many senior and professional-level employees had already been accustomed in their streamlined corporations to working without the benefit of a physical office. They, and their professional contacts, are used to dealing with the "virtual office" of the voice mail, e-mail, and telephones.

In addition, job-search knowledge and first-hand experience with job search are much more widespread. More and more outplacement candidates have been through outplacement before, or, at a minimum, know someone who has. They have "taken and passed the course before," and, increasingly, do not feel the need for traditional outplacement support.

The outplacement professional is no longer the sole authority on job search. There has been an explosion of job-search aid and counsel from many fronts. College alumni associations, professional organizations, job-search clubs associated with churches, synagogues, and libraries have proliferated and are easy to find and pay for. These community-based programs often have the added attraction of a built-in networking function, that may be even better than that available at an outplacement consulting firm, especially if the job support group has a professional or industry focus. Further, the number of job-search books is dynamic and ever changing, as a visit to any bookstore will demonstrate.

The Technology.   Changes in technology now permit additional channels of support for job seekers. There has been a continuing pattern of reduced prices and higher power and performance in the computing, telecommunications, information services, and consumer electronics fields. The rise of Windows®-based computers and programs have made it relatively easy for average people to buy and use computers at home, if not on the job.

Fax machines are affordable for home use and many candidates already have their own. Voice mailing is available at home by purchasing a sophisticated answering machine or by installing a voice mail/fax card in one's PC, or by using an easily acquired service of the local telephone company. For a relatively small fee, local telephone companies can provide additional telephone numbers to one's home, making it possible to have a dedicated business listing and voice messaging to be used in one's search.

Online information is still quite expensive and generally difficult to use at home, but inroads have been made in this area as well. General information services such as Prodigy, America Online, and CompuServe are within the reach of almost everyone with a computer and a modem. Very high speed modems are freely available for less than $100, and are now often included with a newly purchased computer. In addition, CD-ROM discs are becoming commonplace on new computers. These have allowed the packaging and selling of company information products at mass-market prices.

More and more candidates know how to use computers and actually prefer to do much of their word processing themselves. They also use the computer to track information and people in their search. Maintaining their daily calendar and organizing their contact lists are just two examples of how they use computers. Notebook PCs equipped with modems and faxes are more affordable than ever. As such, candidates do not even have to be located at their home or office to be productively engaged in their search. In addition, community libraries have become more useful to job seekers by installing new technology that provides access to more company information, as well as their traditional collections of books and other resources.

The Internet is a siren song to many in our society these days. Now available to anyone with a modem via consumer-friendly services and software, it is providing access to online job leads and bulletin boards. In some cases, corporations are recruiting candidates directly; in others, agencies are scouting candidates on the net. This area of services and opportunities is growing rapidly. Also blossoming on the net or other online services are free career counseling and resumé critiquing. Networking and peer advice is also available online.

A visit to a computer software store will also reveal the broad availability of programs that provide counsel and support in planning and conducting a job search. Within one such program, one could work through goals, skills, accomplishments, be guided and supported in the creation of a resume and letters. The same program will produce a nicely formatted resumé and letters. It will also help individuals organize their searches by including a Rolodex® and calendar. If that were not enough, the program includes a database of information, the Adams Job Bank, on many leading employers.

Do these programs work? Naturally, some are better than others. Taken as a group, they have been improving with time and the increasing storage and multimedia power of the newer computers.

The job-search resources of outplacement firms are increasingly being measured against what is available at home and elsewhere. In increasingly greater numbers, the technological resources of outplacement firms are becoming irrelevant or inadequate compared to those available at home or in one's own briefcase via notebook computer and modem.

WHERE ARE WE NOW?

With respect to the "teaching people to fish" metaphor, we have arrived at a far different place than prior to 1980 when outplacement was itself a relative novelty, as well as the exclusive source of expertise on job search. Stated simply, many outplacement services may be on the verge of being viewed as unnecessary to an increasingly greater number of potential candidates, and might no longer be seen as adequately meeting candidate needs for resources.

Implications for Practice

The outplacement industry and its individual practitioners must do a better job of embracing and employing technology than has been the case to date for four main reasons:

1. Prospective outplacement candidates might use the newly emerging technology and information services on their own and shun the services of outplacement firms and their career management professionals.

2. When individuals do use the services of outplacement providers, their expectations are often more varied and complex than the relatively simple ways of conducting a job search 10 years ago. They often want more than the standard package of typical services.

3. Sponsors continue to reduce their financial support of outplaced candidates. They seek to do this by bargaining with outplacement firms for lower fees and by shortening the duration of services. Outplacement firms and practitioners are expected to achieve much the same results in less time and for reduced fees. Firms will, therefore, expect practitioners to become more productive without loss of quality.

4. Given the intensely competitive nature of outplacement, the pressures for quality and value are higher than ever, despite the increased complexity of desired services and the reduced support for these services.

Guidelines for Becoming More Technologically Skillful

Acquiring knowledge of technology, either as an individual or as a firm, takes continuing effort and financial resources, especially given the rapid pace of change. There is no simple, direct path to growth. What is most useful, in my experience, is "learning by doing" and "learning by observing"—and doing so on a continuing basis.

Learning by doing, means just that. Do something with technology. Buy a computer, if you do not have one. Use one if you have it. Buy or try different types of programs that bear directly or indirectly on job-search and career management. Learning by observing means finding out what others are doing or saying through networking, professional organizations, and reading computer, online magazines, or journal articles on this subject. Also, it is helpful to visit software stores, browse and try new products.

How Are You Doing?

The following self-test will serve to either give some assurances where warranted, or point in directions that will enhance your growth in this area. Give yourself a point for every "yes" answer. Take a point away for every "no" answer. There is no passing score.

- Do I know what the following terms mean? Could I define them to a client at a very basic level?
  - Personal computer
  - Windows
  - Mac
  - Modem
  - CD-ROM
- Do I own a modern computer (Windows or Mac) with a modem? Do I use one at work all the time?
- Can I compose and format standard word processing documents like letters? What about more complicated ones, like resumés?
- Can I load and use CD-ROM based programs?
- Do I have and use an online service, such as America Online?
- Do I have and use an e-mail account (e.g., myname@aol.com)?
- Can I help a client use the Internet to find a job? Such help includes locating company information, job databases, resumé databases, online career counseling, or "meeting places" where professional or other affiliated groups exchange mail and ideas related to a profession or industry?

- Can I recommend specific computer software programs to clients that could help them improve their career or job-search knowledge or skills? Included in this could be software that instructs users on job-search techniques such as resumé development, reference software that, for example, provides access to targeted firms or recruiters, or software that helps clients manage their job search better, such as contact management software. (In order to recommend, you must have personal experience with the product in question, in order to be certain of its essential worth and appropriateness to your specific client.)
- Do I routinely try out new products or services that may be of value to my clients?
- Do I routinely read or otherwise monitor sources of information on new products and services that could improve the cost–benefit ratio of my services?
- Do I engage in continuing education regarding new technology or in using old technology better? For example, have I received training in how to best employ video technology in interview training (when to use it, on whom, and in what way)?
- Am I tired of doing repetitive aspects of my job that a machine could do? If so, have I introduced a technological solution to free myself of it and open my time for more personal, creative interactions with candidates?

In the simplest terms, if outplacement firms and those who practice within them are to survive and prosper in the long term, they must find ways to offer individuals something they cannot find easily or at all on their own. They must also do so in a cost-effective manner. Technology can be the answer here, as well.

If counselors are to survive the increased demands of the field and retain satisfaction in their work, technology may be the key. It will enable them to eliminate or reduce unnecessary labor and free them to do what they uniquely do best: provide personal counsel in an individualized manner. Technology, however refined, can never substitute for that. At its best, and when used well, technology can free counselors from repetitive and unnecessary training and administrative activities, in order to provide the time and energy for the human interactions candidates almost always need, even those who are quite sophisticated about job search. Such needs include active listening, insightful understanding, empathic caring, and constructive feedback.

16 Executive Coaching: Helping Valued Executives Fulfill Their Potential

Kathleen Strickland
The Strickland Group, New York

A PROACTIVE, POSITIVE APPROACH TO HELPING COMPANIES AND THEIR EXECUTIVES MANAGE CHANGE

Consider this recent, actual client experience of mine.

A woman was hired from a manager's position in an operating division in one company and appointed to an executive post at corporate headquarters in another. She moved from a Midwest location to the West Coast. She transferred from a company that was an industry leader to a conglomerate in transition. This woman was extremely competent in her field of technical expertise, and had developed well and blossomed in her old position. In her technical knowledge of the field, she was well ahead of executives in her new organization.

A department head in her new company was scheduled to retire in 12 months, and the woman in question had been hired with the goal of being given his position when he left. However, shortly after she joined the company her managers decided that, unless changes were made, she would not get the job for which she was being groomed.

Why?

It was a matter of "executive presence." In meetings and interactions with colleagues, she talked a little too much, spoke before listening to others, did not ask pertinent questions, and tended to interrupt. At the office, she operated first from a social perspective, and then got around to work. She mixed business and personal affairs too much and too often. In short, she was the same person she had always been, and yet she had never known her behavior to be an issue.

Or, consider another example.

203

A stock trader was extremely successful at a young age due to his knowledge and experience, but also because of his strong intuition and ability to make lightning-fast decisions based on "gut" reactions. However, once he arrived at the executive suite, those same unilateral, quick decisions that served him so well were wreaking havoc in his senior management role. He was not consulting colleagues, working within a "team" agenda, seeking counsel when necessary, or considering the impact his offhand decisions were having on others.

Enter the Executive Coach

Taken together, these two case studies demonstrate the three principal ways in which executive coaching methods can be fruitfully employed.

The first example, the woman manager who lacked executive presence, illustrates that there are countless styles of behavior that, on a managerial level, although perhaps objectionable, are not a serious impediment to career advancement. However, on the senior executive level, these traits are more than stylistic differences. They become veritable roadblocks to success. The executive coaching in this instance was developmental in nature—that is, a matter of cultivating and honing this particular executive's existing skills, and helping her to recognize undesirable behavior patterns in order to increase her effectiveness.

The second example, the impulsive, fast-moving stock trader, illustrates the second kind of executive coaching. It is what I call "fix-it" coaching—targeting and addressing a specific behavior that is causing managerial conflict of some kind. This man's intuitive gifts and "go-getter" enthusiasm were still valued on the executive level. However, such characteristics have to be tempered if an executive is to be successful in a leadership position. (Sometimes, weaknesses are not really weaknesses, just, as I like to say, "strengths gone haywire.")

As it happens, this case study illustrates the third variety of coaching as well, one based on simple career-path assessment. Part of working with this particular executive was helping him assess his appropriateness for a managerial, rather than an "individual contributor" role or entrepreneurial–intrapreneurial role, and plot his career course accordingly.

Enhancing Performance, Resolving Problems, Enabling Change

Simply defined, *executive coaching* is a way of providing companies and their executives with an objective, third-party perspective and a set of coordinated interventions that quickly result in opportunities for change through increased employee recognition of a challenge or problem. Recognition then leads to discussion and resolution of the issues.

Whether triggered by the need for further advancement, corporate restructuring, or simply by a set of behaviors that are seen as problematic in the workplace, executive coaching is much like personal training, in that coaches work one-on-one with executives to foster growth and success. The broad professional definition aside, executive coaching is a recognition that companies frequently need help in resolving complex career issues related to valued employees.

The bottom-line economic fact, of course, is that executive coaching is a far more cost-effective solution to management problems than terminating an employee, and having to hire and train a replacement. Moreover, many complex management conflicts are solvable through the techniques used in executive coaching to the satisfaction of executives, management, and subordinates alike. Performance can be enhanced, problems resolved, and changes made possible.

Is it really that easy, and does it always have a favorable end? Yes—and no.

"Seeing Themselves as Others See Them"

On the most basic level, I define executive coaching as "helping people see themselves as others see them." In other words, helping executives step outside themselves and understand others' expectations, reactions, perceptions, and criticisms. In helping executives accomplish this, coaching assists them in acknowledging and dealing with realities they might otherwise avoid, or deny, or accept with resignation.

At the risk of straining for a metaphor, a good executive coach looks at a management situation or conflict the way one would look at a painting, and then asks questions. What are the relationships among the various elements here? What is missing? What is being communicated and, more importantly, what is being left unsaid in this situation? Why is this executive behaving as he[1] is? Does he realize what he is not acknowledging about himself or about his management style? What is his personal agenda, and what is its relationship to his company's goals?

The proficient coach is a bit of a detective and is able to combine pure business pragmatism with intuitive gifts. He must be sensitive to personality issues, be a creative problem solver, and be able to look at an executive and see the business and personal objectives involved as two equally important sides of the same coin.

How?

Coaching, ideally, is a combination of at least six separate, if complementary, tasks:

---

[1]I am, of course, using the "genderless he." I find saying "he or she" cumbersome and "he/she" awkward. As a female executive myself, when speaking of executive coaches or executives themselves, I am always referring to both women and men.

1. *Listening.* This comes first. My own personal background as a trained psychotherapist has taught me the importance of listening to the client. When you are retained as an executive coach, help the executive tell you, in his own words, what the issues are as he sees them. Chances are, you will be able to clue-in to the focus, the intent, and the orientation of his communication, and thereby "diagnose" the situation clearly from the very words and manner in which he lays out the situation.

2. *Clarifying.* Half the battle in any executive coaching situation is pinpointing and making clear to all parties what the issues are and what can be done about resolving them. The key here is setting mutual goals based on shared expectations and realistic time frames.

3. *Mediating.* The executive coach functions in many instances as a "middle man" between an executive and his senior management, between him and his colleagues, or between him and his subordinates or staff. Intervening sensitively and helping each side, when appropriate, to understand the priorities and appreciate the perspectives of the other, is a key part of the coaching job. Again, clear, focused communication among all parties is key. Coaches must remember also that communication involves process, form, and content. All must be looked at closely. Look not just at what is being said, but how it is being said.

4. *Educating.* Executive coaches are teachers, responsible for educating executives about skills, both management and interpersonal-communication skills, and the impact that their behavior has on others. This involves everything from delegating authority to "executive style."

5. *Training.* Once issues have been clarified and solutions outlined, the coach works closely, one-on-one, with his client helping him to modify behavior, alter managerial style, enact operational or organizational changes, or work on improving problematic relationships within the company hierarchy.

This all-important altering of perspective, or reframing, is the basis of the resolution of virtually all issues. The coach must clarify the executive's existing belief system and self-concept, and then help him identify where the "right" and "wrong" thinking is. On a very fundamental level, thinking can be changed, perspectives reframed, and belief systems revised. This can be accomplished whether faulty patterns were based on incorrect assumptions, conventional wisdom, learned patterns, family pressures, or a host of other factors.

6. *Follow-Up.* Executive coaching can really only be judged as successful in retrospect, after a period of weeks or months have passed. A thorough and professional coaching situation will always include follow-up evaluation and progress review, on both a short-term basis and a long-term one. Immediate results will, assuredly, be seen. However, only a significant amount of time will reveal the true value and lasting benefits of coaching.

Does it always go that smoothly? Of course not.

WHEN EVERYTHING GOES RIGHT

Consider this example.

After working for many years as a brilliant financial executive within a corporate finance department, a woman was promoted to the position of chief financial officer (CFO). Despite her considerable financial talents, 5 years later the finance department was in shambles. It was perceived as having no leadership, no administrative framework, and no responsiveness to other departments in the company. Rife with morale problems, the department was described as a "black hole" of inefficiency.

In this instance, the coaching process involved several levels of intervention. First, we met with the human resources executive to clarify overall goals. Next, we met with the CFO herself to gain her perspective on the issues and learn what she felt needed to be accomplished. Meetings were then held with individual senior executives, as well as with the financial department as a group, to assess individual views of the issues. A detailed questionnaire was developed as an instrument for getting further input.

Following distribution and completion of the questionnaire within the organization, we met with the CFO again to review the results. Next, we interviewed senior executives within the company to get their perspectives, and then met with the entire financial department to review responses. Based on the assessments and reactions of virtually everyone involved, we developed our plans for change, targeting specific issues for individuals as well as for the organization as a whole.

The central issue in this case was one of authority, and the CFO's failure to assume a stance of senior authority in relation to the fellow financial executives with whom she had worked side by side for years. She was quite capable of leadership; she simply had not assumed the role on being elevated. She had continued to act as simply a brilliant financial executive, a colleague to her staff. Hierarchically speaking, this was, of course, a disaster. Once she was able to focus on this "obvious-in-hindsight" pattern, and work on modifying her behavior accordingly, she was able to become a highly effective and strategic manager. Today, the financial department is a model of efficiency and responsiveness.

But Coaching Cannot Perform Miracles

A more troubling case study is presented here.

The director of human resources of a large company had a distant relationship with his firm's chairman, but his subordinate had a close one. This left the director "out of the loop." Several interventions, similar to those previously described, were attempted in an effort to coach the director on how to strengthen his relationship with the chairman. However, in this case the coaching process had a very limited effect. There were several possible explanations. First, the subordinate continued to have the "ultimate weapon," the friendship of the chairman. His view was that he had no reason to want to help make the intervention work. On the contrary, he actively used his friendship to undermine the director. In addition, the human resources director never demonstrated the high degree of motivation and goal-oriented behavior that is typically seen in such executive coaching situations. He did not follow through fully with a number of the recommended interventions. Nevertheless, the coaching process did clarify options, define chances for success, and delineate what was and what was not "salvageable." In that sense, it fulfilled its aim.

TESTING

A wide variety of standardized evaluation techniques and customized questionnaires can be employed as part of the executive coaching process. They include: Myers-Briggs Type Indicator (MBTI), Personality Research Form (PRF), Birkman, "Benchmarks," and others. Tests can be useful in bringing management, leadership, communication, and style issues into sharp relief, as well as bringing to light a particular executive's strengths and weaknesses. Essentially, testing often confirms what a good executive coach already knows. In addition to standardized tests, a helpful means of gaining others' perspectives is the use of 360-degree feedback.

In 360-degree feedback, we use either a standardized instrument or, more frequently, develop a questionnaire customized to the particular situation. Written questionnaires, telephone questionnaires, or in-person interviews are all used in various situations. Focused around a particular individual or issue, the inquiries are aimed at eliciting general perceptions about an executive's strengths and limitations from his peers, subordinates, and bosses within a company. When the questionnaires are gathered, tabulated, and analyzed, the executive coach and executive gain, through specific comments, a clear picture of issues to be resolved. They can review varying opinions on how a problem is perceived throughout the company.

Here's an example.

A young, dynamic, hard-driving executive vice president assumed control of a technology and operations division within his company. He was determined to maximize the division's efficiency and output. The executive coach, together with the executive in question and his human resources professional, put together an extensive 360-degree instrument that incorporated questions about the strategic mission and values of the group, the nature of their customer focus, intragroup communication, and other areas. Each individual within the department sent the questionnaire to 14 executives in a wide range of positions within the division hierarchy.

After the questionnaires were compiled, "team members" individually received feedback from a consultant over a 2-hour session. A week later, the executive vice president and the consultant combined to create a development plan based on what was learned. An unexpected and impressive result was that 9 months after the intervention there was increased team spirit and morale, in addition to a boost in effectiveness and individual productivity.

HOW PEOPLE BENEFIT
FROM EXECUTIVE COACHING

They benefit in a wide variety of ways, particularly when you consider that:

• The executive suite is full of unspoken rules. When a manager is promoted to an executive position within a company, he expects increased responsibility, greater authority, enhanced financial rewards, and the additional perks and pressures that go with the job. However, what he may not be prepared for is the need to learn—in fact, to "decode"—the unspoken rules of the executive suite.

Executive "style," and the rules that govern it, are intangibles. Some individuals almost seem to be born with executive style. Some grasp it instantly and easily. For others, it is a mystery that must be solved and a way of behavior that must be learned. It involves communication skills, ways of thinking and responding (logically vs. intuitively, globally vs. parochially), enthusiasm, confidence, receptivity to ideas, appearance, a sense of humor, and a hundred other things.

The good executive coach can plot a road map for appropriate executive behavior that can, quite literally, make or break an executive career.

• Strengths can be weaknesses. Many executives were rewarded early in their careers for behavior that later tripped them up. In some cases, this particular behavior was the very reason for their early success, so they are unable to "let go of it." The irony is that when they made the transition from worker to manager, the playing field changed, but their behavior did not. The successful executive coach does not just modify the behavior, but reorients the executive in terms of how he thinks about the behavior and the impact it has on others.

• It's well nigh impossible to look at things differently without assistance. "Cognitive restructuring," looking at and evaluating situations in a way you are not used to, is something that even the most psychologically minded among us have difficulty doing on our own. Successful, high-achieving executives, in particular, can be threatened by the idea of letting go of intensely held beliefs about their careers, and long-held notions about their personalities, abilities, and goals. Usually, it is precisely what is necessary in the coaching process.

Again, this reframing, which provides an opportunity for achievement-oriented executives to look at things differently without feeling that their competence or self-esteem are being called into question, is how an executive coach can begin the cognitive restructuring process that leads to self-awareness.

• No one else will tell them what is expected of them. As forward-looking as some corporate cultures can sometimes be, most are simply not set up to support an executive who needs feedback to perform up to par and to reach his potential. In some companies, thoughtful career development and careful "succession planning" is done routinely. However, more often, when an individual is promoted to the executive suite, there is very little clarification of what is expected of him in terms of new perspectives, skills, behavior, or communication style. Ironically, it is not until trouble is anticipated that anyone thinks to discuss these issues. If the executive is lucky, he is referred to an executive coach.

DON'T BELIEVE IT

There are countless myths and preconceptions that keep executive coaching from being sought out as a means of positive change. Based largely on ignorance and inertia, these are mistaken notions that I see contradicted daily in my own professional life. They include:

1. "In the end, people can't really change. They are the way they are—that's that." Anyone who has worked in any area of consulting at executive levels knows that most everyone is capable of change, provided they are motivated and receive coaching.

2. "This person has a severe psychological problem, and it can't be fixed." Ironically, fixing problems, psychological or otherwise, is frequently the easy part. It is identifying them, and getting the parties involved to recognize them as changeable, that is the all-important first step.

3. "The problem has gone on too long to be addressed—there's no way you're going to change things now." Often, it is executives who have behaved in one way for many years who are most in need of executive coaching, and who can most benefit from it. I am constantly amazed at the number of senior executives who simply have a blind spot about the impact certain of their behaviors are having on others. If they can simply be helped to see past the blind spots, and understand the negative effects a particular behavior is having, it is like a light bulb going on in their head.

4. "People don't really want to see themselves as others see them." Actually, my experience has taught me quite the opposite. Everyone wants

to see themselves as others see them, even if it is surprising, and perhaps disconcerting.

5. "Executive coaching won't have any direct impact on the bottom line." In addition to making the executive, himself, more productive, the cost of searching for, hiring, and training senior management continues to rise. As the pool of qualified executive talent continues to shrink, this statement will become even more absurd than it already is.

6. "If people really have motivation and drive, they can alter their behavior on their own." This puritanical notion is the same belief that keeps millions of Americans with personal problems from benefiting from the help a well-trained psychologist, psychiatrist, or psychotherapist can provide.

THE "THREE Cs": COMMUNICATION, CHOICE, AND CHANGE

Executive coaching can be based on timely and appropriate career-path assessment, professional development, or a "fix-it" approach. It can be introduced when an executive is moved into a new position, is identified as a "high potential" whose talents are going unused, or simply when he is seen as someone who can benefit from learning new skills or enhanced styles of communicating or managing. Regardless, when it's done right, executive coaching can be a productive alternative to "sidelining" an employee, or to termination.

Certainly, executive coaches meet with resistance, and individuals can continue undesirable behavior patterns for any number of reasons. It might be that they have difficulty understanding the negative impact it has on others, they believe permanent change is impossible, they feel their personal integrity will somehow be compromised if they willingly change, or they are afraid to fiddle with some imagined "magic formula" for success. This resistance is an inevitable part of the process of executive coaching, and can sometimes dissipate within a very short period of time. The resistance, and the high level of skepticism with which candidates sometimes enter executive coaching, are sometimes necessary for the individual to maintain his own sense of control in the process, especially at the beginning.

In my years of coaching, I've arrived at three conclusions that hold true in spite of these tendencies:

1. Clear, honest *communication*, combined with a well-designed inter-vention, can solve almost any issue. Facilitating that communication is the sum and substance of executive coaching. If a coach is to have one overriding quality, it is the ability to facilitate straightforward, frank dialogue.

2. Two of the most powerful things a good executive coach can do are; (a) help clients recognize, and relax with, who they are and, (b) help them understand that they have *choices* in every area of their lives. It is astonishing how few senior executives are really "comfortable" in their skins. They keep their discomfort a secret. It is equally surprising how empowered an executive can be made to feel when he realizes he has options, both in his work and his personal life.

3. When coaching is performed effectively, the potential for human growth and *change*—and we are talking about meaningful, forceful change—is immeasurable. So are the long-term benefits to the executive and his company.

17 Executive Coaching: A Strategy for Management and Organizational Development

Gary E. Hayes

Executive Development Associates, New York

He is one of our most successful traders. His knowledge and passion for the business are inspiring to everyone on his desk. He says he wants to move up in the organization and we are afraid we will lose him to the competition if we don't promote him soon. Despite his success in completing transactions, senior management is uneasy about his failure to express his opinions in a way that reflects an interest in or grasp of the bigger business challenges the firm is facing. Of equal concern is the perception among traders, who don't work directly on his desk, that he is domineering and dismissive to colleagues and subordinates. The confusing part is that the people who have worked with him for a significant amount of time trust him and cite the ways he has extended himself to help them and contribute to the overall effectiveness of the desk. Why the discrepancy? More importantly, what can you do about it?

So begins a somewhat complicated but rather typical description of a candidate for executive coaching. Whether the words are spoken by a human resource manager or by the employee's line supervisor, the request is the same: Help this employee be more broadly effective in the organization without taking away the "edge" that made him successful in the first place.

This chapter addresses who should be an executive coach, who will benefit from executive coaching, and how the steps of the coaching process are to be applied.

THE COACH

An executive coach must combine a knowledge of human motivations, emotions and interpersonal styles with an in-depth understanding of the complexities and nuances of organizational life. This combination can be

213

found in mental health professionals who have had substantial experience working in, and observing life in, large-scale organizational settings. To have credibility in working with executives, a coach must be able to convey a realistic understanding of the business pressures and challenges these individuals face on a daily basis.

Psychologists, psychiatrists, and social workers can all be effective in this role if they have gained the appropriate level of organizational experience and insight. Sometimes a counselor who is experienced in working with individuals in organizational settings, but who does not have the in-depth psychological knowledge of a licensed mental health specialist, will team up with a member of one of the licensed professions. If such counselors choose to work alone, they should confine their practice within their areas of competence. They need to be able to recognize the issues that, if they arise, require the input of a mental health professional. It should be noted, however, that if personality assessments are to be used, either a licensed psychologist or an individual trained and certified in the administration and interpretation of these instruments must conduct at least this phase of the coaching process.

PSYCHOANALYTICAL UNDERSTANDING

An in-depth understanding of the mutual influences that occur within ongoing human relationships is essential for achieving significant and lasting change in an executive's behavior. Insight into how relationships support and enhance motivation for change and innovation must be employed within the coaching process. Conversely, understanding how certain types of relationships become barriers to experimentation and growth must also be explored and understood.

Several contemporary theories within psychoanalysis stress the relational nature of both human motivation and resistance to change. They can serve as useful backdrops for deepening one's understanding of the impact of managerial relationships on a day-to-day basis. Psychoanalytic orientations such as interpersonal, object relations, and self psychology all highlight the awareness that, at its core, human personality is formed, maintained, enhanced, or constricted within a social matrix. Given this insight, helping managers to improve their relationships with both the individuals to whom they report, as well as with those they supervise, will directly contribute to the overall productivity and creativity of that organization.

Self psychology has provided us with a particularly detailed examination of the bases of self-esteem and the inherently social nature of the influences that determine how we regard ourselves. Two needs have been highlighted as critical for a healthy sense of self and both have obvious implications for organizational life. The first is the need to have our achievements and strivings realistically noted and reflected back to us in a manner that makes us realize we have been recognized and understood. The second is the need to identify ourselves with individuals and organizational ideals that we admire and feel connected to. Taken together, these needs indicate the essential requirement for an organization to provide mentors, not only for junior executives, but also for senior executives, to facilitate an attitude of openness toward learning and growth.

CANDIDATES FOR COACHING

Because our interpersonal effectiveness grows out of what we can draw from key relationships, it can be said that any executives, or executive teams, who face new challenges in their job responsibilities can be assisted through this process. Executive coaching can be of value in addressing these new requirements, whether they arise because of a change in the level, the location, or the function of the individual's job, or in anticipation and preparation for such a change. Executive coaching can also be beneficial for managers who require new people management skills due to the rapid expansion of their organization. Managerial teams may also benefit from coaching to maximize their effectiveness and capacity for innovation.

COACHING TECHNIQUES

Many of the techniques employed in the relatively new and highly customized form of management development, known as executive coaching, have grown out of the long-established activities of outplacement counseling. Although the ultimate objectives of the two processes differ, obtaining a new job in a new organization versus increasing one's effectiveness in one's current workplace, the processes used to accomplish these goals share considerable overlap. The most important of these processes is the attempt to increase the individual's awareness of how his or her actions are being perceived by people at various levels of an organization. In order to help them track these perceptions more accurately, it is usually necessary to help the candidate raise his or her awareness of one's own major motivations, preferred behavioral responses in various situations, and general interpersonal style. With both outplacement and executive coaching candidates, the objective is not to effect fundamental personality change, but rather to help them develop greater flexibility in choosing behaviors from their repertoire depending on the sensitivities and concerns of their audience.

For outplacement candidates, the goal of this increased flexibility is to improve their ability to relate to different job interviewers. It also aids them in highlighting different aspects of their career achievements to present credible and well-rounded executive profiles that address the major needs of different job opportunities.

For executive coaching candidates, the increase in flexibility must be sustained on a more permanent basis and applied in a much wider range of situations. In order for this to occur, the awareness of one's motivations and needs must be deeper, and the time devoted to tracking and understanding the reactions of other people to one's actions and reactions must be longer and more systematic. Most importantly, it must be determined how resistant to change the individual is and what the source of this resistance is.

The type of change required in a candidate that is most easily and comfortably effected by executive coaching, involves helping the candidate realize that some of the very tactics and style that made him or her successful in completing transactions may be counterproductive when he is trying to influence activities where he has less direct authority and where the scope of the influence must be much broader.

To return to the example we started with, the tenacious aggressiveness that our trader employs in completing trades could cause him to appear to be highly abrasive when he is describing his information technology (IT) needs to the director of management information systems (MIS). His quick reactive instincts, developed in his dealings with brokers, could make him seem quite impulsive and lacking in strategic vision when interacting with members of senior management during a policy discussion. In both cases, helping him slow down and articulate the context for his IT needs, and the rationale for his policy positions, will cause him to appear to be more collaborative in his behavior and more strategic in his thinking.

Let us take another example:

A logistics specialist has spent the past 7 years negotiating shipping contracts for her company's national manufacturing operations. Her ability to demonstrate continuously the toughness of her resolve in demanding the highest level of service for the lowest cost, earned her the respect and recognition of her management who recently promoted her to manager of the department. Within the first 6 months, two long-term employees had resigned and another was applying for a lateral move to another department. The new manager was working 14-hour days and yet the overall efficiency of the department seemed to be dropping. It quickly became clear that not only was she micromanaging her staff with the same attention to detail that she used in reviewing logistics contracts, she was also demonstrating the same degree of toughness with her subordinates that she had employed with the representatives of her transportation vendors.

The task of the coaching in this case would be, first, to make her aware of how her behavior is alienating her staff, and then to use her commitment to achieving improved results to consider alternative management procedures. This case might also require another major technique of executive coaching, that is, helping the person to identify and emphasize an aspect of their personality that they have up until now left underdeveloped—at least in regard to the workplace. In the current example, let us suppose that our manager is an ardent athlete playing on both softball and tennis teams. Helping her to translate some of the cooperative and team oriented behaviors, that made her both popular and successful in these activities, into her department could go a long way in helping her to improve the sense of loyalty and morale among her staff.

STEPS IN COACHING PROCESS

Let us now examine in more detail some of the specific procedures that would need to be utilized in the coaching of both of the candidates just described.

Step 1: The Referral Meeting

The process would begin with a meeting between the prospective coach and the member of the organization making the referral. This person, either a human resource professional or a line manager, would describe the developmental goals and current performance needs of the executive that gave rise to his or her company contacting a coach.

Step 2: Initial Meeting With Coaching Candidate

The meeting is followed by an introductory meeting between the coach and the individual referred for coaching. They would describe their understanding of why the referral had been made. This often engages the candidate in a rather emotional and not infrequently angry review of the developments that preceded the referral. Often there is also a mixture of anxiety regarding the real purpose of the counseling (e.g., "Is my company trying to get me to resign?") and skepticism as to what can be accomplished by this process. There are usually pointed and repeated remarks concerning the time pressure the executive lives under, and the additional pressure these sessions will create. The airing and discussion of these feelings by the candidate and the coach are essential if the coaching is to be taken seriously and not reduced to a mere charade.

It is also important that, during this first meeting, the coach describes as concretely as possible the steps to be taken during the coaching and the time frame for these actions. If personality assessments are going to be used, they can be introduced and their purpose described at this point. In my experience, self-assessments by the candidates of their behavioral and motivational preferences are highly useful in creating a common language that the candidate and coach can use throughout the coaching sessions.

This is also the session in which a procedure not commonly used in outplacement counseling may be introduced into the coaching agenda. This procedures involves the gathering of input from the candidate's direct reports, peers, and managers as to how the candidate is being perceived. Sometimes these assessments are referred to as upward evaluations if only direct reports are polled. More frequently, they involve the total circle of the candidate's professional relationships and are therefore called 360-degree evaluations. Although the introduction of this procedure is frequently very anxiety provoking, and often initially resented by the candidate, in many cases it is essential in order to break through the candidate's denial about the seriousness and pervasiveness of his problems.

In the example of the trader, these 360-degree evaluations could be quite useful since we have already observed that the people who work directly for him respect and trust him. His problems lie with colleagues whom he is less directly involved with, and therefore, whose perceptions of him, he is less likely to be aware of. The gathering of this information must be handled sensitively. It is also important that the candidate and the supervisor be in agreement on the choice of individuals to be surveyed.

Step 3: Assessment Feedback Session

The next step in the coaching process is a feedback session during which the data from the candidate's self-assessment is presented and given some interpretation. The most important aspect of this step is to illustrate how particular constellations of motivations and behaviors can be perceived in quite different ways by different members of the candidate's organization. For example, motivations and behaviors characterized as aggressive and dominant can be perceived as intimidating and hostile by subordinates; assertive and results-oriented by a direct supervisor, and reckless and unpolished by senior management. In recognizing these differences, the candidates can increase their awareness of how people are reacting to them and assess where certain behaviors are effective or ineffective.

This is also the step in which significant, but less prominent, aspects of the candidate's personality can be highlighted. In the previous example, if the individual, in addition to being dominant, is also motivated by affirmative and even nurturing feelings, it is important that these are not totally overshadowed by the dominance. Again in the case of the trader, it might be these relational dimensions of his personality that the people who work directly with him see over time, but don't surface, or are eclipsed, in his less continuous relationships.

Step 4: Setting the Developmental Agenda

During this step, a developmental agenda and plan for the coaching sessions must be agreed on. Input from the direct supervisor, the 360-degree evaluations, and the self-assessments must be integrated. It is important that a rather limited number of themes or issues be identified. Rarely can more than three major issues be addressed in the course of a coaching intervention. In the example of the trader, two issues might be focused on, expressing himself in more measured and strategic terms when addressing senior management, and taking the time to convey an interest in, and understanding of, the perspectives of his peers on other desks. In the case of the logistics manager, identifying a plan for promoting teamwork among her staff modeled on her outside athletic interests could promote the overall efficiency of her group, as well as tempering her perfectionist and controlling approach to the tasks the department must accomplish.

Step 5: Counseling Sessions

When a development plan has been drawn up and both the candidate and the supervisor have agreed to it, the counseling aspect of the coaching begins. Sessions are usually held weekly or every other week, and the candidates are asked to describe examples of where they have been successful and unsuccessful in attempting to change or introduce a new behavior or attitude to their repertoire. A discussion of what made the change possible or what interfered with accomplishing the change is pursued. In attempting to clarify what aids and what hinders the process of change, we also gain insight into what other factors might need to be addressed for the coaching to be successful. The possibilities range from the need for continued practice to increase the candidate's comfort and confidence in the new practices to major environmental or psychological barriers to change.

THE POSSIBILITIES FOR CHANGE

Let us examine another example in order to illustrate these possibilities.

In this case our candidate is a 48-year-old, White male marketing executive. He has been extraordinarily successful in launching a new brand of goods in the core domestic business of his consumer goods company, and in dramatically revitalizing a famous, but fading brand in that same area.

Senior management has identified him as a potential successor to the corporate senior vice president of marketing. Reporting into this position are the heads of the core domestic marketing organization, as well as the heads of the marketing function for two smaller but rapidly growing business areas. In addition to these marketing executives, the marketing head for the small, but also rapidly expanding, international division reports into the corporate position. In a succession planning meeting with the general managers from these four divisions, only the marketing executive's own general manager supported his nomination to be the successor to the corporate functional head. The other general managers criticized his lack of team spirit and the international general manager also cited his arrogance and lack of cultural sensitivity.

Assuming that our candidate has received input from 360-degree evaluation confirming these perceptions, what can be done to understand and address this situation?

The simplest type of problem to address would be one of lack of experience and exposure. If the executive has had few opportunities to interact with people from cultural backgrounds different from his own, providing him with information about the perspectives and sensitivities of people from these cultures would supply him with important new tools for broadening his repertoire. He would then need to be coached in utilizing this information in his interactions with members of the international division.

It is likely in this situation that lack of exposure may also be intensified by a certain abruptness of manner because the general managers of the other newer domestic division also held negative perceptions of him. The intensity with which he pursued his goals in his own division made him look disinterested or even dismissive of the needs and concerns of the other divisions. Recognizing this would help him to change his behavior enough to change their perceptions. His motivation to continue to advance his own career, as well as the fortunes of his company, would need to be tapped, to show him the necessity for making these changes.

Although these aspects of the executive's experience and personality may have contributed to these difficulties, it might also be the case that he has been reacting to certain influences within the organization itself. One possibility would be his feeling that some members of senior management at the division level have spent too much time and effort "managing up" to improve their images with corporate and with the senior management of the other divisions. He may have resented this "political" behavior and decided to refrain from "playing the game." In doing so, he may not realize the extent to which he became perceived as being disdainful of the opinions of anyone outside of his own division and, therefore, a poor "team player." In losing his ability to identify with the ideals of his senior management group, he may have lost the sense of validation and reassurance that comes from such an identification. The resentment from this loss can be intense.

Indeed, the environment at the senior levels of his corporation might be quite political and the coaching would then need to help him recognize the negative consequences of his refusing to build alliances for himself with other senior executives. Identifying ways that he could reach out to the other executives that would not betray his sense of integrity would be required. This might involve helping him to see that a focus on clear business goals and objectives must be balanced with building consensus through increased efforts at communication. This increased communication might then allow him to reidentify with at least some members of the executive team, thus enhancing his image as a team contributor, without succumbing to a feeling of sycophancy.

On certain occasions, some internal issue may block the individual's ability to become more open to the input or concerns of one's peers. Sometimes the anger and resentment for what he considers to be past injustices make him or her unwilling to even consider a less hostile approach. Other times, insecurity about one's own ability to operate at the most senior levels of the organization is masked by extreme grandiosity and obsessive attention to detail within his or her own division. In cases like this, exploration of alternative sources of validation are essential. If this fails to offer enough support for the individual to move to a more open and positive stance, it is sometimes necessary to suggest a referral for outside counseling or personal psychotherapy to deal with these feelings. The consequences of an individual's continued refusal or inability to change can be discussed, but the decision to enter into outside therapy must, of course, remain with the individual.

IMPLICATIONS FOR ORGANIZATIONAL DEVELOPMENT

Before closing this discussion of executive coaching, I would like to describe an expanded use of these techniques that can intensify their power and effectiveness for management and organizational development. This use involves extending executive coaching to an entire level of an organization's managerial ranks simultaneously.

This is frequently useful when a company has grown rapidly due to the high level of technical competence of its professional staff. Individual members of this staff may be promoted to managing other professionals based on the rapid growth of the firm's business. Although their technical abilities may be very great, this may not insure that they will know how to effectively manage other people. The technical or transactional focus of these managers may have given them little appreciation for the needs of their young staff members for mentoring and inspiration. In such companies, the bench strength of available managers can be quite thin and therefore the need to develop the managers at hand is very great. The risk of not doing so can include a demoralized workforce and a burnt out cadre of managers who do not know how to delegate and develop their subordinates. These outcomes can result in costly turnover of professional staff and fractious interactions between managers and their direct reports, as well as within the managerial group itself.

Another class of executives that can benefit from executive coaching are employees who are about to begin an expatriate or international assignment. Because the costs to the company of these assignments is quite high, and the consequences of a failed assignment quite grievous for both the expatriate and the company, the justification for this intervention is easy to describe.

In addition to the cost of international assignments, is the opportunity to leverage the assignment to maximize its management development potential. Assessing what aspects of the assignee's personality and managerial style will blend most naturally with the demands of the overseas position and where the greatest development challenges are likely to be, will minimize the risk of a failed assignment and intensify the executive learning that is possible. This process, when conducted periodically throughout the assignment, will reassure the assignee feels that the company is concerned about his or her career path. It will also provide the company with invaluable information about how best to utilize the experience the employee is gaining for a future position.

Whether applied individually for developmental or remedial reasons, or applied simultaneously to an entire sector of an organization's managerial staff, the results can be substantial in improving the present and future performance of the overall organization and its executive team.

CONCLUSION

To be effective, executive coaching must be conducted by professionals who combine an in-depth knowledge of human behavior and motivations with a credible understanding of the complexities of organizational life. The process should be utilized to increase an executive's awareness of his or her own needs and reactions, as well as clarifying how these actions are being perceived by others. New behaviors and styles of interaction can then be experimented with, and gradually adapted to the executive's repertoire. When these objectives are met, the coaching becomes a powerful tool for raising an executive's managerial competence. It also contributes to a higher level of satisfaction, communication, and cooperation throughout all levels of the organization. In this way, executive coaching becomes a powerful tool for achieving organizational development through management development.

18 Career Management: It's Not Just for the Outplaced

Charles W. Cates
EnterChange, Atlanta, GA

Our very young profession of outplacement is at a crossroads of crisis. One avenue leads past buggy whips, record stores, typewriters—outplacement as a curious antiquity. The other road leads to even greater opportunity for career management professionals.

It is more and more difficult to convince senior managers that fees for outplacement are worth the value. There are a number of possible explanations. It could be that managers are driven by budget necessity to spend limited dollars on people remaining, rather than people leaving the organization. Or, it could be that the last 15 years of job slashing have desensitized corporations to the pain of losing one's job. Or, it could be that we, as professionals, have failed to demonstrate our true value because so much of our work is done outside the sight of the organization, or that the competitive nature of our profession has resulted in price cutting and diluted services. One thing is clear. Fees are down, and profits are lower. Outplacement has joined its customers with a need to reengineer, streamline, and seek new market opportunities.

CAREER DISILLUSIONMENT

The 1980s and 1990s have been a period of chaos and crisis in the lives and careers of millions of workers. Downsizing, layoffs, reengineering, streamlining, delaying, restructuring—whatever the terminology, it is clear that the old bond and contract of employer job security exchanged for employee loyalty is broken.

The outplacement profession has responded to the needs of millions of employees who have been cast out and discarded by companies changing to meet tomorrow's challenges. The outplacement profession has prospered by providing job-search knowledge and skills to the displaced workers.

223

This movement in and out of organizations will continue, but there is a new crisis facing business and industry today. It is the career unrest and disillusionment of individuals inside organizations.

There are millions of workers inside organizations who see their careers in turmoil and shatters. They have seen coworkers shoved out the door. They have been saddled with more work and less pay. Streamlining erases traditional career paths and opportunities for upward advancement. Technology changes so fast there is no opportunity for job mastery or competence. They see no chance for career satisfaction or fulfillment. They focus from payday to payday, taking fewer risks for fear of losing their jobs. They feel powerless in managing their careers. These employees are the career disillusioned. They have lost their vision, their enthusiasm, and their commitment to their job and their employer. This survivor mentality results in low morale, increased absenteeism, and reduced productivity.

Many companies are wrestling with what to do to reengage these disenchanted employees. They are seeking to "rehire" their employees. Companies are also struggling with how to replace the loyalty–security bond that was the implied employment contract for decades. How does a company gain the commitment of its employees when it can no longer provide guarantees for continuous employment? How can both the employee and employer meet their needs in this climate of constant change?

NEW CONTRACT

Today's employees must shift their thinking from "job" to "employability." Employees must forget about holding on to one job, one company, and even one career. What is critical in today's constantly changing workplace is having competitive skills and the know-how to find meaningful work. Companies, likewise, must be constantly retooling their work force. Skills and competencies needed to meet ever changing market demands must be hired and updated. A company that does not forecast the competitive skills needed by its workforce is a company that will find itself constantly lagging behind the competition.

This mutual demand for both employees and employers to constantly upgrade and retool skills and competencies provides common ground for a new type of bond—a commitment–opportunity agreement.

The basic terms of this new agreement are that the company provides an opportunity for meaningful work and an opportunity to develop new skills and competencies in congruence with the company's future needs. The employee commits to work diligently at the meaningful work provided and to continuously learn new skills and competencies. This agreement keeps the company competitive while keeping the employee marketable. When circumstances change and the organization can no longer provide meaningful work, or the individual no longer finds meaning in the work, both parties agree to part company. Certainly, individuals can be sad about leaving friends, familiar work projects, and surroundings, but the employees are not so traumatized that they cannot get on with their careers.

Although this new contract sounds idealistic, some enlightened employers are attempting to develop such "career resilient" employees. Waterman, Waterman, and Corland (1994) reported this in their *Harvard Business Review* article at the Career Action Center. They are developing workers who are committed to life-long learning, who understand the need and opportunity to move from employer to employer, and who see themselves as portable business ventures with dynamic, portable skills, not just as workers doing a job in a company. Although much of their work has been in high tech companies with technology professionals, more traditional companies are also seeking solutions to deal with their "career disillusioned" employees.

EXPANDING OPPORTUNITIES
FOR OUTPLACEMENT PROFESSIONALS

Providing these solutions offers a tremendous opportunity for career management professionals. Jesup (personal communication, April 23, 1995), the human resource director for Sarah Lee, stated, "Those career management professionals that provide tangible solutions, and show positive return on helping companies deal with the career unrest of their people, will certainly be on the cutting edge and be in an enviable position to compete for business." The International Association of Career Management Professionals (IACMP), formerly the International Association of Outplacement Professionals (IOAP), recognized this opportunity by adopting the career management title to reflect the expanding role of the outplacement consultant.

Do professionals who work as outplacement consultants have the skills and knowledge to help companies deal with the career disillusioned? How can career management professionals help organizations develop a career resilient workforce? Perhaps the solution begins with what outplacement consultants do best—provide counseling support for their candidates.

A first step for any counselor working with a candidate is to help build the self-esteem of the individual. Individuals who have recently lost their jobs are filled with self-doubt. The individuals feel angry, sad, betrayed, out of control, and directionless. They lack confidence and feel trapped and often helpless. The career disillusioned inside organizations display similar symptoms. They feel a lack of self-esteem. The same model of counseling that rebuilds the self-esteem of outplacement candidates can rebuild confidence in career disillusioned employees inside companies. The other type of activity that has always been central to the success of outplacement consultants has been the ability to consult to business organizations about meeting their human resources challenges.

Certainly in today's organization, a key challenge is to have not only the right number of people, but to have those people with the right competencies to successfully do their jobs. Outplacement consultants need to move "inside the organization" and assist the organization, "our other client," deal with career management issues. Outplacement consultants have an opportunity to help the companies identify the skills and competencies needed. Effective career management programs can best be tied to the human resource needs and competencies critical for the organization's future success. The model, shown in Fig. 18.1 can serve as a guide for career management professionals who anticipate working with employees inside companies.

INFORMATION ABOUT SELF

As with outplacement candidates, one of the initial efforts in working with internal employees is to help them gain a sense of their employment assets and liabilities. Many workers have lost confidence in their abilities and

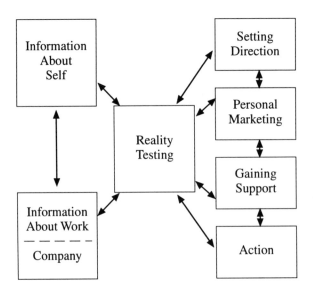

FIG. 18.1   Career development model.

have no clear career direction. A systematic career assessment process can help individuals gain a sense of their worth, as well as identify gaps in their skills and competencies. Many of the career assessment tools used with candidates can provide information about career interests, values, occupational personality, skills, and achievements. Whether working individually or in groups, a combination of self-discovery exercises and assessment instruments yields rich information for interpretation and feedback. In some organizations, peer, personal, and boss ratings, applied against specific objective competencies, provide specific feedback for both developmental needs and internal career opportunities. One vital self-dis-covery exercise is to help individuals develop their personal definition of success. For many employees, success has been equated with job promo-tions, more pay, upward mobility—climbing the corporate ladder. With today's corporate ladder shorter and more crowded at the top, employees must redefine their ideas of success. Self-assessment is a critical first step in helping employees to reclaim a sense of worth and value.

CAREER INFORMATION

If companies are committed to developing career resilient employees and workers who take charge of their own career development, they must be open to providing up-to-date business information. All employees, not just top management, must be involved in shaping the company's future.

Likewise, employees can best shape their own future when they are clear about the company's strategic direction. Anticipating future skills and competencies enables employees to plan for development needs as well as internal opportunities. It also helps employees anticipate the need to seek external opportunities.

This open sharing of information will be "business as usual" in some companies, but for most it will be a new and challenging activity. Career management professionals can develop practical models for helping com-panies begin this business information flow. Both structured and unstruc-tured methods can be used to facilitate communication. Weekly staff meetings can focus not only on the usual operations issues, but also on strategic issues. Focusing on how various business units are performing and what future plans are anticipated not only provides a better under-standing of what future competencies are needed, but also conveys a sense of trust to employees. Understanding future directions conveys a sense of what parts of the company may be shrinking or expanding. This type of information is vital in internal career planning. Some companies utilize electronic media as a part of this structured meeting. A video message from the president or other senior executive can give messages credibility and visibility.

Information about market trends, competition and an understanding of the skills and competencies needed now and in the future is vital. Creative communication vehicles are necessary. One alternative might be "brown bag lunches" where a manager or representative from another department might educate the group on work tasks, types of jobs, skills needed, future directions, and opportunities. One innovative manager regularly took 20 minutes of department meeting time and invited representatives from other departments to talk about the rewards and challenges of work done in the other business units. The result was that his employees had been exposed to all areas of the company in 6 months. He felt his employees had a much keener sense of the big picture of the entire business.

Shadowing or intern opportunities can be arranged for individuals with specific interests. Vacation fill-ins, temporary, or project assignments in a new business unit give employees a keen sense of "what the work is really like."

Some companies have developed a career library. The library has collections of books, tapes, and videos of career and industry information. This type of information is certainly familiar to career management professionals and can provide important data to job seekers and others who are attempting to learn about certain positions and careers.

Rich information resides with the people who do the work. One company has created a network of more than 360 employees who have agreed to talk to any employee who wants to learn about the nature of their work. This career information network can be a vital link in providing insightful information for those employees seeking to learn about other jobs. Essential in this information exchange is accurate and credible data on job openings inside the company.

Job openings should be equally available to all employees. All employees need to be informed of inplacement procedures. A successful inplacement program promotes movement within the organization. Although not always upward, these career moves allow employees to grow and develop new marketable competencies. Many companies are reaping the value of "recycling" employees through development and active inplacement programs, rather than discarding their valuable human resources.

Career management professionals must play a critical role in this business information exchange between employer and employee. In many situations, this open communication must be "sold" to senior management who is often more comfortable "holding information close to the vest." Orientations with senior management that include this "need to communicate message" should be a part of every career management project. Consultants can help with drafting of messages, providing communication models, and educating management on the kinds of information necessary for employees to proactively manage their careers.

Consultants can also help companies develop resources for career information, as well as personally conducting information sessions.

SETTING DIRECTION, PERSONAL MARKETING, GAINING SUPPORT

Managing one's career in today's organization requires employees to have focus and direction. No longer can individuals leave their careers to chance or to the whims of the organization. Organizations are challenging individuals to take charge of their own career direction. To do so requires employees who have career direction focus and skills and the know-how to navigate the internal career waters.

Successful individual assessment and accurate information about work and the company can equip employees to identify potential jobs and careers inside the company and the skills needed for these jobs. Having this type of mind-set, helps the individuals plan developmental opportunities, project assignments, and other opportunities that expose them to their potential assignments, and helps them add skills and knowledge to successfully compete for and perform in these jobs. Some employees are able to identify specific internal jobs to pursue, but for most, especially in this climate of constant change, identifying a department and a collection of needed competencies is sufficient. This enables the employees to focus, but remain flexible.

For most companies, career direction is limited to opportunities within that company. Other companies, however, provide individuals with separation support services when it is clear that the individuals do not see future opportunities inside the company. These "transition volunteers" leave the company, but with a mutual agreement between company and employee.

A career management program helps employees develop a personal marketing plan and the skills and know-how to implement the plan. Internal personal marketing plans are similar to the job-search marketing plans familiar to outplacement consultants. Career management consultants should educate employees about using the company job posting system, but should also help the individuals become more proactive.

An internal networking plan is vital for the employees to gain information and exposure. Networking skills are critical for finding out about other departments, job duties, and potential and current openings. The "hidden job market" so familiar to outplacement consultants exists inside companies. Career management consultants can help employees tap into this key source of information. One telecommunications company provided internal job-search seminars to all of their employees. Each employee developed career targets, resumés, marketing plans, and improved internal interviewing skills. These "Taking Charge of Your Own Career

Development" seminars, although voluntary, were attended by 90% of the workforce.

Before individuals begin active networking, it is very important to gain support from key people inside the organization. The obvious key person is the individual's manager. Career consultants can help employees learn how to initiate career discussions with their managers. Such discussions allow individuals to share insights about their strengths, values, skills, and liabilities as determined through self-assessment. They provide opportunity to discuss future ambitions and directions. They are vehicles for the employees to gain feedback, address concerns, and to test the reality of their career plans. The employees can solicit the support of their managers for developmental opportunities and gain commitment toward career action plans.

Just as training for employees to initiate career discussions improves successful outcomes, training with managers to become "developmentally focused" pays dividends. Managers can be taught how to use every day work situations as developmental opportunities for employees. Temporary assignments, interdepartmental projects, and task force participation that are congruent with developmental desires of participating employees are the vital building blocks of a "learning organization." One insurance company provided "Managing Your Development" workshops for employees in tandem with "Managing Development" seminars for managers.

Often, there is initial resistance on the part of managers to support and develop their employees, as they are concerned that the employees will be more inclined to move out of the work group. These managers tend to focus only on their work area and not on what is best for the larger organization or for the employee. For such managers, the time and effort spent in recruiting and training replacements seems to outweigh the value of a crosstrained, committed, and motivated workforce. To drive home the critical importance of development, more and more organizations are including development accountability as a significant part of a manager's performance. People development is a vital part of a learning organization. To reinforce this initiative, compensation and rewards must be tied to success in developing people. As an added incentive, one company gives one share of stock for each employee that a manager develops to the point of transferring up or out to a new assignment. By rewarding this type of behavior, developing people comes to be seen as a vital part of a manager's job.

CAREER ACTION PLAN

Some companies have used career action plans for years. However, in many cases these plans have not had the commitment of the individual or the organization. They have served little purpose. Many of these career plans were the responsibility of management, with the employee a passive participant at best. For a career action plan to work, it must be the committed product of the employee. It is the employee's career; it should be the employee's plan. Certainly it is developed within the reality factors of the company, but its ultimate success rests with the individual.

Career action plans that have the commitment of both employee and employer, coupled with the personal marketing know-how of the individual are vital to create the new employment bond of "commitment for opportunity."

During the 1980s and 1990s, outplacement consultants met the career needs of millions of workers who were on the outside looking in. Today, that need is shifting. Outplacement consultants must widen their vision and become career management consultants. They must take their skills inside organizations to help those career disillusioned employees develop self-esteem, self-confidence, and a sense of power and control over their careers. We must catch this wave of the future.

REFERENCE

Waterman, R. H., Waterman, J. A., & Corland, B. A. (1994, July–August). Toward a career resilient work force. *Harvard Business Review*, pp. 87–95.

19 The Evolving Workplace: Its Implications for Outplacement Practice

Murray Axmith
Murray Axmith & Associates, Toronto

Changes in the workplace are having a very substantial impact on the practice of outplacement. Those in the outplacement business who aspire to survive and optimize their opportunities will need to pay very close attention to what is happening and what is likely to happen in the future.

Nobody can claim 20/20 vision with respect to the future. What follows represents my personal thoughts including the assumptions I am making about the changes that are occurring and what this all means for the outplacement industry.

CORPORATE RESTRUCTURING

Assumption

Businesses, in order to respond to the rapidly accelerating pace of change in an increasingly competitive global economy, will require flexible management, flexible structures, and flexible utilization of people. The passwords for corporate survival will be *change, flexibility, mobility*, and *speed*. Corporations will need "to turn on a dime" in order to respond to changes in the marketplace.

In order to control costs and make more flexible utilization of people, corporations will pare down to a "core" group of key people and utilize an increasing number of personnel on a short-term, interim, contractual, and contingency basis. The galloping pace of change will result in shorter service and more rapid turnover of personnel in both the core and project groups.

233

Implications for Outplacement Practice

Corporations that employ people for shorter time frames will feel less of an obligation to departing employees. This will result in more time-bound, modified outplacement programs and lower fees per assignment.

Many people in project groups will not be offered outplacement services at all. Outplacement firms will enter the "retail" market in order to service the growing number of contract, project, and contingent personnel. The fees will be paid in their entirety by individuals without corporate sponsorship.

EMPLOYEE BENEFIT PROGRAMS

Assumption

In order to compete with emerging economies in Asia, India, China, and South America, we will need not only a better educated and trained workforce, but also a cheaper workforce.

With shorter employee lengths of service and competitive pressure to reduce costs, corporations will gradually, over time, reduce their commitments and contributions to employee benefit programs.

The gap will be filled by industry and professional associations that will, over time, assume more commitment to, and offer benefit programs including, insurance and pension programs.

I wrote an article entitled "The Work Force: How it Will Change" for Career Options—*The Graduate Recruitment Annual*[1] magazine, which highlighted my views on the subject of corporate benefits. Following the article's publication, the editor conducted an informal survey among the organization's corporate members and concluded that the majority of those contacted concurred with my position.

Increasingly, industry and professional associations will offer a range of employment services to their members, including job banks, networking opportunities, placement services, career management, and outplacement services. These associations will both employ outplacement professionals on staff and contract out these services to outplacement firms.

For example, the Association of Professional Engineers in Ontario and the Association of Professional Social Workers in Ontario have both begun, on a relatively small scale, to provide services in this way.

---

[1] A professional publication representing the Canadian Association of Career Educators and Employers (CACEE), an organization that brings together career consultants on university campuses with corporate recruiters.

EMPLOYEE ADJUSTMENT

Assumption

The accelerating pace of change in which work and roles will continually be redefined, and the swelling ranks of contingent professionals, will result in "work life" becoming a "series of assignments" for many.

This will have an unsettling affect on many people with accompanying anxieties, difficulty focusing and concentrating, and perpetual uncertainties. For those undergoing this transition, who require a great deal of external structure to meet their personal security needs, the fallout will be a negative impact in performance. Those who do best will develop self-management skills and thrive on the change associated with the ever-present prospect of new assignments.

Implications for Outplacement Practice

Recognizing the turbulent workplace and its potential impact on people adjustment and productivity, many progressive and enlightened employers will offer career management services to their employees.

Employers will recognize a multiple payoff in doing this. Career services will assist employees to expand their perception of areas in which their skills and knowledge can be potentially utilized, both inside and outside the company. This will have a settling effect on employees, improving their concentration, focus, and productivity on the job. The confidence gained from being able to perceive more options for themselves—in terms of the application of their skills and knowledge—will be empowering and result in employees identifying new ways and areas in which they can contribute to corporate goals.

Many enlightened and progressive temporary employment agencies will offer career management services as a value-added service to the growing population of "temps" at technical, professional, managerial, and executive levels.

Just as training enhances the employability of temps, career management services will do the same. These services will assist temps to discover new areas to apply their skills and knowledge as well as keep them focused and productive for longer periods of time.

Temporary employment agencies that offer outstanding training and career management services will be able to attract the "best" people and have a significant competitive edge in the market. The risk of losing some of their best trained and outstanding performers to attractive new opportunities elsewhere is always there. However, this will be more than offset by the agencies' continuing capacity to attract good high-potential people based on their reputation in both skill and career development.

Temporary employment agencies will become major employers of career management professionals as well as contracting these services out to outplacement firms.

LEVELS OF UNEMPLOYMENT

Assumption

Driven by competitive pressures, increased use of technology, and corporate de-layering, organizations in all sectors—service, manufacturing, high technology, and the public sector—will all become less labor intensive.

Predictions that the demographic impact of retiring "baby-boomers" will result in a scarcity of skilled people through the year 2000 and into the 21st century, will be overridden by the application of technology and by the competitive drive for corporations to become less labor intensive. This will result in a global surplus of skilled people into the 21st century. Richard Barnet, of the Institute of Policy Studies in Washington, supported this position in his article published in *Harpers Magazine* in September 1993, entitled "The End of Jobs; What the Global Economy is not Making."

Implications for Outplacement Practice

Outplacement firms will need to go well beyond teaching candidates job-search skills and providing career counsel. Higher levels of unemployment and an increasingly difficult job market will put competitive pressure on outplacement firms to increasingly offer proactive assistance to candidates.

Popular forms of proactive assistance will include job banks, the increasing utilization of job developers to identify job opportunities for candidates, and plugging candidates into the outplacement firm's alumni network for information and job leads.

Outplacement firms will need to offer more "do fors" to compete, particularly for "shoppers" whose corporate sponsors have allowed them to select their own outplacement firms.

To lure senior-level shoppers into selecting their firm, outplacement firms will offer to make contacts on behalf of candidates—"I will personally put you in touch with the CEOs of 50 major corporations."

Senior-level shoppers will also be offered budgets derived from the outplacement fee for such items as:

1. Advertising their availability in selective business publications.

2. Expenses associated with networking luncheon meetings.
3. A budget for purchasing off-site private office space and administrative services.

The growing outlay of funds associated with the provision of these additional services will cut deeply into the profit margins of outplacement firms.

RECRUITMENT FIRMS TAKE ON
THE OUTPLACEMENT INDUSTRY

With the combination of outplacement usage of job banks, job developers, and alumni networks, the distinction between outplacement and placement will become increasingly blurred. Search, recruitment, and placement firms will develop strong resentments to outplacement firms cutting into their markets through the utilization of highly proactive support to assist candidates in identifying and filling job opportunities.

Recruitment, search, and placement firms will retaliate by entering the outplacement market with services of their own. They will compete very aggressively in the marketplace with offers such as: "Give us your search business and we will offer you our outplacement services at substantially reduced prices." The offer of substantially discounted outplacement services will be made possible by the higher profit margins in the search business.

Deeply discounted outplacement services offered by recruitment, search, and placement firms will further saturate the outplacement market and put even greater pressure on already thinning profit margins in the outplacement field.

OUTPLACEMENT FIRMS SEEK REFUGE
IN DIVERSIFICATION

With the entrance of recruiters onto outplacement turf, a maturing industry for its services, lower fees, and increasingly thinning profits margins, many outplacement firms will look to diversification to replace lost revenues and enhance their bottom line.

Outplacement firms will make forays into human resource consulting, change management, performance coaching, training, and recruitment. Most will fair very poorly in this diversification. A few will manage this well.

A Recipe for Failure in Diversification

Firms that manage diversification poorly will approach the new service as a sideline without employing highly experienced, specialized staff in the new areas. Their resources will be spread too thinly over the new offerings and their outplacement service line. With the loss of focus on the enhancement of outplacement services, the firm's core service area will gradually erode with accompanying confusion in the marketplace as to "Who are they? What are they really good at?" This drift into mediocrity across all its service lines will inevitably result in (a) the firm's loss of reputation and business in the original core niche it has established in outplacement; and (b) failure to establish a solid footing in the new service areas.

A Recipe for Success in Diversification

The few outplacement firms that manage the diversification well will hire specialized, experienced staff with "leading edge" reputations in the new service areas. Separate identities will be established for these services either in the form of separate companies or specialized divisions within the overall consulting group. Within these structures, the staff will devote all of their time to their specialty. Continuous honing of leading edge knowledge, skills, and programs combined with marketing and public relations programs, which are totally separate from the firm's outplacement thrust, will gradually pay off and carve out a flourishing business and a reputation for the firm in the new service areas.

On Becoming Leading Edge and Thriving in the Outplacement Business

Outplacement firms that "do best" in the changing marketplace will "stick to the knitting." While other firms are preoccupied with diversification, those firms that focus their resources on developing leading edge programming relevant to the major career transitions required in the evolving workplace, and develop some special niches within the outplacement and career management spheres, will gain a very substantial competitive edge in the marketplace.

Each of the following career transitions requires substantial expertise plus supporting programming and research to provide leading edge service.

Most outplacement firms are providing "seat-of-the-pants" counsel and "winging it" in these areas. Relying on the instincts and intuition of individual outplacement consultants based on their personal cumulative experience is useful, but what is lacking in most firms is substantive research-based programming. Firms that can demonstrate real substance in their programming will have a substantial edge over competitors.

SOME MAJOR CAREER TRANSITIONS
IN THE EVOLVING WORKPLACE

Up to this point, the focus of this chapter has been on major general trends and their impact on the outplacement industry. The following career transitions, which individuals will need to make in the changing workplace, will require that outplacement firms develop very substantial programming to support each one of these transitions.

Some major changes occurring in the evolving workplace include making the transition from:

1. Being a full-time employee to working on a shorter term contractual, project, interim, or contingent basis. This transition will require substantial self-management skills and significant changes in individual expectations. With work life becoming a series of assignments for an increasing number of people, there will be a pressing need for workers to learn to position and market themselves as a service center—a microbusiness—with their employers, at any given point in time, being their customers.

To prepare for downtime between assignments, the need to invest in further education and training, and to be in a position to pursue a "transitional job" to acquire additional specific skills and knowledge, workers will need to keep their personal overheads low.

2. Being an employee to being in business for oneself. This transition will require an entrepreneurial programming stream to:

- Help assess individual suitability to be in business for oneself;
- Assist with the development of feasibility studies and business plans;
- Provide information on how to seek out business opportunities and the management and funding of existing business prospects and "green site" start-up situations.

3. Working in a large organization to working in a much smaller organizational setting. Large organizations will undertake major restructuring yielding to smaller organizational units that will be more flexible, mobile, and able to respond much quicker to changing market conditions. With opportunities in larger corporations drying up, the career transition to smaller organizations will require individuals to expand their role expectations—to be prepared to "wear many hats," to fulfill their responsibilities without the support of large groups of staff specialists found in larger companies, and to temper their expectations with respect to base salaries and benefits.

4. Public sector employment to private sector employment. To compete in the global economy, the business community in each country will

require the support of more "competitive government." Substantial re-structuring will occur at federal, state, and municipal levels to cut the cost of government and focus on important public service priorities as these relate to the competitive needs of the business community. Helping individuals make the transition from the public sector to the private sector will require specialized knowledge and programming. Programming will focus on the cultural differences between the public and private sectors, role expectations, and the transferability of specific skills and knowledge gained in the public sector to specific functional and industry areas within the private sector. The shift to the private sector for public servants with long service will require changes in attitudes, expectations, orientation, and focus.

5. Focusing career management on one person's career to focusing on multiple persons within the context of a relationship ("partners in life" or family). The job market will require individuals to be increasingly mobile and, in turn, will necessitate that people manage their careers within the context of the career management needs of family members and other significant people in their lives. Specialized programming will be required to focus on this constellation of career management needs and to facilitate a process in which individuals negotiate adjustments in their career plans with each other. The need for increasing career mobility will create family tensions and be very stressful on relationships. Out-placement practitioners will need to be sensitive to family strains and make referrals as required to capable family counselors.

6. Focusing career management on a local, regional, and national basis to focusing on a global–international basis. In a global economy, goods, services, and people will move more frequently and much easier across international boundaries. The search for suitable job and project opportunities will transcend international borders and require special-ized programming in terms of how to conduct an international job search, differential approaches to job search inherent in other business cultures, and how to "do business" and make effective adjustments on the job in the context of different business cultures throughout the globe.

7. Employment to retirement. Career/life and financial planning, along with other specialized programming, are required to assist individuals to meet their ongoing needs for achievement, satisfying and productive activity, and social interaction. These needs do not cease to exist for individuals on retirement, but rather carry over into their new life situations and demand fulfillment.

Outplacement firms that can clearly demonstrate their capability, based on substantive programming and research to respond to the entire constellation of career transitions specified above, will be in a superior competitive position.

Smaller outplacement firms with more limited program development capacity could select niches within the above constellation and "by doing one thing and doing it better than anybody else" compete very effectively with the larger firms.

Some More Niche Markets for Outplacement and Career Management Specialists

1. There will be a need for career assessment and management focused on an individual's potential for retraining, and linking this to retraining programs and opportunities in the marketplace. For example, machinists and tool and dye makers with experience in heavy industry, such as the manufacturing of farm machinery and refrigerators, have the potential to be retrained to work on the development of precision components for the automotive supply, aviation, and aerospace industries. Critical shortages of skilled people in these latter areas have forced corporations in North America to import trained workers from England and Germany. Identifying technical training resources and transitional job experiences to map out an entry strategy to these high-demand areas will provide exciting and rewarding new opportunities for workers who have been displaced, or potentially face displacement from industry areas where their skills are in less demand.

There is a huge potential market here directed to corporations, unions, governments, and industry and professional associations. There are currently very few resources with the capability of doing an outstanding job in this area. An enormous business could be built around this niche.

2. Assisting organizations to identify how the critical competencies in specific key roles in the organization are changing in relation to the changing needs of the organization's customers. Research and analysis could focus on the future needs of customers, inside and outside the organization, as these relate to the critical competencies. Individual career management programs would focus on assessment and development plans tied to the changing critical competencies and their requirements.

3. Career assessment and counsel focused on the career management needs of professional, managerial, and executive personnel who become disabled. There is a substantial market here as a supplier to insurance companies and both public and private rehabilitation centers.

4. Career assessment and counsel focused on the career management needs of high potential upwardly mobile individuals. Identifying executive leadership capability with potential for application in a highly competitive fast-moving global economy will be a service in very great demand in the corporate world. A service that helps corporations make optimum use of these high potential people and provides accelerated career development opportunities will command a substantial premium.

5. Career assessment and counsel focused on the career management needs of professionals whose careers will move on a more horizontal plain. With the trend toward corporate de-layering and the elimination of middle management jobs, an increasing number of professionals will need to hone their skills and knowledge, look for new areas in which they can make a contribution, and enhance their employability. This population will represent a substantial market for career services.

THE UTILIZATION OF TECHNOLOGY BY OUTPLACEMENT AND CAREER MANAGEMENT FIRMS

Access to information is very critical to career management and job search applications.

1. Computers will provide candidates access to all aspects of the job search process 24 hours a day.
2. Computerized job banks will provide access to local, regional, national, and international opportunities.
3. Computers will provide candidates access to the alumni network of an outplacement firm by function and industry and cover local, regional, national, and international markets.
4. Computers will match specific skills, knowledge, experience, and industry exposure to specific career opportunities on a local, regional, national, and international basis.
5. Computers will identify the transferability of skills, knowledge, and experience to other related careers that, in turn, may require transitional job experiences and training to access. The latter requirements will be identified along with the specific prospective career areas.
6. Sophisticated computer programs will match an individual's specific skills, knowledge, experience, forte, niche, orientation, and achievements to the needs, problems, and priorities currently prevalent in specific industry areas and companies.
7. Career channels will emerge on the information highway providing interactive access on a pay-for-view basis to job banks, and all aspects of the job-search process, including differential approaches to career management tied to the differences inherent in specific business cultures throughout the world.
8. The public sector will provide computer access available to all job seekers and reemployment consultants on unemployment benefits, retraining eligibility, income support sources, and requirements for retraining, and job banks at the blue-collar, technical, and professional levels.

These services will either be available free or, in some cases, on a user-fee basis.

Does some of all of this sound like "science fiction?" It is all very imminent. Items 5, 6, and 7, for example, are already in the development stage. At AOCFI's annual conference held in Atlanta in October 1994, a number of specialized suppliers of computer services to the career management field made presentations covering these three areas.

I predict that all of the services outlined earlier will be fully available within the next 3 years and in extensive use by outplacement and career management firms within 5 years.

A TURBULENT TRANSITION FOR OUTPLACEMENT AND CAREER MANAGEMENT FIRMS

The research, program development, and technology requirements relevant to the evolving career transition needs in a workplace, characterized by a rapidly accelerating pace of change, will be beyond the financial capacity of all but the very largest firms in the industry.

Small and medium-sized firms will merge or form alliances on a regional, national, and international basis to finance super corporate groups that will either make, develop, or acquire the programming they need from specialized suppliers.

There will still be plenty of room in the marketplace for small firms to remain unaligned and not only survive, but flourish, in the market. The important determinant of success for these firms will be the focus of their resources and marketing efforts on specific niches. "Doing one thing and doing it better than anyone else" in their area of operation will be their lifeline.

Every single firm in the outplacement and career management field will need to think very strategically about the changes that are occurring in the evolving workplace. What does this mean for their programming? Do they need to merge or form alliances with other firms to acquire the programming resources they need? Do they make or buy these services? Should they, indeed, become a supplier of a specialized service to other outplacement firms? How do they plan to position themselves in the marketplace? What niche or niches should they pursue? Should they remain small or become part of a larger firm or group of firms? Should they diversify beyond outplacement? If so, what areas beyond outplacement should they pursue? How should diversification be structured—fully integrated within the firm, as a separate division within the firm, or as a separate entity outside the firm?

Welcome to the world of our corporate clients! If the pace of change, the formidable decisions to be made, and the gut wrenching uncertainties in the marketplace are somewhat frightening to people in the outplacement and career management fields, the Irish writer Oscar Wilde has some reassuring words of wisdom for you—"the basis of optimism is sheer terror."

Index